War Is Coming

THE ETHNOGRAPHY OF POLITICAL VIOLENCE

Tobias Kelly, Series Editor

A complete list of books in the series is available from the publisher.

WAR IS
COMING

Between Past
and Future Violence in Lebanon

Sami Hermez

PENN

UNIVERSITY OF PENNSYLVANIA PRESS

PHILADELPHIA

Published by
University of Pennsylvania Press
Philadelphia, Pennsylvania 19104-4112
www.upenn.edu/pennpress

Printed in the United States of America on acid-free paper
1 3 5 7 9 10 8 6 4 2

Library of Congress Cataloging-in-Publication Data
ISBN 978-0-8122-4886-9

In Memory of
Teta Samira Merizian Hermez
and
For my parents,
Samir and Velma

Contents

PART II. RECOLLECTION

Note on Translation

The *International Journal of Middle East Studies* (IJMES) Arabic transliteration standards have been used in this book. In some cases, the Lebanese dialect rather than Modern Standard Arabic has been used in the transliterations with minor adjustments. For example, endings with /a/ have sometimes been replaced with /e/, /al-/ with /el-/, and /q/ with /ʾ/. All translations are my own unless otherwise stated.

Timeline of Key Historical Moments

1838: Druze-Maronite fighting in Mount Lebanon

1845: Another spell of Druze-Maronite intercommunal fighting

1860: Druze-Maronite fighting in Mount Lebanon

November 1943: Lebanon gains independence from France; unwritten National Pact (*al-mithāq al-watanī*) forms basis of multi-confessional political system

May 1948: Palestinian Nakba begins

July 1958: Civil war between forces for and against pro-Western Baghdad Pact

December 1968: Israel bombs Beirut International Airport

November 1969: Cairo Agreement between Palestinian Liberation Organization (PLO) and Lebanese army

April 1973: Israel attacks PLO in the heart of Beirut and Sidon

April 13, 1975: Clashes between Phalange party and PLO mark beginning of Lebanon's war

December 1975: Black Saturday when Christian militia massacre Muslims in Beirut

January 1976: Karantina and Damour massacres

Summer 1976: Tel al-Zaatar massacre

February–April 1978: 100 Days War between Syria and Christian militias ends ceasefire

March 1978: Israel occupies South Lebanon

October 1978: Arab League Summit imposes ceasefire with entrance of Arab Deterrent Forces

July 1980: Bashir Gemayel unites Christian militias under Lebanese Forces (LF)

Summer 1982: Israel occupies and besieges Beirut; beginning of Lebanese Resistance Movement against Israel

September 1982: Assassination of Bashir Gemayel; Sabra and Chatila massacre

May 17, 1983: Israeli-Lebanese peace agreement under leadership of Amin
    Gemayel

February 6, 1984: Intifāda (uprising) of Amal Movement and Progressive So-
    cialist Party (PSP) against Lebanese army in West Beirut, wresting con-
    trol of West Beirut from army.

May 1985: War of the Camps begins between Amal Movement and Palestin-
    ian factions. Concludes in July 1988.

March 1985: Internal intifāda within LF—Elie Hobeika takes party leader-
    ship from Fouad Abu Nader

March 1985: Collapse of Israeli-Lebanese peace agreement

December 1985: Tripartite Agreement between LF leader Elie Hobeika, Amal
    Movement's Nabih Berri, and PSP leader Walid Jumblatt under aegis of
    Syria.

January 1986: Internal *intifāda* within LF—Samir Gaegae takes leadership
    from Hobeika and annuls Tripartite Agreement

March 1989: General Michel Aoun wages "War of Liberation" against Syria

October 1989: Taif Agreement (National Reconciliation Accord) signed

January 1990: "War of Elimination" between LF and Lebanese army under
    leadership of Aoun

October 13, 1990: Aoun defeated, marking the end of Lebanon's war and
    sending him to exile.

April 8, 1996: Israel attacks Lebanon for sixteen days in Operation Grapes of
    Wrath

May 2000: South Lebanon liberated from Israel

February 2005: Former prime minister Rafiq Hariri assassinated

April 2005: Syria withdraws its troops from Lebanon

July 2006: Israel wages month long war on Lebanon

Summer 2007: War in Nahr al-Bared Palestinian refugee camp between
    Lebanese army and Fateh el-Islam

May 2008: Battles in Beirut between March 14 and March 8 coalitions; Doha
    Agreement signed to end hostilities

June 2009: Lebanese parliamentary elections

Major Political Parties
and Political Blocs

Between 1975 and 1990, there were more than one hundred political parties or organizations, most of which were armed and not all legally registered with the government. As of 2007, there were eighty-one political parties or organizations, not mentioning those that were not registered, like Hizballah, for example (Information International 2007). It is beyond the scope of this work to list and describe all of them. Below are descriptions of the political parties most cited in this book and may not include some prominent ones that are represented in government (as of this writing):

Amal Movement (Amal) was established in 1975, originally as the military wing of Musa Sadr's Movement of the Dispossessed. In 1980, two years after Sadr disappeared in Libya, Nabih Berri became the movement's leader and remains so today. Amal fought alongside the Lebanese National Movement (LNM) in the 1970s. In 1985, the movement launched a military campaign against the Palestinians, in what would be called "War of the Camps," and later against Hizballah. Hizballah took over much of the area previously controlled by Amal after these deadly battles.

Free Patriotic Movement (FPM; also known as Aounists) is led by former commander of the Lebanese army General Michel Aoun. After being exiled from Lebanon for fifteen years after the "War of Liberation" against Syria in 1989, Aoun returned to Lebanon in 2005. The party is officially secular but perceived as a predominantly Christian party.

Future Movement (also known as Al-Mustaqbal from the Arabic *ṭayyār al-mustaqbal***)** was founded by Prime Minister Saed Hariri in 2007, and after the assassination of his father, Rafiq Hariri. Rafiq Hariri had built much of the party's structure, including a newspaper and TV station, but never had a formal political organization. The movement is said to be secular but most of its base is Sunni.

Hizballah (Party of God) is the Islamic Resistance in Lebanon against Israel. It was officially established in 1985 but is widely held to have been active as early as 1982. Its political wing, represented in parliament, is called Loyalty to the Resistance Bloc.

Lebanese Communist Party was founded in 1924. During the 1970s and 1980s it fought alongside other leftist, Muslim, and Palestinian factions as part of the LNM. Its membership came predominantly from a Greek Orthodox, Armenian, and Shi'a base. The Communist Party was also part of the Lebanese National Resistance Front (LNRF).

Lebanese Forces (LF; also known as ʾuwet from the Arabic al-ʾuwet al-libnāniye) was founded as a militia in 1976, by Bashir Gemayel. Although associated with the Kataeb Party during the 1970s and 1980s, the Lebanese Forces became an independent unit after the assassination of Bashir Gemayel. Samir Gaegae assumed control of the LF in 1986. It advocates a Christian nationalist agenda.

Lebanese National Movement (LNM) is the coalition of left wing movements formed in 1975 and supported by the Palestine Liberation Organization (PLO).

Lebanese National Resistance Front (LNRF) was an underground alliance of left wing movements that came together in 1982 to oppose Israel's invasion of Lebanon and siege of Beirut.

March 8 is a coalition of parties that formed on March 8, 2005 after a large demonstration that day. It came together initially to thank Syria for its presence in Lebanon as it was pulling out, but later grew as an opposition to the March 14-led government. It has close ties to Syria and Iran, and its main concern is in opposing U.S. and Israeli agendas in the region, as well as ensuring that Hizballah is disarmed only after there is no need for a resistance movement. Some major parties of the coalition are: Hizballah, FPM, Amal Movement, and the Syrian Social Nationalist Party (SSNP).

March 14 is a coalition of parties that formed on March 14, 2005, one month after the assassination of former prime minister Rafiq Hariri. The coalition has strong ties to the United States and Saudi Arabia, has opposed the Syrian presence in Lebanon, demanded an independent investigation into the assassination of Rafiq Hariri and other assassinations that followed, and called for the disarmament of Hizballah. Some parties included in this coalition are: LF, Kataeb Party, Progressive Socialist Party, Future Movement, and al-Ahrar.

Movement of Independent Nasserites (Al-Murabitoun) was formed in

1958 by Ibrahim Koleilat. It played a significant role during Lebanon's war in the 1970s and 1980s, fighting alongside leftist factions and the Palestinians until it was crushed by the PSP and Amal Movement in 1985. The Murabitoun were a secular Arab movement and their flags began to appear again during the time of my fieldwork, but it has not had an impact since it was disbanded in 1985.

National Liberal Party (al-Ahrar) was established in 1958, by former president Camille Chamoun. It was part of the Christian nationalist block during the war years. In 1980, fighting broke out between them and the Phalange Party, after which the militia was brought under the command of Bashir Gemayel and the LF. It survives as a party till today and was aligned with the March 14 coalition during my fieldwork.

Phalange Party (also known as Kataeb from the Arabic *ḥizb el-katā'ib*) was founded by Pierre Gemayel as a nationalist youth movement in 1936. It was a main Christian nationalist player in the beginning of the 1975–1990 war and was opposed to Palestinian resistance in Lebanon. The party had close ties to Israel during the war and its leadership went on to form the LF.

Progressive Socialist Party (PSP; also known as *ishtirākiye* or Socialist Party) was founded in 1949. It is officially secular and nonsectarian but effectively the party of Druze leader Walid Jumblatt. In the 1970s and 1980s the party was aligned with the leftist LNM.

Syrian Social Nationalist Party (SSNP; also known as *'awmiye* from the Arabic *ḥizb al-sūrī al-qawmi al-ijtimā'ī*) was founded in Beirut in 1932 by Antoun Saadeh; it strives for the unification of a Greater Syrian state and a nonconfessional Lebanese entity. It was on the side of leftist forces between 1975 and 1990.

List of Characters

The following is a biography of major characters in this book. Other minor interlocutors are not listed. Names, and in some cases descriptions, have been altered to ensure the anonymity of my interlocutors. As the research for this book has taken several years, I have described people as they appear in the ethnographic moment even though age, relations, and occupations have changed and continue to do so.

Although kinship structures are very relevant to both anthropological research and outcomes, I have encountered difficulties in finding the balance between describing my explicit kinship relations and responsibility to the anonymity of interlocutors. This balancing act says something of the way kinship is negotiated, silenced, and affected in conflict zones. Thus, I have used the ambiguous term "relative" to refer to both consanguineous and affinal relations, rather than describing explicit connections.

Basil is thirty-nine years old, a father of three girls; he works as a driver. He is originally from the south but moved to Beirut in his early youth, in part a consequence of urbanization and in part due to war. He fought with the Lebanese Forces in the last three years of the war when the militia was engaged primarily in inter-Christian battles. Basil is a tall, well-built man with fair skin and black hair; he has homemade tattoos on his arms. He is also very jovial, but can sometimes overdo his comedy.

Dima is an architect and grassroots activist. She dresses casually, is fair skinned, and has dark hair and gentle features. The two of us often engaged in passionate conversations about war and her observations of the world were always framed poetically. She lived abroad during her childhood but also experienced significant periods of war from 1975 to 1990. She still recalls such things as the arrest and torture of her relative by the Syrian army. She is from Tripoli but lives in Beirut and teaches at the American University of Beirut (AUB). She is related to Rasheed.

George is my relative. He was twenty-one at the start of my research. George had lived his entire life in Lebanon and was now a university student at the AUB. He is a Maronite from the North but grew up in the northern suburbs of Beirut.

Jad is a relative of mine. He is in his late forties, medium build and clean-cut. He began carrying weapons in 1975 with the al-Ahrar Party at age fourteen while continuing his schooling. He stopped fighting about two or three years later after completing his high school diploma. He is an engineer by training, once owned a factory, but is now a businessperson with unsteady work.

Jana is a woman in her thirties, a filmmaker, and not affiliated to any political party. She is from a home with a religiously mixed marriage, though her parents are now divorced. Jana lived in Lebanon all her life until she moved overseas for some years to complete her master's degree and take on various jobs. She experienced the entire period of the war in the 1970s and 1980s before leaving in the early 1990s. She identifies with being both Muslim and Christian.

Jihad is in his forties, tall and tanned with light brown hair and dark piercing eyes. He fought with the Communist Party in the 1980s mainly in operations against the Israelis, although he did take part in several internal battles. Jihad is now a political activist who uses his animations to tell his story and works with other activists like Dima. He lives near the Mousaitbeh area of Beirut.

Nabil is a relative. He is in his early fifties. He has a large build, is slightly balding and has soft eyes that betray much emotion. His son speaks highly of him though he is a stern father. Nabil has a private business and did not finish university. He took part in some armed fighting in the early war years from 1975 to 1976. He is Maronite, and generally supports the positions of the Lebanese Forces, although he is not a party member. He never joined any political party but was closely affiliated for some time with the Kataeb Party.

Rasheed is a fair-skinned man with dark brown hair and in his early thirties. He is an engineer, though secretly a poet. Rasheed was raised between an Arab Gulf state and North Africa. His parents are divorced, and he was largely cared for by his loving grandparents. He comes from a well-to-do Sunni family. He is a committed political activist and related to Dima.

Rola is a relative of mine, married to Jad. She is tall and dark skinned, a housewife and mother of four children. She is originally from the North but her father moved to the Greater Beirut area in the early 1970s. She has nine siblings and comes from a landowning family, but her father's business was severely crippled during the war years with his factory burning and finally shutting down. She lived through the entire years of the war and is now a strong supporter of the Free Patriotic Movement. Because she is married she no longer votes in her home village as she follows her husband, but had it been otherwise she would have supported Suleiman Franjieh, at least in elections, as her family is traditionally indebted to him through a patron-client relation.

Zuzu (short for Joseph) is in his early forties, a dark-skinned, balding man, of medium height. He is strong and bulky and has a belly. He is a mechanic. He is married and has four children with another on the way, and comes from a large family as his father was twice married. He is from Beirut, and of Greek Orthodox faith. He is a close old friend of Basil. He began fighting with the Kataeb Party at twelve. He was an active member with the party at least until the end of my fieldwork. His engagements in battle are extensive. He had siblings who also fought; one was killed in the 1980s. He did not take part in armed combat after 1988 and married in 1992.

Chapter 1

In the Meanwhile: Theory and Fieldwork in Protracted Conflict

The Hamra neighborhood of Beirut was a very busy place during *ḥarb tammūz* (the "July War" in 2006). Many displaced people from the South had made their way to the city, escaping Israel's incessant bombing of that part of the country in an ineffective attempt to destroy Hizballah, the Lebanese resistance movement against Israel.[1] The displaced were staying with relatives or in school compounds, underground garages, unoccupied apartments, and other vacant spaces in the city. On this particular afternoon, Dima and I decided to take a break from our relief work and have lunch at Roadster Café, a local American-style diner. I came to meet Dima during this period of relief work in the July War, and with her and others I would take part in various forms of humanitarian and political action during the course of my fieldwork. Dima is an architect and grassroots activist originally from a town near Tripoli. She mostly lived abroad during her childhood, though she recalls significant periods when she experienced the 1975–1990 war.

We walked down Hamra Street, busy with people but not so jammed with cars as one would usually expect. We passed the popular fast food restaurant, *malek el-baṭāṭa* (King of Potatoes), and crossed the cobblestone street to our destination. There, we ordered our food. As we sat lazily at the bar, waiting for our food to arrive, we got into what would be one of our many sad and fervent conversations about war, its future possibilities, and our past memories of it. Although we did not begin by defining "war" (*ḥarb*), we understood the grammar of our conversation about it in the context of the July 2006 war. It was certainly not an abstract talk of war, for we were living and hearing it. This was the case in many of my conversations with interlocutors: even

though we had an idea what war was when we spoke about it, and although
it was a concept that had and continues to have meaning for people, the term
always seemed to remain somewhat porously defined, contested, ambiguous,
and incommensurable in our attempts to represent it. This grayness was reflected in my experiences asking people directly to explain or define war and
in their inability to produce clear limits and definitions. Simply to understand
the grammar of such conversations about war did not resolve war's ambiguities, even as it brought meaning and form to the concept. In this book,
through conversations and debates, I will reflect on the ambiguities of political violence that complicate any possibility of producing a fixed definition of
war.[2]

Dima and I sat at the bar waiting for our burgers, Dima sipping water
and I lemonade. At one point, she turned to me in her intense and heartfelt
voice and said, in English: "Our lives are like superhero comic strips. You
know how in the comics when there is fighting going on, oftentimes the next
slide says 'In the meanwhile.' Well, that's us. We are 'In the meanwhile'; we
live 'In the meanwhile'." While the war went on above and around us, while
the displaced tended to their lives, "in the meanwhile" we ate at Roadster,
had meetings, went out for a drink, worked on humanitarian relief operations, and conducted our everyday lives the way we saw fit.

If "in the meanwhile" was a way people lived through conflict, for me it
became a lens through which to think about social life amid political violence
and the protracted nature of conflict that has existed in Lebanon. Dima, it
seems, meant to say that in the interstices of war, people still live their lives
and take their breaks; indeed, war can intensify social life, as she later told me.
I, too, lived my life during this war. I spent days and nights in conversations
and debates with family, I watched the war live on TV, and I enjoyed nights of
drinking with new friends. In this war, I also found time to love. War, whatever war, does not necessarily erase either daily actions or emotions, and it
certainly does not erase feelings of love. War re-shifts and reconfigures, but its
processes are not very good at total erasure. It tries, but it cannot destroy our
human emotions or our connections to the techniques of everyday life that
came before the war—and are transferred down generationally.

So people continue to live in the meanwhile of war in ways that can sus-
tain a sense of everyday normalcy, and that may resemble, if only ever so
slightly, the way life was lived prior to a given outbreak of war. This meanwhile suggests a temporary state between two longer periods before and
after, and as an informant once told the journalist Anthony Shadid, the solu-

tions to war themselves "amount to a meanwhile" (Shadid 2007). This is not surprising if we are to consider that people live these solutions—these meanwhiles—as temporary periods within a longer war.

Death, like life, goes on as well. I mentioned to a friend and filmmaker, days after the end of the July War in mid-August, about the passing away of a friend's father. He reflected back that many forget people die from non-combat-related deaths during a war. "Life goes on," he concluded, and so does death. He made me think of the many events and emotions, too many to recount, that go on in their seemingly normal trajectory in times of war: new life, death, laughter, happiness, and sadness. All this goes on, affected in huge ways by the war, while people try to maintain normalcy. Cancer still kills in war; it doesn't wait, nor does a heart attack, old age, or a car accident.[3] Death goes on in its taking of lives away from the bombs and the fighting in South Lebanon.[4] War is, after all, as much a private affair as it is public and collective,[5] and we live it through our own personal experiences as much as through the public narrative.

Thinking about life "in the meanwhile" came around the time that I also began to think about the anticipation of political violence. While spending one night in military jail, I had begun to think about anticipation as an affective site of research, and one where political power operates. I had been picked up during the 2006 war by the Lebanese army for taking pictures too close to a military base, and they suspected me of spying for Israel upon finding out that I had been in Palestine only a few days before.[6] During that night in prison, I was told that other convicts had been evacuated because military locations were in danger of being bombed by the Israelis. I spent the night in my cell, hearing the bombs in the distance, and wondering if the next would hit my cell. Fear struck me as I anticipated the bombs and heard the explosions, followed by the momentary calm of knowing this time my location was not the target. I was exhausted, and soon, despite the fear, I fell asleep on the humid ground, separated from it by a thin, hard, rancid mat. Something about the bombings made them both absent (over there) and present through their sounds and the potential to annihilate me at any moment, an absent presence that I managed to acquaint myself with enough to sleep through much of the night. That night, I felt myself as living "In the meanwhile" and in "anticipation of political violence." Later, this became an axis to question and critique forms of absent present political violence, and to think about the little nooks and crannies present in war that would bring forth a deeper understanding of people's lives in such unstable times, and that would deconstruct a homogeneous idea of what war is and isn't.

This absent presence suggests there is an act of recollection of past violence and imagination of future violence,[7] and a sense of people living in between past and future violence, remembering one, anticipating the other. Whereas the physicality and perpetration of war is often felt as absent—or in the past or future—talk of war, imagining it, sensing it, being tense and frustrated by it, feeling despair, resignation, fear, and hope by it, these are some of the ways that war remains constantly present (conceptually and not necessarily physically) as a structuring force in social life. In this way, recalling Carl Schmitt, war is solidified as a crucial component of politics, and undergirding political life for people in Lebanon. Yet, unlike Schmitt or even Thomas Hobbes, this is not an ontological statement about the relation between war and politics but rather a statement that war (like peace or peacemaking) is one byproduct of politics, and once war emerges as a possibility, politics becomes the mechanism by which to intensify or deescalate war. Contrary to Hobbes, politics (and the Leviathan) is not what keeps the threat of war at bay, but actually, following Michel Foucault, politics establishes and ensures the continuation of the structures and relations of power embedded in war (Foucault 1997).

The July 2006 war lasted thirty-three days. For most of the time after that and during my fieldwork, the bombings, gunfire, and armed confrontations between political groups were seemingly absent. In such times, I was struck by people's preoccupation with the idea that a war, in its vaguely defined terms, was on the horizon.[8] El-ḥarb jāye (the war is coming) or raḥ tūlaʿ el-ḥarb (the war is going to ignite), and their various derivatives, were phrases I would regularly hear in a family dining room, around a restaurant table, or at a local political party office. It is the sentiments behind such phrases that affect everyday life in Lebanon, making past and future war very much lived in the present, that I investigate in this book.

In Part I, I look at the anticipation of political violence and how it could be sensed in the meanwhile of physical conflict as well as in its absence. What kind of strategies do people employ in order to live in this meanwhile? How were people in Lebanon living and experiencing the aftermath and in-betweens of war, assassinations, bombings, and the various other acts and events often grouped together as political violence?[9] How could one rethink this other than in terms of resilience, a recurring theme that seemed to produce forms of Lebanese exceptionalism (that somehow Lebanese were uniquely resilient for the way they conducted their lives during and after war)? People were living in the midst of armed conflict or in the shadow of threats that war might ignite, and I wanted to foreground their experiences. It is one objective of this book, then, to explore how people live in this midst, "in the meanwhile," of political conflict and instability, and to do so in a way that does not totalize and sensationalize the experience of violence, or make violence and coping with it the only concern of people in a conflict zone (Lubkemann 2008).[10]

Moreover, I ask how society is reconfigured in periods of political violence and subsequent calm, and how the possibility of future war inscribes recollections of past civil conflicts into everyday life. Such experiences lead me to study political violence through its "practices of anticipation" to better understand how the memory or expectation of impending political violence shapes social interactions and political relationships with the state. By practices, I mean mundane acts, gestures, conversations, psychological states, and interactions. A focus on practices of anticipation exposes ironies, contradictions, and political antagonisms present in the spaces of daily life.

Memory emerges as another fundamental part of this story and is the focus of Part II. The anticipation of political violence cannot be extricated from recollections of past war, and we should see the passage from past to future in Lebanon as a seamless duration where recollection and anticipation are simultaneous processes that meld into each other (Bergson, 1946). The flow of memory between past and future, how people experience this, and what they do with it is crucial to our understanding of how political violence is experienced, especially in its invisible forms. In Part II, I am especially concerned with how people in Lebanon consciously forget (tanāsī) past war, how their spontaneously lived memory works as a strategy for dealing with everyday life, and how this memory connects the past to the future.[11]

No Victor, No Vanquished

To a large extent, the politics of "No Victor, No Vanquished" (lā ghāleb, lā maghlūb),[12] which was first invoked by former prime minister Saeb Salam after the 1958 civil war,[13] forms the undercurrent for this book. In its basic form, and reemphasized after every conflict, this politics implies that no political party or sect in Lebanon can eliminate any other party or sect, and that all political groupings must be represented in the political system. This is to ensure *al-'aysh al-mushtarak* (coexistence) and *al-waḥda al-waṭaniyya* (national unity), and to preserve Lebanon as a place that is tolerant of diverse religions (*al-tasāmuḥ bayn al-adyān*). The sense that no winners or losers emerge from any single conflict contributes to the idea that causes remain unresolved. I argue that this lack of resolution practically guarantees that past political violence remains a central concern in the present and facilitates the feeling of its reemergence in the future.

The politics of "No Victor, No Vanquished" and its implications on life in Lebanon have not been seriously interrogated or analyzed. Some have taken this policy as promoting a state-sponsored politics of forgetting, but like Volk (2010), I call for us to think of this policy as one way "culturally plural societies may work toward reconciliation after periods of violence" (2010:23). Here, political elites lead the process of reconciliation and can "publically appropriate, narrate, and circulate violent pasts for the benefit of present and future generation" (23). Volk pushes us to question the meaning and process behind this coming together of political elites. In this book, I consider the everyday life that is set into motion by this type of supposed elite reconciliation process, and the way such a "No Victor, No Vanquished" politics can facilitate the melding of past and future violence in the present.

Robert Meister describes a relation to past war when he says that evil in the age of human rights is no longer understood "to be a system of social injustice that can have ongoing structural effects, even after the structure is dismantled. Rather, evil is described as a time of cyclical violence that is past—or can be put in the past by defining the present as another time in which the evil is remembered rather than repeated" (2012: 37). In Lebanon, there has been an attempt to think of war in a similar way, as something in the past, without ongoing structural effects, and should be remembered as past so as not to be repeated in the future. The problem is that it is not past: not physically as its presence is felt continually, nor in the structural outcomes as they manifest persistently in the present.

To a large extent, the discourse and actions of political elites, in advocating a consensual politics represented in "No Victor, No Vanquished," and in forgiving their wartime opponents for their supposed crimes, are working in the spirit of liberal transitional justice, which is primarily concerned with whether the demands of victims will "return society to the logic of revolution and civil war" (29) or bring society to civil peace. This reconciliation among the political elite, a "justice-as-reconciliation," is a process whereby the rest of society is asked to reconcile with continuing inequality as a morally acceptable alternative in the aftermath of violence. In this justice-as-reconciliation, the ultimate fear is the idea that distributive justice will lead to a retributive component in societies emerging from (or still embedded within) protracted conflict, and the process of transition "presents itself as a period of grace in which redistributive claims in the name of victims are indefinitely deferred" (29). In this way, through the power-sharing function of a policy of "No Victor, No Vanquished," violence is averted in favor of *al-silm al-ahlī* (civil peace). The politics of fear that emerges leads to a politics of compromise. It is an essentially liberal politics motivated by a Hobbesian project of keeping violence at bay, whereby politicians seek ways to prevent the always (according to them) inevitable war that will destroy the country, instead of practicing an ethical politics of seeking good for victims.[14]

In Lebanon, this Hobbesian view dominates how politics is perceived. This produces a kind of zero-sum game where politicians announce that any act destabilizing the status quo, their power, or the current structure of power sharing embodied in the policy of "No Victor, No Vanquished," will inevitably produce war, thereby, in one and the same breath, reminding people of the devastation of past war and the possibility of a future one. Thus, society is faced with an ultimatum: either it accepts the compromise where past perpetrators are given amnesty or it faces war (or threat of war). However, rather than this zero-sum game, it might be more effective to think of politics as a dialectic between threat and mediation (Caton 2006). Processes of mediation and negotiation are always taking place alongside possible threats of war, but it is when these processes lose intensity that the possibility for political violence might appear. This differs from the Hobbesian view in that it is political mediation, negotiation, and forms of diplomacy that, when they lose intensity, produce the conditions for and relations of power embedded in war. Rather than war driving politics, it is the compromise of the beneficiaries of war that drives politics, and any threat to this compromise is said to bring about war, which these beneficiaries (politicians), in any case, would be the ones to organize, fund, and implement.

As we will see in later chapters, civil society in Lebanon has called for the implementation of techniques of transitional justice like developing memorials and instituting truth commissions. These techniques are not a panacea for keeping war in the past, but in fact can work to entrench the status quo of beneficiaries of past war and injustice. Meister tells us that these techniques "aim to convince beneficiaries that their ongoing advantages will not be denounced as continuations or revivals of past injustice. When such techniques succeed, passive beneficiaries of the old order will join with former victims in opposing a return to the politics of fear itself—their new common enemy." The potential result is to assure beneficiaries of past oppression that they will be permitted to keep the unjustly reaped fruits they currently enjoy (Meister 2012: 31). Indeed, few would argue that this was not the result of the "transitional" process in Lebanon, where former warlords turned into politicians. Telling, too, is that civil society continues to advocate for these transitional techniques by addressing their grievances to the beneficiaries themselves (former militia leaders and politicians for example); if only the beneficiaries would institute some of these processes, the logic seems to go, the country would be saved and the beneficiaries redeemed. The beneficiaries are only too willing to oblige so long as it does not threaten their benefits. Of course, this threat happens to be in most cases, at which point one can usually hear calls from politicians to stand down on the basis of the preservation of civil peace (*al-silm al-ahli*).

It is my contention that the constant anticipation and recollection of political violence, and living in the perpetual coming crisis, are a result and reinscription of this politics of "No Victor, No Vanquished." In a sense, this is a top-down use of the discourse of human rights, where the political leadership speaks in the name of tolerance, coexistence, and both individual and group rights. In describing the lives and experiences of people anticipating and recollecting political violence, this book offers a critique of such politics. What processes of accountability do a politics of compromise make absent? How is this absence of accountability translated into people's lives, experiences, and conversations? And what are we asking people to live with when we call on them to subscribe to a discourse of tolerance in light of such a politics of compromise at the leadership level?

Between the two parts of this book, in exploring the way people live in an environment of constant anticipation and recollection of political violence, I hope to show the urgency and necessity for a new politics that would be able to reflect the moral imperatives of protecting minorities with the practical implications of building a state for *all its residents*. Must people in Lebanon remain captive to a politics of "No Victor, No Vanquished" as the only model for sustaining political life?

An Approach to Political Violence and the State

When thinking about political violence, there is often a tendency to be more attentive to its visible forms, where it is physically and publicly present. I took another approach, thinking about the invisible forms of political violence that usually go unnoticed. A good example of this kind of fetishism with the physical presence of violence can be seen in perceptions of the public spectacle of the death penalty as having been more violent than when the spectacle transitioned to a private and secretive matter, where the prisoner dies in front of a few chosen witnesses and is even stunned so as to feel less pain (Foucault 1979). Such absenting of violence from public life does not eradicate it, although it may feel that way for many people. Similarly, the so-called end of war with the signing of peace agreements is meant to send a message to a population that violence, and evil, is past. My project comes as a critique to this, and to call on us to question the way political violence continues to structure our daily lives in supposed peacetime.[15]

Since the founding of the state, but more pronounced since the 1970s, people in Lebanon have witnessed various wars and occupations. Political parties have taken up heavy and light arms to battle each other for internal political control and to combat invading armies to liberate their communities (this history is taken up in Chapter 2). The founding of the modern state is implicated in this political violence; thus, the state is constantly present in this book as a subtext. It serves as the backdrop for which many negotiations and frustrations, debates and experiences take place, and as a central focus in the enactment of violence. The Lebanese state is perhaps best defined "as the sum of communal and political party leaders using national and local institutions, networks and resources, to provide and facilitate access to public services, secure people's dignity, and act as power brokers and protectors for their constituencies" (Hermez 2015). In this state, the Zu'ama, or communal leaders, play a large role and manipulate the functions, institutions, power, and meaning of the state, and use it to advance their clientalist power.[16] During my fieldwork, the state was caught up between those that sought a primarily pro-American neoliberal state and those that called for a supposedly anti-imperial state that rejected American-controlled globalization (it was not always clear with the latter if it would also follow a neoliberal path or not). This, at least, and in a nutshell, was the dominant discourse.[17]

The Lebanese state was, and continues to be, perennially susceptible to fallout from regional instabilities as Israel, Syria, and global powers take advantage of internal Lebanese rivalries and conflicts of allegiance. Within the modern international state system, old communal and feudal structures remain entrenched, though drastically changed. Here, personal and communal priorities have become inflected with concerns raised by the structures of international diplomacy and modern bureaucratic state mechanisms. Making claims about the state in Lebanon must then be done from within such contexts.[18]

Like war, which is often unclearly defined, violence, too, is fraught with deep ambiguities—in what it is, where it is, and how it is experienced and lived. These ambiguities of violence are another thread that connects this book together. Not just the meaning and experiences violence carries, but the term itself is ambiguous, and is used to represent a wide range of experiences in everyday life. These experiences get folded under the category of violence, but the category is felt and experienced as profoundly subjective so that it hardly means anything (analytically or otherwise) to remark that people experience violence. They see an explosion; they hear bombs or gunshots; they smell corpses. The social scientist tries to make sense of these experiences and the ambiguous meanings they produce by subsuming them under the category of violence. Yet, the category of ʿunf (violence) is itself not so prevalent in daily conversations and usage in the field. People have other words they use for violence, such as qatl (killing), damār (destruction), ḥarb (war), qaṣf (bombing), and this may suggest that they are more descriptive in the way they remember and converse about the phenomena included under the term violence.

Violence is brought to life, made tangible and experiential, when one begins to specify what it is and define its content by exploring specific acts, practices, experiences, impacts, and behaviors. I am left troubled by the category, as I believe it obfuscates the ability to understand people's lived reality and unique experiences of war, and obscures an already ambiguous set of experiences. It is muddied precisely because it has come to signify such a diverse set of practices and experiences that have filled it to the point of emptiness. I say this to argue that we may have to rethink the very notion of an abstract ethnography of violence as a discrete body of thought. What I found in the field was that people were constantly grouping together different acts of political violence so that what they experienced as a series of bombings or a series of armed confrontations, was categorized by them as war, battles, or "the events" (al-aḥdāth). And essentially, part of studying and understanding

the meaning of these acts was to get into debates with people over their categorization and naming. So long as I, the researcher, used the catchall term
of violence to group these acts and experiences together, and constantly tried
to make them fit into a more universal concept, I would find myself perpetually missing the specificities of given situations. Ironically, the more I focused
on violence as a general category to encompass all the acts my interlocutors
experienced, remembered, and communicated to me, the more obscure violence became and the less I felt I could understand its influence and meaning
in social life.

Thus, I have tried my best to begin my points of inquiry with a set of
specific terms picked up from conversations in the field. In my case, this has
meant, to some extent, doing away with the word "violence" as a category of
general investigation and to think of "war" (ḥarb)—its diverse implements,
outcomes, feelings, and material effects—real and imagined, as a local category that people invest with meaning and emotion. Certainly, what can be
said about violence can be applied to the similarly porous and ambiguous
term "war," but I prefer the latter because despite its complex meaning and
referents, it remained a prevalent term in conversations in the field.

Whenever I do speak of violence in the abstract, I use it as a synonym for
political violence, which I further define as subjective and physical, and incor-
porating those actions that take on a political meaning at a level higher than
the neighborhood (ḥay) or village (dayʿa).[19] I do understand, however, that
shearing off violence from the political is impossible, and like Jeganathan, I
believe that "what counts as violence, and what does not, its very emergence
and the location of that emergence, and then given its emergence the texture
and quality of the category itself, can only be known with and through the
politics that constitute it" (Jeganathan 1997: 222). Still, it is important to
note that my reference to political violence does not include family feuds and
blood revenge, even though these could have political implications in the
country. Rather, I have in mind such things as war, assassinations, bombings, and other forms of armed conflict that take place at the level of the state
and between political parties, and that people in Lebanon, and around me,
consider as violence of a political nature.[20] My concern is with everyday life in
the midst of these forms of violence and conflict, and how the event and the
ordinary might be reconceptualized to move away from thinking purely in
terms of ruptures, suspensions, and interruptions of conflict.[21]

The Event and the Ordinary

In her book, *Life and Words*, Veena Das suggests "the event [violence, Indian Partition] attaches itself with its tentacles into everyday life and folds itself into the recesses of the ordinary" (2007: 1). For Das, Indian Partition serves as an unambiguous, momentous, and politically violent event that her inter-locutors struggle with, and that folds into the ordinary. However, in my field site, there is a sense that political violence is not necessarily eventful, nor does it always constitute an event in itself. Moreover, there is no singular event, like Indian Partition, that catalyzes a national psyche in some extraordinary way. People may talk about *al-aḥdāth* (the events) to refer to the fifteen-year period of war between 1975 and 1990, but it is not viewed as one event, and people contest which episodes in this period are most important. So, while Das makes a powerful point about the relationship between violence and the ordinary, the context of Lebanon opens a space for me to think further about the ambiguity that often constitutes the division between the event and the ordinary.

One cannot, of course, deny the possibility of the "event," even if at times it is unclear how it might be constituted. There are moments, experi-ences, and actions that happen that impact our lives in serious and drastic ways. An "event" makes the idea of the "before" and "after" possible. There are incidents that happen in our lives that create a separation between the "before" and "after," and whether we call this separation a rupture, break, or fissure is unimportant; what matters is that life before and after is no longer the same following such moments. For example, my interlocutors spoke of how the July 2006 war changed our lives, created new friendships, tested old ones, and altered the way we lived in Lebanon before and after the war. As this shows, events do not have to occur over the span of a few moments or a day, they can occur over a longer span of time—a month or a year.

Other incidents are more instant. The Sabra and Chatilla massacre,[22] Black Saturday,[23] and the Damour massacre[24] are examples of happenings that occurred over a day or several days and signify events for the communi-ties and people who experienced them, and for the nation that remembers them and continues to reference these events. Bombings of various kinds would also have an eventful impact for the families who lost loved ones. There is a clear material difference, for example, between my day to day, with all its moments and mundane happenings, the day one's child is born, the day one loses a loved one, or the day one's house is demolished by military orders. But what constitutes this difference? Why, whether they occur over days, months, or years, do we call some occurrences "mundane" and others an "event," or eventful? In part, borrowing from Alain Badiou, it is the intensification of "subjective energy" (emotions, meanings, people's desires, and memories, to name a few) that socially constructs events, turning them from mundane to eventful (Badiou 2012). While certain happenings involve real measurable material loss, what makes them events is that they intensify subjective energies. Thus, insofar as loss will almost always intensify emotions, experiences, and senses, it becomes inseparable from our understanding of the category of the event, and makes certain circumstances instantly felt as eventful. In other cases, however, actions, incidents, and experiences are felt as continuations and meld the before and after.[25] They are constituted as events in hindsight as they gain intensity of what Badiou calls "subjective energy"—which, in some cases, can be the result of enough accumulated moments (like a series of bombings or political maneuvers), felt or remembered as related, that consolidate into a grand moment or event. In this way, what was thought to be mundane can become eventful, and what may have felt as an event in the moment may lose intensity and become uneventful. The event itself is never fixed. It is a precarious category threatening to become mundane.

Intensities of Political Violences: Between War and the Normal

People who live through various forms of wartime and its aftermaths come to experience political violence as a type of normality. This leads to a common ambivalence as to what is considered the normal by which people measure their present up against (Maček 2009). My interlocutors, if heard carefully, were always articulating this tension, confusion, and ambiguity. They often held multiple standards of normalcy in mind at the same time, and felt their experiences in ways that were simultaneously normal and incomprehensible (or abnormal). In this way, their experience with violence cannot automatically make them objects for the representation of violence, for they are themselves struggling with the representation of their own world, and positioned both inside and outside the violence that supposedly makes them its objects.

With my interlocutors, I grappled with these tensions, much as Ivana Maček (2009) did in Sarajevo. What was the normal to which they often measured their current state against? How did the normal get intertwined with forms of violence? Important here is that local categories don't always help. They should not be mistaken for a bible, for they are themselves unfixed and shifting. One may gather a certain kind of knowledge or meaning in a category in one instance, and then learn how it is contradicted in another. The question of the "normal" is a great example of this. People use the terms *ʿādī* or *ṭabīʿī* (normal) to mean various things. Sometimes, people can be heard complaining that their situation is not normal, nor is the sense of war on the horizon. At other times, they are clear that their situation has become normal (or at least normalized), and they go about their lives as though everything were so. A friend's cousin, on vacation after having emigrated from the country, once told me about how the sandbag barricades (*mitrās*) in her building's entranceway had become normal and she found it weird when they were finally removed after the war was supposedly declared over. She spoke of the war as normal and that it was out of the ordinary to live without the sandbags. Yet, local and global meanings intersect and bind together to complicate a pure understanding of a local category, and this is no better witnessed than in ideas of the "normal."

Questions of the "normal" continued to haunt many of my interlocutors and me for the entire period of my fieldwork and through this writing. There always seemed to be a discrepancy between, on one hand, what people believed about the "normal"—they had complex analyses about its fluidity and its meaninglessness as a category in the changing contexts of everyday life—and on the other hand, how they produced the idea of the "normal," and reinscribed its discourse by setting it up against an ambiguously defined conflict that was then imagined as "abnormal." The "normal" was something "out there" that people aspired to, even as the present situation, "right here," was itself admittedly normal.

One possibility to untangle the normal is in the subtle difference between the normal (*ʿādī* or *ṭabīʿī*) and the normalized—or what has become normal—expressed as *ṣār ʿādī* or *ṣār ṭabīʿī* (literally, "became normal"). This latter construction (*ṣār*—became) assumes a separation between what is "normal" and what is political violence, in that political violence is in need of a process of becoming normal (a process of normalization) in order to assert its normality. "In the meanwhile" of war was such a period where this process of war "becoming normal" took place, and where the absence of violence in a person's everyday life was actually caught up with its presence. In this period, even though violence may be absent by not necessarily seeing or hearing a bomb, it was visible in personally "knowing" the bomb was falling, and it was felt intersubjectively and caught up in people's senses (Staudigl 2013). The time of the meanwhile is meant to be temporary and fleeting, a time betwixt and between two wars or two moments of political violence. Yet, the meanwhile can itself become the norm as waiting for war, rather than war itself, becomes the permanent situation, and ongoing acts of political *violences* are rendered invisible.

Living in the meanwhile can refer to two different time periods. The first can be said to be "in the time between two wars," where a peace agreement is said to have ended the first war and the second has yet to begin. This is the time of normalcy and making life normal. At this point the second war is not an actuality, just an anticipated inevitability. The second period is "in the time of war," where one lives between one bombing or act of political violence and the next. This period of living in the meanwhile can also be characterized as "making life normal," but it is lived differently from the previous period in that there is no illusion of actual normalcy. In this time of war, living in the meanwhile can be a way of coping, where the meanwhile serves as a liminal moment—for example, in the fresh breath one takes knowing one is alive in the reprieve between hearing one bomb and the next.

I want to suggest that in contexts of protracted conflict, as in Lebanon, we are always already embedded in political *violences* in such a way that neither the ordinary/normal nor political violence has any meaning without the other. People are embedded in a plurality and diversity of violence, which also speaks to its ambiguity. I am not collapsing violence and the ordinary here. The key to avoid this is in the plurality—*violences*—where people are experiencing all kinds of emotions and are subjected to various material realities. The key is also in the idea that political violence is not a homogeneous event experienced in homogeneous time, and impacting everyone in similar, simultaneous, or chronological and clear ways. By suggesting that there are always already political violences of sorts, I am not saying that war or political violence is totalizing, or that it consumes everyone. Rather, I am suggesting that this means we cannot talk about the absence and presence of violence, the normal, or the ordinary. Instead, violence lurks in invisible realms, and when it becomes visible, with barely a moment's notice, the ordinary becomes defined in and through it. And, more important, war and political violence can be visible in the ordinary, or seemingly normal, in ways people don't always want to vocally admit.

Thus, in the protracted conflict space of Lebanon it did not seem useful to focus on the distinctions between violence and the normal, or the ordinary and violence. Nor was understanding the impact and embodiment of violence in everyday life necessarily a matter of drawing a line from the event to the ordinary, or vice versa, or about the simple continuity of political violence. Rather, my approach was to think about political violence as a question of scaling and intensity. We might, then, begin to think in terms of intensities of conflict or even "intensities of political violences," as that which is always being enacted in social life. What is eventful and what is life shattering are matters of scale and intensity, and for that reason violence is further open to ambiguities.

Scale is rather straightforward. However, by intensity I mean the emotional and experiential intensity of political violence as it is felt viscerally. In some cases, one's distance—whether in space or time—from an event such as a bombing or armed combat might define or determine one's intense relation to violence. At other times, the intense relation might be determined in the way a person relates to those who are being targeted, or how one understands oppression, or how much a person would rather ignore politics in favor of a capitalist consumerist culture—concerned with going out to the newest club, café, or shopping center.[26]

The "intensities of political violences" refer to the differing ways people feel, experience, and locate themselves in a particular violent event. The intensification, to borrow from Sara Ahmed, is how political violence materializes and takes shape, how it is embodied, and how its borders and surfaces are produced and made visible for the people who are in its midst (2004: 24). A theory of political violence must take into account the way these intensities are felt and received, experienced and embodied. Such a theory can also shift our thinking about violence as being either absent or present, to considering intensities of presence and thinking in terms of the visible or invisible.[27]

We are in the realm of affect here.[28] Affects can escape us. As potentialities they are often beyond the grasp of easy interpretation, and in their fluid intensities they become difficult to categorize. To say that conflict is delimited through intensity is to remark on the way both territory and time are felt and folded to bring us closer to or farther from events (Massumi 2002: 15). Massumi writes that a "matter-of-factness dampens intensity" (25). People are able to imagine themselves out of a conflict through appearances of normality and matter-of-factness, and this is especially easier when physical destruction is either absent or made invisible to the subject. The normal mutes intensity and masks conflict. In this way, what researchers, journalists, military strategists, combatants, and civilians call the frontlines can be complicated. These lines are constructed and are lived through intensity. The anticipation and recollection of political violence become other markers of this intensity, as they persistently keep past and future war accessible.

A Phenomenological Journey

Traversing through the chapters, I want to take the reader on a kind of phenomenological journey to encounter everyday experiences and the way they lend themselves to thinking about the intensities of political violence, both visible and invisible. This book, therefore, does not follow people, or even a concept. It does not follow war or political violence, or even the object of anticipation. Rather, I follow the conversations and experiences of people as they appear to me in everyday life,[29] and it is in this sense that my project can be said to be phenomenological.

Pursuing a phenomenological knowledge is to consider all aspects of a given experience from various perspectives so that one accounts for the spontaneous ways of acting in response to a given situation (involving violence in this case), as well as to the order of actions, and the response and views of interlocutors to these actions (Hammoudi 2009: 248). Phenomenology, as it was understood by Maurice Merleau-Ponty, is an understanding of the lived world, embodied, and coming before the construction of things as objects of pure knowledge. As such, for Merleau-Ponty, the body is the source of perception and from where social relationships with others arise. Merleau-Ponty uses the metaphor of a football field to show how a field of play constantly shifts and is modified as a result of the changes in players and their shifts in perspectives, so that the same playing field is reconfigured as players and audiences change and move. In order to grasp this field seriously, and in order to think about specific forms of political violence phenomenologically, we need to think more carefully about what Hammoudi calls "communicative configurations" (2009: 211). This approach entails "sustained presence and prolonged interlocution with people," which would "help us produce—in discussion and argument with them—a claim to truthful knowledge, knowledge on which we can rely for an understanding of the current transformation of cultures and societies" (245). This entails an attention to the inconsistencies, contradictions, complexities, relationships, and other details in the lives of our interlocutors, who resist simple correlations we might try to make as we write in their absence.

By theorizing the encounters, gestures, conversations, deep discussions, and experiences that I had in the field about political violences, I capture the moments of contact in Merleau-Ponty's "playing field," those instances we, as audience, might miss as we watch from the stands or through the camera's lens. The winks, the taunting or friendly conversations that occur on the field and off camera, or as the ball is dribbled, are the spirit of what I hope to capture—the "communicative configurations" as I understand them.

The Pub Brawl

Let me illustrate with a brief example how one would begin to think phenomenologically about an experience. This episode also lends itself nicely to thinking of the gendering of political violence. In September 2008, I went to a pub with Zuzu, Basil, and Basil's wife Josiane, as we had been doing regularly for a few months. The two men were former fighters with the Phalange Party and Lebanese Forces, respectively; Josiane was a school teacher. The night got off to a good start, and by 1:00 a.m., Zuzu and Basil had drunk a good amount of whiskey. The pub was quite empty. There was a live singer and his keyboardist playing Arabic music. Other than our table of six located close to the band, there were two tables of Zuzu's friends and a couple we did not know at the other end of the pub. Zuzu's sister Mariana was working as hostess and three of his brothers and a sister had joined us at our table that night. The owner of the pub was a friend of my interlocutors. Everyone in the pub was a supporter of the Lebanese Forces (LF) except for the couple no one knew, who supported the Free Patriotic Movement (FPM), a rival Christian political party with differing political opinions and positions.[30]

At one point in the night, the singer got carried away and while singing, screamed in Arabic, "I dedicate this song to the beautiful Lebanese Forces." Everyone clapped and cheered, which encouraged the singer to repeat this phrase a few more times over the next minutes.

Unbeknown to me at the time, the couple, a man and a woman, were beginning to get angry and upset, and were slowly becoming vocal about it, complaining to the staff. Zuzu had left our table to find out what was going on and returned to tell me the woman was getting aggravated. He continued with some fancy expletives of what he wanted to do to her, and that all she had to do was keep up her attitude and threats.

Eventually, when she had calmed down, the singer repeated his phrase again, which served as a final blow of honor to the two FPM supporters. The woman started screaming and everyone ran to her, Mariana at their helm. Shouts and threats ensued. I understood that the singer *mas bi-karāmta* (had touched or hurt the woman's dignity or *karāme*—here also understood as honor or *sharaf*). Her pride was being attacked and, unless she defended it, she would lose her dignity. Although the woman was not being attacked personally, and no one would have known she was an FPM supporter if she didn't speak up, she seemed to feel that she had to act as defender of the political party, which was being shamed, in turn producing an emotion of shame in her. Her shame pushed her to screams, violence, and revenge.

As the brawl continued, Mariana got involved. She was prevented by her siblings from throwing a punch as the woman tried to throw her own fists in the air. Unable to do so, the woman picked up a glass and threw it. It hit me on the shoulder. The customers were now all ganging up on the woman and her husband. Zuzu, who earlier had threatened he would practically kill her, had jumped into the middle of the fight and was attempting to break everyone up, pulling his siblings away and preventing punches from being thrown. Basil had taken Josiane outside to be away from the fight and was now back inside but watching from a distance. His back and forth speaks to the ambiguity of violence. On one hand, he takes his wife outside in anticipation of violence, but then he returns, perhaps because he doesn't know where this violence will head and can only know by observing it. Or maybe for the chance to inject himself into the conflict, as either fighter or mediator, whichever had a higher chance of turning him into the hero of the conflict.

Zuzu's acts also deserve attention, for they show the complexity of the brawl. Zuzu, who had been threatening to be the first to throw a punch, turned into the mediator and the conflict resolver, trying to regulate the potential for violence, and eventually taking the couple outside and talking sense into them—the former armed militiaman who had taken part in a fair share of brutal acts had become temporary peacemaker, a man of reason, and in the classical sense, a politician attempting to build consensus. The different possible roles Zuzu (and Basil) struggled with are an indication of how violence can produce equivocal and negotiated meanings and positions. As the eldest of his siblings, it is as if Zuzu had to protect the family and be the force of reason among those who were acting spiritedly and emotionally. There was certainly a discourse of honor at work. It was seen in the need for each side to defend the honor of their political party, and in the respect Zuzu and those around him tried to show the man accompanying the screaming woman—who was in turn dismissed in gendered terms as irrational and crazy. Zuzu expressed to me later that he thought it wrong to hit the woman in front of her man; and while this would have shamed the man (much as it would in any bar fight),[31] it does not explain why Zuzu did not fight him instead. This part might be better explained by thinking of the gender dynamics that played out, primarily in the way the women took the lead and escalated the conflict. Zuzu, and the other men in the room, had little control of the escalation and the sequence of actions. And they may have calculated that they could break up the fighting women, whereas if they got involved there would be greater blood and destruction to property, something Zuzu's relative would be responsible for as the pub owner.

In this brawl, we see how the women start, employ, and escalate a politically laden violence; how they force men into this violence on their terms; and how men try, somewhat unsuccessfully, to reassert their control over (and regulate) this violence.[32] Women are not just the objects or subjects of violence, they are not just controlled by it or participate as willing subjects in men's designs, they do not simply have agency in violence in what is otherwise often assumed to be the domain of men (both in Lebanon and broadly in the literature). Rather, they can also lead violence, plan it, establish the ideological foundations for it, anticipate and recollect it, and, perhaps most important, as in this case, show us how the politics of violence, perceived as being in a male-dominated realm, is not necessarily so, and is made and remade through gendered negotiations in which women play a central role.

There were clear contradictions between what was being said by the men around me before and during the quarrel and what actually ensued. The fight amounted to a tug-of-war, with each side, primarily the women, responding to the threats of the other with more threats, rather than a disdain and refusal to respond. Surely the couple knew they had no chance among a group of fifteen to twenty people, but they could not retract their threats and anger now that it had been made public. They must have known, however, as the quarrel grew, that someone would intervene to prevent the escalation from turning into a lynching, as this argument, initially political and in defense of a political party, had more or less transformed to a more personal defense of kin.[33]

This violence *reveals* itself in the moment. It is lived in a glass hitting my shoulder, in the spontaneous contradictions between what is said and what is acted upon, and in the fleeting smiles exchanged between people steps away from the main event. The violence did not appear, but rather became visible through its intensification. It did not begin with the shouting and the punches, perhaps not even with the singer complimenting the LF, but was arguably embedded in the existing forms of political violence oscillating in intensity in the country. It did not simply materialize from thin air, but grew with an almost natural, if quick, intensity that built on political and gender markers present that night.

There is far more one can describe in the sights, sounds, and smells, and the experience of being there, the pain in my shoulder, the screaming woman, the onlookers, and the objects used. In some ways, the fight escapes full description and any attempt to do so would reify what is otherwise an ambiguous and unfixed experience. It is for this reason that I have stressed the contradictions in Zuzu's actions, and that the incident did not end there but continued into my conversations with him about it the next day, and a week later when Basil joked in front of others about how they made me experience a fight. This violence may follow certain structural patterns like being motivated by a sense of pride and feelings of shame and humiliation—all felt most viscerally by the women in this case. But the way these are felt by those present manifests itself in the moment in unexpected ways.

This was a pub brawl. But we already begin to see the complexities and multiple layers that carry into a war between state and nonstate actors, and we begin to observe the workings of an anticipation of political violence in everyday life. We see this, not least, in the loyalties of the participants to political parties that form a basis from which dignity is derived, and where the state of macro-political tensions—locally, regionally, and internationally—becomes the catalyst for the woman's anger and the singer's taunting chants. The brawl took place in 2008, at the height of internal political instability and immediately after the May 2008 battles in Beirut, in which Hizballah and its allies, also allied with the FPM, battled against the Future Movement and the PSP, allies of the LF. There was general fear and expectation that the aggressive political language exchanged between the FPM and LF on a daily basis might result in violent confrontation, and each side was accusing the other of colluding against the state. The woman's defense of the FPM in the face of the ridicule of people, drunk and enjoying their night out, should be seen within this larger context where partygoers become political opponents. The Israeli-Palestinian conflict, the alliances of Syria and Iran, the resistance of Hizballah, and America's strategic designs in the region, to name just a few factors, influenced the participants of this brawl. Through participant observation, ethnographies of violence are able to capture both micro and macro events to understand the way local and global politics play out in everyday life. One way to do this successfully is for these ethnographies to remain deeply phenomenological; in other words, the ethnographer must be attentive to perspectives of knowledge, to experiences, and to dialogic communications and relations with interlocutors.

Lebanon's War: The Problematics of Naming War

Jill Lepore writes, "acts of war generate acts of narration," and every narration needs to be named; "How wars are remembered can be just as important as how they were fought and first described" (1998: x). Indeed, every battle, every war, has a name. For the people affected by the violence, these names can trigger memories; they can also serve as metonyms for entire histories of life, death, oppression, and struggles of everyday life. These names are fundamental to producing a genealogy of specific pasts, and to communicating about past war in the present. The 1975–1990 war in Lebanon has no agreed upon name, and one could argue that the political conflict over past truth begins here, with a lack of common naming of war to begin producing a coherent genealogy of the last half century.

Names are assigned, and the contours of political violence (its beginnings and ends) are defined as war and perceived as an event often only in hindsight. In the moment, people tend to wonder if a specific violent event is *the one* that will begin the war, whereas *the one* usually only becomes determined later. Ascribing war to events of the past is a way to represent that past but says nothing of how that past may have been felt, lived, and experienced at the time. For example, the "events" in Lebanon from 1975 to 1990 have come to be defined as one continuous war commonly known as the "Lebanese Civil War" (al-ḥarb al-ahliya), but they were actually a series of battles, each called a war, that people in Lebanon refer to specifically by name: Two-Year War, 100 Days War, War of Elimination, and so forth. The way people have come to reference each battle during the fifteen years signals that war was not lived and experienced homogeneously throughout. Another example is how April 13, 1975, has become the official date for the beginning of this war, even though major acts of political violence began months, if not years, before.[34] In fact, it may very well make more sense, as a way to express the ambiguity and diversity of moments and experiences in those years, that this period has come to be collectively known as al-aḥdāth (the "Events") in Lebanese parlance.

The different names for the same war allow me to see variability in the way people experienced the past and anticipate the future. The way war is named and referenced also highlights the fact that while war was continuous, political violence was often invisible, and that because of this invisibility, even in war, much of society lives its everyday, even enjoys it, in anticipation of political violence to come.

Al-ḥarb (war), in a sense, and as written about here, is perhaps more a metaphor for uncertainty rather than having a monolithic definition or bounded meaning. It figures more prominently in common parlance than the word violence (*'unf*) to represent various events and experiences. In many ways, war is often personified as the big bad guy who is blamed for everything, while the people who perpetrate it or politicians who command it are given free passes. War, with no clear definition, becomes the culprit and it is always to come, out there, rarely ever in the here and now. It is perhaps thought of more as a period of time—in the past or future—and less as a practice, process, or ultimately, logic that can be playing out in the present.[35]

An understanding of war becomes differentiated by the various ways and intensities people experience and anticipate it. A coming war can refer to a war with Syria or Israel, or internally between Lebanese political factions, and the conflagration of such a war can itself be perceived variably. In fact, war need not begin in Lebanon for it to become physically present. People also spend time anticipating how war in other parts of the region, and how America's wars in the world may spill over into their daily lives in violent ways.

Although no single name for the years of war has acquired the status of a social fact, "Lebanese Civil War" comes close. However, when speaking in general about the totality of that period (1975–1990), I have decided against using "the Events" or "Lebanese Civil War." The first is too vague and implies a near refusal to acknowledge that there was a war, while the second assumes that the entire period was only a war between Lebanese, and does not take into account the contested meanings of the term "civil war" (Kalyvas 2003). Civil war also obscures the fact that significant aspects of the violence were not war between equal parties, but a counterinsurgency operation by states (including but not limited to Syria and Israel) to root out guerrilla groups (Lebanese and Palestinian) (Khalili 2012: 50). Journalist and politician Ghassan Tueni coined the phrase "the war of others" (*ḥarb al-ākharīn*), but that relinquishes the Lebanese role and complicity in the war (Tueni 1985). For a time, I used the construction "Lebanese Wars," but this implied a type of Lebanese identity, a sort of "made in Lebanon" that denies the foreign component; it also fed into the idea that there were many wars during this period, when in fact they were battles within a larger war narrative.

Thus, in this book I propose *ḥarb lubnān* (Lebanon's war) as an alternative, and in a sense borrow the title from an Al-Jazeera documentary (2001) about the war. My reasoning is that this captures the geographic landscape, acknowledges that people in Lebanon were always involved, but leaves room to recognize the foreign and domestic elements, and considers that, much as in the construct of the "Lebanese Civil War," the entire period was a series of battles in the same ongoing war. This claim is possible because, although battles were ignited for different reasons, the underlying causes throughout the period were constant. The war was about how to share internal political power and how to adopt a posture vis-à-vis the Palestinian cause of liberation. The war was sustained in some form or another so long as one or both of these factors could not be temporarily resolved.

To be sure, to talk about *ḥarb lubnān* among people in Lebanon might raise a confused brow. However, I hold onto it as a way to articulate this project in a way that I find to be far more accurate and expressive than "Lebanese Civil War." Among many interlocutors, neither of these terms would really mean much. People would often ask me, especially if I spoke generally about *al-ḥarb* (the war), which war I was referring to. They would be more exact and speak about specific battles, mostly referring to them as wars, like *ḥarb al-jabal* (the war of the mountains). Formerly armed interlocutors would also reference battles, especially when talking to each other, like a time over drinks with formerly armed Christian men, when I heard about *ma'raket balaunyā* (the battle of Bologna) between the Kataeb and SSNP. For some Kataeb ex-fighters I spoke to, any reference to *al-ḥarb* (the war) was specifically a reference to *ḥarb el-sinteyn* (the Two-Year War between 1975 and 1977), when they claim to have been fighting the Palestinians. This difficulty over naming often made it very hard to identify which period someone was talking about, and which year an incident took place. As Haugbolle says, the period between 1975 and 1990 was "so long that it often fails to make sense as a whole to the people who remember it" (2010: 50). To add to this, I would often be told that there were distinctions between earlier and later wars (55), specifically divided between pre-1982 and post-1982. The distinction within these periods went so far as to lead one ex-communist interlocutor to say that fear was experienced differently in those two periods.

The other point to be made concerns the way people named individual battles. In most cases, names did not include the year a battle or war took

place. The "July War" (*ḥarb tammūz*), for example, follows such a conven-
tion, similar to the naming of many other wars and battles. To the foreigner,
ḥarb tammūz might not be fixed temporally, nor is *ḥarb al-taḥrīr* (War of
Liberation), which took place in 1990, *ḥarb al-ilghāʾ* (War of Elimination) in
1989, *sabʿa ʾayyār* (May 7) in 2008, or even the more ambiguous term of *intifāda* (uprising). However, to those concerned, these names are clear: they
reference specific stories and memories, and situate the particular war within
a national narrative, and sometimes even more narrowly within the narrative
of a specific political party. The reference to the *intifāda* is a case in point.
When one speaks to a former combatant fighting for the Christian Phalange
Party in the 1980s, the *intifāda* can refer to the *intifāda* of Samir Gaegae
against Elie Hobeika and his Tripartite Agreement in 1985,[36] whereas for a
member of the Communist Party, the *intifāda* might refer to the uprising by
the Amal Movement and its counterparts against the army in 1984. In these
references, there is an assumption that the interlocutor, being familiar with
the details of Lebanon's war, knows which conflict is being recalled. I try
throughout to provide the necessary context for the reader to follow the
naming of different battles I reference, but it should be noted that so much
of this knowledge of context, in the field, is assumed by interlocutors as they
converse and interact in everyday life.

Navigating Fieldwork

Doing fieldwork about political violence between bursts of armed conflict is
both tricky and emotionally draining. There came a point when I began to
feel like an "ambulance chaser,"[37] pursuing violence to gather data and analyze
it for research by spending several months in the South after the July 2006
war, then in the North during the war on the Nahr al-Bared Palestinian refugee camp, and, in between, gathering impressions from scenes of explosions
around Beirut. I was consumed by the armed conflicts and assassinations that
it became difficult, at times, to look for deeper meaning.

I began my research in February 2005, spending two weeks in Lebanon
after the assassination of former prime minister Rafiq Hariri, and followed
this by a summer of fieldwork that same year. I returned in the summer of
2006 during the July War with Israel, but did not start formal fieldwork until
the following May, around the beginning of the Nahr al-Bared war. However, this was supplemented, and complicated, by a lifelong personal and

familial connection to Lebanon that provided me with experiences and narratives that predated those I collected during fieldwork.

The question of being local or "native" is actually interesting here because it came up often in the field (Narayan 1993). In August 2006, after the war ended, my Lebanese interlocutors (increasingly becoming my friends) and I went to the South to operate a relief center for refugees returning to their destroyed homes. Initially, we assumed our common national belonging would situate us as insiders in the community in the South, but it was not long before we realized that there were ways of drawing differences. We were not from the South, we were not returning refugees, we had certain privileges, and some of us had lived many years abroad. These were all ways to complicate positions of being inside and outside a community. One had to be attentive to the question of "native to what?" and "inside which community?" Being Lebanese or local versus foreign both had their advantages and disadvantages, and negotiating this was part of a more common struggle over positionality ethnographers often face.

One of the chronic problems I encountered was the home blindness one experiences as a local ethnographer, whereby a lot of what I observed seemed trivial and not worth recording. Home blindness also affected my ability to notice rumors for what they were rather than normal social discourse, or to observe practices of anticipation of war as more than regular social practices. The major concerns with "being native," however, came late in my fieldwork, when it dawned on me that I had rarely ever been asked to meet the families of my interlocutors. It was often assumed that I knew the culture, when in actuality this knowledge was partial. It was also assumed, rightly, that I had my own family to feed me, that I ate more or less the same food, and that Sundays were reserved for family time. Thus interlocutors rarely offered to feed me, to accompany them on family outings, or generally to take care of me. I also never got lessons in basic cultural practices, even though the diversity of practices across religious sects, geography, and class means that I, and other people in Lebanon, certainly do not know or grasp many of them. I assumed this would be different for other researchers who had arrived to Lebanon for the first time and had no familial connections. Yet, a disadvantage here was compensated with advantages elsewhere. Whereas my interlocutors assumed much of my knowledge, and doors to their family homes were less accessible as a result, this same knowledge meant I was privy to deep conversations, and to the steady pace of their lives without their need to slow down and explain or articulate the grammar of their practices.

Most of my research was conducted among three categories of people. The first were those I met through an engagement in political activism that was committed to social justice and the Palestinian cause. These people would later become close friends, and had spent their lives, like me, between Lebanon and other countries. They came from diverse class backgrounds, were of varying religious sects, and had different occupations, such as university professors, filmmakers, doctoral students, NGO workers, and lawyers, to name just a few.

How to deal with their sect, in specific, posed a problem because I didn't want to reinscribe the same sectarian tropes about Lebanon by identifying my interlocutors by sect, as if that was how they always self-identified. Thus, I often approached interlocutors with what one might call sectarian blindness (or a false sense of it), and refused to ask about sect backgrounds.[38] In one case, I am still unsure how my interlocutor identifies, and she refuses to say. In the case of Dima, I never asked, but remember finding myself trying, implicitly and reluctantly, to place her in a religious category, if not by sect. I leaned one way because she spoke French (invoking the sectarian notion "she acted Christian"), and another way because of her association with her boyfriend, whose sect I knew. Six months later, perhaps inevitably, the conversation about sect was brought to center stage when someone asked her about her sect background in front of me and she announced she was Greek Orthodox. After the person left, I turned to her, and with hesitation said, "It's funny, I didn't realize you were Greek Orthodox." I was embarrassed because after all this time, spending almost every day together, it was expected I would have known this.

Dima laughed, "Sami, I'm not Greek Orthodox. I just like to pretend sometimes, and it's none of the person's business. Did you really not know my sect after all this time?" I thought I knew, but always doubted myself and wondered if an opportunity would come up to learn what I never wanted to ask directly because I, too, believed it was not really anyone's business.[39] The episode, however, highlights an anxiety around everyday sectarianism that I wrongly tried to resolve by not making sect an issue.

In this book, the reader will notice that in some cases, especially when interlocutors were otherwise secular, I do not provide the sect as a marker. The problem with my approach, as I reflect on it years later, is that, whether I liked it or not, my interlocutors often identified with their sect, and even when they didn't, their sect (even as a supposedly absent marker of identity) affected where they lived, who their friends were, how they traversed the city, and the politics they subscribed to. Importantly, it also influenced how they spoke to me and what they might tell me. Of course, their sect was not the only factor determining any or all of these things, and often it wasn't even the prevailing factor, but it also shouldn't be written out as I tried so hard to do.[40]

Looking back, I realize I had mistakenly taken the social construction of sectarianism to mean that sect identification and sectarianism didn't exist in reality or shouldn't be an issue. In fact, in a political system that conditioned political power on sectarian identification, it was all but inevitable for people to identify themselves and others along sect lines, and it was necessary for people to be counted as part of a sect in order to negotiate better access to political and social resources. In other words, sectarian identification was very real now that it had been constructed as such (see Chapter 8 for more on this construction). I learned this quickly, but it was always a source of frustration as I tried to play down my sectarian identity, and as I traversed between a secular community of political activists and other interlocutors who prioritized their sectarian identity.

In this first group of interlocutors, there was a stratification by age as well, and people ranged from their late twenties to late forties, which meant that their exposure to Lebanon's war varied from participating in it, to experiencing and remembering firsthand accounts entirely, to experiencing and remembering very little. I also came to connect with the wider networks of these interlocutors, which ultimately allowed me intimate channels through which I could observe everyday life in Beirut. With them, I conducted recorded interviews, attended countless activist meetings, participated in various political and social events, took part in demonstrations, met with political leaders, organized relief efforts, and experienced three wars.

The second category of people were those who, between 1975 and 1990, and then again during battles that took place during my fieldwork, had carried arms for a militia. I spoke with more than fifty such people—men and women from different political parties, sects, and echelons of society. Admittedly, however, my earliest and most solid connections were with male former fighters, and it is they that appear more centrally in this book.

With this group, sect was pervasive and hung over our political conversations like smog over Beirut. My fieldwork with them consisted of recorded interviews, outings with their families, attending political, religious, and social events, engaging in seemingly mundane activities, as well as hanging out at political party offices. Much of my work with them has opened ways of thinking about society and its relation to the past and present. However, since the focus of this book is not on specific people, my research with this group is used to provide further sets of experiences of everyday life thinking about past and future violence, and to further explore and give depth to my analysis. Therefore, as the reader will see, rather than treat them as a separate community, these former fighters enter and exit scenes in this book as other noncombatant interlocutors do.

Finally, the third category included members of my extended family. I used my observations, conversations, and recorded interviews with relatives to supplement my other ethnographic data, and because I could not deny this personal and intimate access I had, and the networks it connected me to. Besides allowing for another insight into social life in Lebanon, my reason to engage family is that it is a kind of paradigmatic one if we look at a list of possible wartime transgressions and traumas that can be inflicted on people (for such a list see Khalaf 2004: 254). My relatives included a number of armed militia members and some who lived on the green line that separated East and West Beirut for much of the war years. They straddle a variety of class backgrounds, being middle, upper-middle, and even upper class if wealth, property, job descriptions, and social connections are considered, and have seen various levels of upward and downward mobility depending on the decade—all this makes class an unfixed and fluid category.

Much of what I know and have experienced that relates to war has come in the form of narratives transmitted to me by relatives over the years, as I visited from abroad during summers. I have been critical of family political opinions and beliefs as far back as the year 2000, when my own political leanings began to form. This allowed for critical engagement during research, but it also meant that relatives may have often watched what they said around me (perhaps unconsciously), or tailored their language, if not thoughts, in an effort to maintain a sense of understanding and civility. My work and accounts with family are, thus, filtered through these politico-ideological critiques and disagreements, something I imagine many in Lebanon will identify with. I engage these accounts precisely because they add an important dimension to my own position as ethnographer and interlocutor, and because my field site deserves to be communicated from all possible angles available to me in order to attain, as Panourgiá writes, the "ever-elusive heteroglossic and polyphonic texts we desire" (Panourgiá 1995: 13).

Together, these three groups inform my use of the category of "people" in this book, as in "people in Lebanon." To be sure, the "people" presumes some coherence and homogeneity in a population where often there is in-commensurability, and where "the people" are in fact diverse, multivocal, gendered, classed, and sectarian. My experience is primarily drawn from and informed by people that ranged the spectrum from lower-middle (some fighters and Palestinian refugees) to upper-middle class (some friends and family); they were mixed in gender and sect, and mostly, but not exclusively, in and around Beirut.[41] My ethnography draws on women and men of various backgrounds to tease out a general sense of how people anticipate, recollect, and live with political violences. However, for the most part, and to some degree, like in the pub brawl, in this book, I take the women and men as "people in Lebanon" to think of them as co-conspirators of political violence, making and remaking it through their mutual acts of anticipation and recollection. As such, the gendered ways in which they participate in and experience this political violence differently is left implicit for the most part, and here there is much room for further exploration.[42]

To understand how I maneuvered my field site, the reader should note that all these interlocutors were somehow tied to Beirut and its suburbs either through work or residence, and my community was, therefore, defined geographically. Even in those times when I was "chasing violence," I did so with my networks from Beirut, who went to the South or North for their professional work, relief work, or out of their own curiosity. I rarely left the city for research without my Beirut interlocutors, so that my knowledge and analysis is informed through their perceptions of Lebanon's centers and peripheries.

I have always wondered how other ethnographers take notes and conduct themselves during fieldwork under extreme conditions of uncertainty. The field site in which I operated was experiencing instability and various forms of political conflict during the years of my research, so I was often not able to take notes or openly carry a notebook when I was talking to people. The situation was too tense and suspicion would run high that it was not only access I was worried about, but also my own safety. It did not help that the U.S. military was hiring anthropologists for its Human Terrain System program,[43] and that during my fieldwork a two-part article was released in one of the Lebanese Arabic daily newspapers on the anthropologist as spy.[44]

I was able, however, to record many conversations, though only in certain activist circles and in formal interview situations. For the most part, once I was home I would write down from memory sequences of events and conversations I had. Sometimes, though rarely, I would sneak away to a bathroom or away from the crowd and jot down notes, though my paranoia of being perceived as insincere, or as a spy, prevented me from doing this on most occasions. The lack of on-the-spot field notes, however, means that the writing process later on has been, in part, a product of my own framing and (mis)understanding (Gilsenan 1996: 58).

The Book That Follows . . .

This book is divided into two parts. The first is primarily future oriented, dealing with questions around the anticipation of violence, how people live with this every day, and the issues it engenders in Lebanon. The second is directed toward the past, trying to think about how people in Lebanon live with the memory of Lebanon's war, and bringing this to bear on both the present and the future. But first, in the next chapter, I write a brief and select history of contemporary events in Lebanon to provide the context in which the book was conceived. The chapter explores the ways past events (assassinations, armed battles, war, and political violence of various kinds) weave into present events (an election) through ongoing encounters and conversations occurring in everyday life—in this case a lunchtime encounter with relatives. Through this process, what is eventful and what is ordinary are blurred, as the ordinary is visible from within the recesses of the event itself. This chapter is meant to have the double purpose of highlighting the local knowledge needed to engage in daily conversations—complete with the ambiguities this knowledge can often produce—as well as showing how the past is very much in the present, more of which will be examined in Part II of the book.

Part I is divided into three chapters. Chapter 3 takes several experiences in and around the Nahr al-Bared war in 2007 to set out the main theoretical argument on the anticipation of violence in Lebanon. I analyze the intersections between violence and the ordinariness of everyday life, as well as the connections between certainty and uncertainty. My claim is that these binaries are not mutually exclusive states of being. In Chapter 4, I extend my analysis to include the vantage point of several periods of violence I witnessed during fieldwork: the 2006 war with Israel, the 2007 war on the Palestinian camp of Nahr al-Bared, the 2008 battles in Beirut, and the period of indiscriminate bombings that overlapped with my fieldwork. Each presents itself with various questions regarding anticipation. This chapter reads as a narrative of a critical part of my time in the field and the intimate experiences I

encountered. It looks closely at the way an anticipation of violence is related
to people's identity and interests, and together with the previous chapter,
forms the main theoretical intervention of this book to understand the concept of anticipating violence. Chapter 5 builds on the previous theory by ex-
amining the way politicians, the media, and people in general (such as artists),
manage and utilize the feeling of anticipation of violence in a way that orders
and controls this anticipation in everyday life. I will discuss the formation of
hegemonic moods and attitudes that arise from a convergence of different
social forces, each trying to make sense of the world and establish a sense of
security for itself. The result is security and insecurity imbricated into a national feeling.

I then turn to an examination of Lebanon's experience with past war in
Part II, also divided into three chapters. Chapter 6 hopes to rescue a meaning
of the past as being lived every day, and memory as spontaneous rather than
needing to be archived and commemorated. The analysis is built on my argument that there was no amnesia in Lebanon after the war, but that people
have continued to remember the war while still living in its midst. I rely here
on the Arabic notion of *tanāsī* to think about active forgetting as an agentive
process that complicates our relationship to past war. This chapter reinforces
previous ones by showing how people deal with their past and present in the
context of protracted conflict. I do this without necessarily creating a causal
or neat trajectory between past, present, and future. In Chapter 7, I continue
with an ethnography of memory and violence in order to elaborate on the
argument of "No Victor, No Vanquished." Here, I highlight a "Human
Rights Discourse" that claims evil must be remembered in the past so that it
does not repeat.[45] Some of my interlocutors, especially former fighters, subscribed to this if only to appease the general public that supposedly believed
it. I argue that memory does not serve as a panacea for staving off armed
conflict, and that we must be more attentive to political processes to resolve
issues that can lead to violence. Chapter 8 takes on the issue of amnesty as
another piece of the debate between memory and violence. Amnesties are
meant to signal reconciliation and a movement forward, and to put past
crimes in the past. Through discussions with interlocutors, I write about how
amnesty in Lebanon has served to entrench the status quo, strengthen sectarian attitudes in the political sphere, and ensure that the past continues and
overlaps with the present to produce the constant anticipation of violence.

Finally, I conclude with a chapter to tie together the two parts of the
book and the different arguments regarding the way past and future violence

impacts social life in Lebanon. In this final chapter I also think of the broader implications for a phenomenological study of violence and the way an anticipation of violence can be thought to bear on other locales and shape our understanding in the wake of political impasses.

In the chapters to follow, the reader will notice a switching back and forth between the ethnographic present and past. I do this deliberately, and borrow from Ana Tsing, who argues that the ethnographic present can exoticize, but at the same time the past tense "suggests not that people 'have' history but that they *are* history, in the colloquial sense" (1993: xv). She explains that "I cannot escape these dilemmas; I can only maneuver within them." And so, like her, I remain most comfortable in inconsistency, finding uses for both "the historical past and the ethnographic present" (xv). This jumping back and forth, at times, is symbolic of the interconnection between past and present in the daily political struggles of people and the way they live the wars of the past in the now. It is also meant to highlight my own political action during my ethnographic fieldwork and the persistence of this action into the present.

Overall, in reading the chapters together, the goal is to deconstruct certain dominant narratives of sociopolitical life circulating among people in Lebanon (among both academics and non-academics). The goal is also to get a sense of how everyday experiences are informed by and inflected with both the anticipation and recollection of political violence. As people in Lebanon go on with their days, as they reflect back on their past, they continue to sense that the war is coming. Political violence is mostly invisible, but it pervades their lives and gathers intensity—and visibility—through their anticipation and recollection of war. How, then, do they get on with their lives?

Chapter 2

War, Politics, and Lunch:
Conversations of Everyday Life

Historians will tell you that the writing of history is a deeply political affair. Where in time one begins, the words one chooses, the events one decides to retell, all these decisions are not neutral matters and are informed by a writer's politics and motivations. Every day, history is told and retold, interpreted and reworked—discerned.[1] People mold and mangle it to reinforce their political decisions, win an argument with friends, or create meaning for the way they understand themselves and their surroundings in the flow of their everyday life. Daily conversations and events can tell a lot about the underlying histories people understand and, perhaps unconsciously, hold onto. In this chapter, I narrate a political conversation over lunch with my relatives along with the essential but concealed history that is meant to explain my encounter with them. The narrative will highlight a sense of the intertwining of war memory with the present. People don't give this form of memory much attention, but it speaks to the ways the past is present in the daily lives of people in Lebanon, and how the past and present are co-experienced and co-endured.[2] The way I tell this history is itself important, as I experiment with a method of narrating history that emerges from discussions with interlocutors.[3]

One goal of this narrative is to give the reader a sense of the implicit historical indexing employed in daily political conversations, whether these are in extended conversations, or shorter one-off remarks people might make in their days. To be able to employ and follow this indexing requires, in Riskedahl's words, "some social understanding of bygone days, as well as current days, in order to make sense of the historical talk" (2007: 308). Experiences and events of the past produce shared signs, symbols, abbreviations, and knowledge that together become part of the grammar of everyday conversations that lies beneath the surface, and which people use to read, decipher, and make sense of their present social and political world. This grammar is shared between interlocutors (including myself), subjectively produced, and is essentially the historian's historical knowledge interpreted and used in the messiness of people's daily conversations and analysis. Like the grammar of language, this grammar can give form to content of the past, but it can also expose ambiguities, debates, and misinterpretations.

In the proceeding narrative, I use italic text to signal the conversation over lunch, the present-tense lived reality and my engagement with interlocutors. The non-italic, regular font sections are meant to signal a break from this lived reality, and they provide three types of information. First, in these sections, I elaborate on the shared symbolic references and on what would otherwise be unsaid—in other words, on the historical indexing that is necessary to understand the present conversation that is in italics. Second, I include "objective" historical background because these historical accounts, which might be objectively real for historians, can be read, interpreted, and employed differently by people, and transformed into personal stories and memories. Indeed, this transformation is what happens during the lunch encounter I narrate, and this episode is one context from which to read the historical accounts and the symbolic meaning they acquire with my interlocutors. Third, and finally, I include my own personal reflections as a witness to some of these historical and political events. These three elements are fused together in the non-italic parts of the text. In combining this information in these sections, I wish to highlight the interplay between the historical record, the subjective reality of this history as lived by my interlocutors, and the way I witnessed, and to an extent, experienced this past. I also wish to locate my interlocutors and me in this past.

The non-italic text is meant to turn our attention to the implicit knowledge required to follow political conversations and lived events—therefore, if I have done my job well, those knowledgeable about Lebanon should be able to skip the non-italic text in this chapter and still understand the narrative and all the historical indexing before reading the conclusion. Crucially, as the conversation evolves, the reader will notice that historical events actually become the topic of conversation and are being narrated, debated, and clarified during the present lunchtime encounter; hence, they remain in italics.

The following encounter also shows how political views do not cut simplistically across sectarian lines, as one may glean from international (and

local) news reports on Lebanon. Rather, political tensions and differences
split through families, and views transform, but also solidify, through the
buildup of conversations, debates, arguments, and encounters occurring in
the mundane spaces of everyday life.

Presenting Pasts

*Monday, June 8, 2009. There is not much traffic in the streets of Beirut. It is
calmer than the usual Monday on this day after parliamentary elections. Most
people have the day off. The calmness is primarily because the media, government,
and political parties have spent weeks scaring people about the possibility of a conflict breaking out during the elections or after them, depending on the outcome. In
anticipation of this trouble, people are hardly venturing out.*

*I drive from Hamra to my Teta's (grandmother's) house for lunch. I haven't
seen my relatives for quite some time. Teta's house is about twenty minutes from
Beirut, close to the foot of the mountain and tucked behind some hills. From her
second floor balcony you can see all of Beirut and its suburbs. The view can be
breathtaking at sunset, not so beautiful when the city's smog hovers over the day's
sky, and outright terrifying when bombs fall on the city in full view, as I've witnessed. When I arrive, five of my relatives are already there, Teta is preparing
lunch, and they are chatting on the balcony, drinking Almaza beer, and munching
on salted mixed nuts. There is Leila, an unmarried school teacher in her late fifties; Jad, her brother, an engineer in his late forties turned business consultant; his
wife, Rola, who is a stay at home mother; Lara, who is Jad and Leila's sister and
is a store manager; and Nabil, her husband, in his early fifties who is the local
agent for some industrial machines, and is also Rola's brother. The women are
chatting, but I cannot make out the subject. When I walk out on the balcony they
joke about the outcome of the previous day's election. They generally hold strong
views, but tend to defer to the men in these conversations. In the case of Lara, her
political views diverge to some degree from her husband's. Leila is soft-spoken in
these settings and is more introspective. Rola agrees with her husband. In family
settings the women often tend to jump in and out of political conversations but
don't bother, or take a minor role, when the men begin to argue with each other.[4]
So far, however, Jad and Nabil are both relatively quiet. They hold opposing
views, and it seems they are only willing to talk about the election outcome when I
join them. Here is a clear case of my position as researcher, citizen, and family
member colliding to influence the trajectory of a conversation, but also, perhaps, to*

moderate a space for discussion on a topic they might otherwise deflect on their
own. "Shū ra'yak" (What's your opinion?) Nabil asks to get me going.

On June 7, 2009, Lebanese citizens went to their voting districts to elect
a new parliament. Many were hoping this would pave the way to a new era
and move politicians to resolve longstanding conflicts. In the lead-up to the
elections, I had spent my days with independent political activists and political party members. In the three prior days, I spent it with members of the
Phalange Party at one of their offices in the predominantly Christian neighborhood of Ashrafieh as they campaigned to get their candidates elected.
During this time, I listened to my interlocutors argue about the outcome,
speculate on the winners, and discuss the possibility of war should anything
go wrong with the elections.

My mind races through my encounters of the previous days as I am asked for
my opinion. I did not vote in these elections. My relatives know this. But I am still
shocked by the outcome and Nabil is trying to hide his satisfaction, knowing well
that I have no love for the coalition that won and which he supports. I remark that
I'm not sure "anything will change" as an outcome of these elections, in which, al-
ready, there are signs that the winners will share power with the losers. "hek
ḥayetnā," (this is our life) Jad concurs after a brief exchange.

The phrase *hek ḥayetnā* is a common one I hear when confronted with
political disillusionment, or in the face of some bombing or attack of sorts. It
is meant to capture (or assert) a sense of the ordinary, and to remind us of
the ongoing crisis of our time and the frustration of being unable to change
a never-ending political conflict. It is a cynical nod to the idea that the conflict of the past remains in the present and will continue into the future.
Those of us listening are meant to understand this history of conflict and
share in the frustration that things will not change.

We had all lived through the parliamentary crisis of the last few years
that the 2009 elections were supposed to resolve. The government had been
in crisis since at least December 1, 2006. That day, ministers from Hizballah's
political bloc walked out, citing that the government had gone back on the
ministerial decree agreeing to preserve and secure Hizballah's weapons for its
resistance to Israel; this effectively removed confidence in prime minister
Fouad Siniora's government. Jad had supported this walkout and had briefly
participated with the protestors in the streets in those early December days.

This crisis between Hizballah and its political opponents actually dates further back to at least February 14, 2005, when former prime minister Rafiq Hariri was assassinated. Yet, even this date should not be taken as a fixed beginning, since many people in Lebanon would perceive their lives to be mired in a more protracted political conflict. The struggle over the Lebanese state's foreign policy direction and strategy has been a constant fixture of Lebanese politics in the post-independence era, albeit in different forms and involving different parties (in the 1970s, for example, Hizballah did not exist and the conflict revolved around Christian and Palestinian armed factions). The Hariri assassination serves as a new period of crisis because one could argue that, aided by Syrian control over the country, he had reached a temporary compromise on matters of economy and foreign policy during his roughly fifteen-year domination of the Lebanese political scene, ten of them as prime minister. In the aftermath of his assassination, this politico-economic compromise was up for grabs and thrown into flux. It was, however, the long-standing conflict and the ambiguity and inability to really define when all this began that led people to conclude, "This is our life," with the implication that this life is filled with political violence. This is sometimes said with disillusionment and desperation, sometimes with remaining hope, as witnessed in high voter turnout, but almost always with a degree of cynicism.

Despite Jad's comment, Nabil and he are interested to get my opinion on the elections, why I didn't vote, what I observed, and the outcome.[5] I tell them I spent the day before in Ashrafieh, which happened to be part of the "Beirut 1" voting district, and one of the hot spots and most heated election battles.[6] I recount for them, vaguely, some of what I observed before the March 14 candidates won later in the night. They had swept all the seats in this district, to the surprise of many.[7] My relative, Jad, supports the opposition March 8 coalition and is trying to show Nabil, a March 14 supporter, that he is not so upset, although I know from other March 8 supporters that the defeat is devastating. Some people I know have cried, others have told me they do not want to answer their phone. "maʿlesh, raḥ yifūtū bi ḥukūme weḥde waṭaniye" (Never mind, they will enter into a national unity government), Jad rationalizes. Nabil does not challenge this. Jad is trying to remain content in the knowledge that a future government could not be formed without the March 8 political bloc, and that this bloc received an absolute majority of votes in the country.[8] There is also talk and speculation of vote buying, but overall, the conversation between us remains without accusations or attacks.

The March 8 and 14 coalitions emerged in 2005 after Rafiq Hariri's assassination. Jad and Nabil were both in Beirut at the time of his killing; I returned a few weeks later. We all participated in a series of demonstrations and sit-ins that took place in the wake of the Hariri assassination directed against the Syrian regime and its de facto control of Lebanon. These protests were held spontaneously at first, but soon began to be planned by political blocs that tried to steer the popular outcry. Hizballah and other groups with good relations to the Syrian regime planned a protest in opposition to all this on March 8, and it turned into the biggest protest the country had seen yet. In response, a week later on March 14, the groups who had been demonstrating since the death of Hariri on February 14 came out in strength, potentially equaling or surpassing the size of the March 8 demonstration, expressing their anger at the Syrian regime and, in cruder moments, their hatred of Syrians.[9] In April that year, Syria, under local and international pressure, was forced to withdraw its military from Lebanon, thus ending a long period of de facto Syrian control of the country. In the process, new polarized political coalitions were formed, named after the big days of protest.

The March 14 coalition was formed one month after Hariri's assassination, and continues to be a coalition with strong ties to the United States and Saudi Arabia. It has opposed Syrian presence in Lebanon, demanded an independent investigation into the assassination of Hariri and other assassinations that followed, and called for the disarmament of Hizballah.[10] March 8 takes its name from the protests that occurred a week prior to March 14. It came together initially to thank Syria for its presence in Lebanon as it was pulling out, but later grew as an opposition to the March 14-led government. As a coalition, it has close ties to Syria and Iran, and its foreign policy concern is in opposing U.S. and Israeli agendas in the region (the Hizballah-Syrian-Iranian axis is referred to as anti-imperial, the resistance front, or *mumāna'a* in Arabic). Internally, the coalition has packaged itself as supposedly reformist and wishing to ensure that Hizballah is disarmed only after there is no need for a resistance movement.[11] Unlike the March 14 coalition, March 8 does not have a formal structure and does not hold public or high-profile conferences under the banner of March 8.[12]

After the March protests, the Syrian military withdrew from Lebanon. Following this, the country was witness to incessant bombings, assassinations, and assassination attempts; I was present to observe reactions for a few in 2005 and all those in 2006–2008. (See Table 1 for a list of bombings. I have highlighted in gray those that appeared to be random bombings for all but

Table 1. List of Bombings (shaded) and Assassinations, 2005–2008

Name/Location of Bombing or Assassination	Date
Rafiq Hariri assassination	February 14, 2005
New Jdeideh bombing	March 19, 2005
Kaslik bombing	March 23, 2005
Sad al-Bouchrieh bombing	March 26, 2005
Broummana bombing	April 1, 2005
Jounieh bombing	May 7, 2005
Samir Kassir assassination	June 2, 2005
George Hawi assassination	June 21, 2005
Elias Murr attempted assassination	July 12, 2005
Monot bombing	July 22, 2005
Zalka bombing	August 22, 2005
Ali Ramez Tohme attempted assassination	September 15, 2005
Jeitawi bombing	September 17, 2005
May Chidiac attempted assassination	September 25, 2005
Gebran Tueni assassination	December 28, 2005
Pierre Gemayel assassination	November 21, 2006
Bekfaya bombing	February 13, 2007
ABC bombing	May 21, 2007
Verdun bombing	May 21, 2007
Aley bombing	May 23, 2007
Grenade in Beirut	May 27, 2007
Sad al-Bouchrieh bombing	June 4, 2007
Walid Eido assassination	June 13, 2007
UNIFIL attack	June 24, 2007
UNIFIL roadside bomb	July 16, 2007
Antoine Ghanem assassination	September 19, 2007
François Al-Hajj assassination	December 12, 2007
U.S. diplomatic vehicle in Karantina	January 15, 2008
Wissam Eid assassination	January 25, 2008
Tripoli army bus bombing	August 13, 2008
Saleh Aridi assassination	September 10, 2008
Tripoli bombing	September 29, 2008

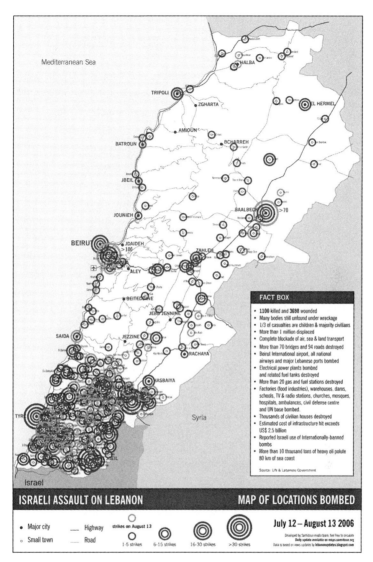

Figure 1. July 2006 war map of Israeli bombings.

the planners.) The March 14 coalition blamed Syria for all these acts, but there was little substance to this beyond speculation at the time.

In July 2006, Israel used the pretext of a border attack by the Lebanese resistance movement, Hizballah, in which several Israeli soldiers were captured, to wage an open war on Lebanon, and to attempt to eliminate Hizballah. This war lasted thirty-three days and targeted much of the country (see Figure 1). In the aftermath, rumors emerged that in private diplomatic channels the March 14 coalition had been promoting the continuation of the war. These rumors were later revealed to carry truth in WikiLeaks documents published years later in 2010.[13] In the months after the war, however, these remained rumors that created a serious crisis of confidence in the March 14-led government, which led to the resignation of March 8 ministers in December 2006, and to subsequent street mobilizations against the government.

On December 1, people in Lebanon from all walks of life took to the streets in what supporters of the March 14 political bloc called a Hizballah-led coup. For the hundreds of thousands who protested in the streets it felt like a real opportunity for change. And in those early days, walking in the crowded downtown streets and talking to protestors, there was a feeling of euphoria among them that their March 8 coalition would unseat the government. People initially transformed downtown from what is otherwise an elite space with brand name high-class shops, expensive restaurants, and private security, into a pseudo-public space with street vendors, public lectures, and creative political graffiti (see Figure 2). The feeling of change (not revolution, because at best it would have been a coup between the various power brokers) was evident in the posters and comparisons of Hassan Nasrallah to former Egyptian president Gamal Abdel Nasser and Venezuelan president Hugo Chávez (see Figure 3).

At the time, I questioned in my field notes the discrepancy I felt between the goals of people mobilized in the streets and the March 8 leadership. I wrote:

> With what seems to be a 50,000 strong daily demonstration, reaching almost 1 million on the opening day, one would think they [March 8] are actually calling for the total downfall of the government, an end to the Taif Agreement, significant social change, and a complete takeover of power by the opposition. One would expect the leaders of the demonstration to set their demands high: the exile of corrupt leaders, a new constitution, resisting

Figure 2. Street vendor and graffiti in the square.

Photo Credit: Author.

Figure 3. Poster on downtown tent comparing Nasrallah to Abdel Nasser and Hugo Chávez.

Photo Credit: Author.

Israel, and a more equitable economic system. These are just a few demands that come to mind when I see the demonstration before me from my perspective standing on top of the Fouad Chehab Bridge looking upon the masses of demonstrators. The irony of where I stand is quite fascinating. It is Chehab's name that I hear over and over today: "What we need is someone like Riad el-Solh or Fouad Chehab."[14] General Aoun's supporters believe Aoun to be that man today, but he is too divisive.

While the impression one gets from the street would lead one to think March 8 is calling for revolutionary change, the coalition is simply calling for a National Unity government in which they would command one-third-plus-one voices in the cabinet.[15] This demand is in order to block any laws and resolutions the March 14 majority would like to pass against the resistance. They are also calling for a renegotiation or disbanding of the Paris III agreement (related to debt structuring and neoliberal economic policies), and for setting the terms of an international tribunal to investigate the assassinations of the last year. I might agree with the opposition on some points, but are these demands worth a destabilization of an already weak economy, or worth the rising tension and anticipation of violence by the people?

The demonstrations continued, Prime Minister Siniora did not budge, and in time, with the prolonged sit-in, downtown became a tent city largely emptied of people except for a few diehard political party members.

Although Siniora remained the outgoing prime minister, he was unable to constitute a new government, and the country remained without one for eighteen months until May 21, 2008. In the meantime, in summer 2007, the Lebanese army waged a war on the Palestinian camp of Nahr al-Bared, attempting to eradicate the militant group Fateh el-Islam. The Lebanese army was perhaps more successful than the Israeli army as it accomplished its goal while also annihilating the camp and forcibly dislocating 40,000 of its Palestinian residents. Unfortunately for Palestinian refugees, no tribunal for the army's crimes will ever be held and there was little outcry, as this "war on terror" (as it was called) was backed by world powers such as the United States.[16]

In November 2007, the term of the president of the republic, Emile Lahoud, expired and the parliament was unable to appoint a new president until May 25, 2008. This was days after the Doha Agreement was signed, which ended a two-week battle between the March 8 and March 14 coalitions that had been the source of the political impasse in government.

The government that formed in May 2008 was an interim government. Parliamentary elections were scheduled for June of the following year to appoint the new government. People waited for a year, and were told that the election outcome would decide the fate of the country in the near, and possibly far, future.[17] On June 7, 2009, the March 14 coalition emerged victorious, taking home 71 seats with the March 8 opposition taking 57. Saed Hariri, son of the assassinated former prime minister, was soon after named prime minister. It took him several months to form a national consensus government. Such a government, remaining faithful to the politics of "No Victor, No Vanquished," was what Jad had predicted in our discussion on the balcony the day after the elections. It sealed any hope for overcoming the political impasse in favor of either coalition, and eventually collapsed on January 12, 2011.

Jad and Nabil exchange their views on the outcome of the elections; they are frustrated. I try, for once, to keep my own analysis to a minimum, mainly so as not to reveal too much about my informants on the campaign trail. I am also aware that their opposition in this election and in the current political climate is quite entrenched, so I don't want to rock the boat too much, and I attempt to listen more than speak.

Besides the context of protracted conflict recounted above and the March 8 and 14 divisions, Jad and Nabil's disagreements have another important layer to them that are rooted in intra-sectarian politics of the Christian community. These politics were often visible in relations with my extended family. Jad and Nabil's larger March 8/March 14 coalition differences were partly a result of being on different poles of specifically Christian party politics. At the time of this conversation, this meant, in general, supporting General Aoun's Free Patriotic Movement on one hand, and Samir Gaegae's Lebanese Forces, or Amin Gemayel's Kataeb Party, on the other. All these parties are focused on politically uniting the Christians and in protecting their rights in Lebanon. However, the leaders of the FPM and LF have been at odds at least as far back as the 1989 War of Elimination (*ḥarb al-ilgha'*), when Aoun tried to eliminate the LF from East Beirut, followed by Gaegae taking the side of Syria in its 1990 battle to eradicate Aoun's military resistance to Syria. In their most recent challenge to each other's legitimacy, Aoun has sided with March 8 and Gaegae with March 14.

Jad supports Aoun, while Nabil simply thinks very little of Aoun rather than being a hardline Gaegae supporter. Still, for this reason, I expect the conversation to turn into teasing and taunting by the winner once we get deep into the discussion, analysis and speculation. Although there is some taunting, especially between Nabil and Lara, who is closer politically to her brother, the conversation for the most part is calm and I hear both Jad and Nabil say, killo mitl baʿdo *(it's all the same thing).*

Although conversations can get heated and tense, I often notice time and again that among my family, when politics is discussed, we conclude by re-sorting to a common statement that "*killo zeyt el-shī*" or "*killo mitl baʿdo*" (it's all the same thing), or the topic is somehow changed altogether, or turned into a joke. This is usually said or done for the purpose of solidarity within the family, and often comes after shouting over each other's heads and trying to convince each other of a political position. In an effort to remain on good terms, interlocutors will oftentimes agree that all sides are equally complicit, and that it is the fault of all politicians, or the fault of the people themselves. Such rhetorical statements might transition a conversation or deescalate an argument, and while members in my family might believe that all politicians are the same, to an extent, they certainly do not act as if they are, continuing to support some over others. I imagine some families might be more confrontational, but among acquaintances, business colleagues, and strangers, one often hears these comments, "it's all the same," or *kil hal siyāse wa-hal siyāsiyīn mitl baʿda* (all this politics and these politicians are the same), as deflections to maintain civil and loving relations.

From Elections to Assassinations

"el-ghadā ḥader. Yalla!" (lunch is ready, get up!), my grandmother yells from inside for a second time. We were too engrossed in the political conversation to pay attention to her the first time around. "Yalla, jayīn" (Ok, we're coming) Jad re-sponds. We get up, they grab their beers, and we move the conversation inside to the lunch table, now talking about specific outcomes in the districts, and speculat-ing about how things might turn out after the election results are finalized.

The discussion goes through various pauses as we take our seats and pass around the food. We move momentarily away from politics when my cousin, who has just joined us, comments, "el-ʾakl mish ṭayeb" (the food isn't good). We laugh.

Teta waves him off with a chuckle "lā, wallā, shū mā btifham" (Oh really, you don't understand [your taste]). She is used to her kids and grandkids teasing her and knows how to shoot back at us; we all know the food is fantastic. On this day she has made Kheibat (Middle Eastern dumplings), in addition to a few other dishes. Kheibat is a dish I have only seen Teta make, and with great pride and patience, but it is most likely from Southern Turkey, from places like Mardin, where my grandmother originally hails from. The dish looks similar to Asian dumplings, but the dumpling is made from Semolina (smīd), bulgar wheat, and water. It is then stuffed with minced meat and boiled, and must be eaten quite hot, usually with a good dose of squeezed lemon.[18]

As we enjoy lunch, the discussion turns to the Zgharta voting district in the north because Nabil votes in that district. We talk about the election of Suleiman Frangieh, a Maronite Christian communal leader in the north allied with March 8. Lara makes fun of Nabil because although he won overall as a March 14 supporter, his coalition lost in Zgharta.

"Haha, inta khsirit! (you lost)" she teases, followed by Nabil's silence and wry smile. He knows he has ultimately won because it is the March 14 bloc he wanted to see victorious, so he gives his wife the pleasure of thinking the Zgharta loss was a big one. By playing this game and trying to tease him, she is essentially holding onto whatever victory she can, being herself more of a supporter of the FPM, part of the March 8 coalition.

Nabil, like scores of other people in the country, voted against his political beliefs (March 14) in favor of Frangieh, the candidate who would preserve local patron-client networks. Such networks help maintain status and security for him and his family in his village in the district of Zgharta, and they are far more important than short-term and precarious political victories.[19] In many cases, people's cliental networks drive their national politics, but in cases when they don't intersect, voters find themselves with the hard decision of biting the hand that feeds them, as the saying goes. People could often find a compromise by voting for their patron, in Nabil's case Frangieh, but not their patron's entire political list.[20] This can still be a source of family conflict but far less than dropping the patron altogether.

From Zgharta, the discussion turns to the Metn district and I tell them that the official results came out an hour ago, giving Sami Gemayel, son of former president Amin Gemayel, and Michel Murr, a businessman and politician who has led several key ministries over the last few decades, the only March 14 victories

*in the Metn area. This is more than the March 8 opposition had expected to con-
cede.*[21] *Although March 14 lost so many seats to March 8 in the Metn district,
where Nabil lives but does not vote, he takes solace in one fact, responding that:
"el-mohem inno Ghassan al-ʾAshʾar mā rebeḥ" (what is important is that
Ghassan al-Ashar did not win). Nabil is relieved that al-Ashar lost because, as he
says, he is ʾawmi (shorthand for ḥizb al-sūrī al-qawmi al-ijtimaʿī or Syrian Social Nationalist Party—SSNP).*

This was probably the seamless and unconscious moment of transition
from the present to the past for all of us.

*"lesh mā btiʿfī ʿanhum" (Why don't you forgive them?) I respond. Since
Lebanon's war saw bloody confrontations between all the different political parties
and across all sects, I continue, "why is it specifically this party that you cannot
forgive when others also massacred Christians, and in some cases friends and
relatives?"*

In my line of questioning about forgiveness, I am referring to the amnesty law passed on August 26, 1991, that pardoned all political leaders and
militia fighters.

Nabil responds that "the ʾawmiye,[22] *being Christian, should be people who
will stand with us [the Christians], yet, they are always against us. It is a case of
people within your community who are against you. So I will never forgive them
for assassinating Bashir Gemayel." The mention of Bashir Gemayel is like a specter that further brings the past into the present.*

To understand the ensuing conversation, the SSNP, and the reference to
Bashir Gemayel, one has to return to the beginning of Lebanon's war. Jad
and Nabil were both teenagers when the war first began, and both participated in defending their communities in various ways, at least during the
Two-Year War, and shortly after.

Lebanon's war in 1975–1990 is commonly, and in hindsight, cited as beginning on April 13, 1975, and ending with the defeat of General Aoun's army
by the Syrian military, on October 13, 1990. This, however, is a simplified
designation of the beginning and end of the war. It leaves little consideration
for the role of planning, preparation, and the conditions necessary for its
emergence. It also assumes no variability of physical violence and calm in the

fifteen-year period, and does not consider the way war might continue after the signing of peace agreements like the Taif Agreement, ratified on November 4, 1989.[23] To consider the conditions that set 1975 into motion, one might take the war to have begun in 1973 with the Israeli undercover raid into the heart of Beirut, in Verdun, followed subsequently by a confrontation between the Lebanese army and Palestinian armed factions; or in 1969 with the signing of the Cairo Agreement that allowed Palestinians access to stage a resistance against Israel from Lebanon (see Appendix 1); or even, arguably, in 1948, with the expulsion of hundreds of thousands of Palestinians, many of whom came to Lebanon, and with political factions in Lebanon not agreeing on how to posture themselves vis-à-vis the new Israeli state, or how to take care of this influx of politically mobilized refugees. There are far more incidents between and alongside the ones mentioned (the brief civil war in 1958 is one example), but so far as history is told diachronically, these events and stages mark significant moments.

In 1975, the war began as a confrontation between the LNM and right wing Christian factions, where the LNM was challenging the status quo of Maronite power and demanding changes in civic and political life.[24] The LNM were effectively confronting nationalist Christian political groups to seize power from them, redistribute this power, and bring about more social justice.[25] However, there was another dimension to this war, and observed from a Christian nationalist perspective, the war began as a battle between Christians and Palestinians, who, according to the Christian factions, were supported by Muslim political forces (the LNM was ultimately viewed as a Muslim-led coalition). For these Christians, their fight was against Palestinians who were not only staging operations against Israel from Lebanese land, but also trying to create a Palestinian state in Lebanon.[26] In this way, what leftist Lebanese forces saw as a demands-based conflict over resources, Christian factions had packaged as a war against Palestinians and Muslims; only in hindsight today do many Christians, in an effort to find common ground and consensus, frame their battle purely against Palestinians. In the mid-1970s, with Muslims and Palestinians fighting alongside each other, Christian factions often considered their identities similar and interchangeable—take, for example, the 1975 incident of Black Saturday, when Phalange Party members massacred Muslims near the Beirut port.

In this way, the conflict came to be seen both by foreign observers as well as many in Lebanon, as a sectarian battle in the first degree,[27] and could then be connected to a discourse about sectarian and ethnic conflict being of a primordial nature. This has led to a longstanding argument, commonly found in reference to ethnic conflicts, that Lebanese have always been and will always be embroiled in internal conflict.[28] It is also crucial to understand that the war had a significant foreign element as well. Battles with Syria and Israel took place, with the former entering Lebanon in 1976 and the latter officially in 1978, though Israeli cross-border bombing and interference began in the early 1970s (and even earlier, with a massacre committed in the village of Houla as far back as 1948). Israeli and Syrian troops were positioned in Lebanon, either as occupiers or "protectors," until 2000 and 2005, respectively, and certainly long after the alleged end of the war in 1990. Israel had advanced as far as Beirut and besieged and occupied the city in 1982 for several months, and it continues to directly occupy the Shabaa Farms in the south. Moreover, there was intervention by American and international forces, which left after successive bombings on their embassies and militaries in the mid-1980s.

In 1975, Bashir Gemayel was a young man in his late twenties, already the head of an elite unit in the military wing of the Kataeb Party known as "*bī-jīn*" (P.G), named after the founder of the party, Pierre Gemayel. In 1976 he became president of the Kataeb military council after the death of William Hawi in the Battle of Tal el-Zaatar.[29] Bashir was the son of Pierre Gemayel, and is credited for uniting Christian militias under one army, the LF. He was elected president of the republic in 1982 and assassinated by a member of the SSNP just twenty days after his election, prior to ever taking office. Bashir, among other things, was known to have collaborated closely with the Israelis and had a hand in the Israeli invasion of Lebanon in 1982, which saw the Israeli army reach Beirut and besiege it.

Antoun Saadeh founded the SSNP in Beirut in 1932. This is the party to which Ghassan al-Ashar, the losing candidate in the 2009 parliamentary elections, belonged. The party strives, at least in ideology, for the unification of a Greater Syrian nation and for a nonconfessional Lebanese entity. It was on the side of leftist forces between 1975 and 1990. The SSNP and the Phalange have been foes of an almost existential nature, with a brief alliance in 1958—an alliance some critical SSNP members today claim is one of the biggest mistakes in the party's history. The liberation of Palestine has been one of its key concerns, and it takes a strong position against any collaboration with Israel

By 1982, the Phalange Party collusion with the Israelis had become quite evident, and Bashir Gemayel's role in opening channels with the Israelis, and receiving weapons and training from them, was known to the LNM. On

September 14, Habib al-Shartouni, a member of the SSNP, whose sister lived in one of the floors over the Ashrafieh Kataeb Party headquarters, detonated a bomb that killed Bashir. Bashir had gone to the headquarters for his last weekly Kataeb meeting, as he was soon to take the position of president of the republic. Al-Shartouni was caught but never tried. He was released in 1990 to Syria, and cited Bashir Gemayel's ties to Israel as the reason for the assassination.[30] The Kataeb have not forgotten this.

These are the broad strokes of grammar that are implicitly present during our conversation. If Nabil's emotions toward the SSNP and the loss of al-Ashar in the elections were the first reference to a history of Lebanon, then my line of questioning about amnesty served as a second. This back and forth worked as a kind of collaborative archeology into our contested knowledge of the past. Nabil's anti-SSNP sentiment took us into the war. Without knowing the history of Lebanon's war, his interlocutor (me in this case) would have been confused. Subsequently, by raising the issue of amnesty in response to his anti-SSNP sentiment, I was focusing on a specific moment in that war, and alluding to the political assassination of Bashir Gemayel without having explicitly to say so; Nabil understood this and followed up with the explicit mention of Bashir. Once this had been raised, the internal logic of the conversation that led from our talk of election outcomes and speculation about the country's future political trajectory to talk of war was easy to follow, and in hindsight, unsurprising. The issue was not that the conversation descended into war talk, but that the feelings generated by a war that supposedly ended twenty years ago still carry on with us till today, and they interfere with elections and amalgamate with the flow of a daily conversation.

"Bashir could have saved the country," Nabil expresses to me. Many Christians, and indeed, many Muslims, see Bashir as having been a potential savior. But the dirt on him starts to emerge as we continue our conversation. After Nabil mentions his name, I raise the issue of his collaboration with Israel, and Jad follows by saying, "he really split the Christians by assassinating Tony Frangieh."

Tony Frangieh, son of former president Suleiman Frangieh and father to the current communal leader of Zgharta, Suleiman Frangieh, was killed along with his wife and daughter in June 1978 in what would be called the "Ihdin Massacre." This event had a role in the rise of Bashir Gemayel's LF, which gradually came to unite Christian arms.

Traboulsi (2007) tells us that Bashir had rightfully gauged the growing dissent of a new social class to the traditional ruling notable families. This group, largely involved and vocal in the war, was comprised of fighters, middle-class professionals, and disenfranchised families of villages, among other groups (2007: 208). Bashir, himself from a notable family ruling the Phalange Party, had difficulty directly imposing himself on the party. He sought to do this by placing the Phalange military command under the structure of the LF, which was to become the umbrella military organization for all Christian groups, with Bashir at its helm. To do this, he had to break the hold of traditional Christian leaders in places like the north and the Beqaa valley. The attack on Ihdin in the north was part of this plan.

Ihdin is the home of the Frangieh clan, which has historic ties with Syria. In 1978, Suleiman Frangieh left the Lebanese Front in protest of Phalange collaboration with Israel, and this resulted in a conflict between his Marada Party and the Phalange. In June, around two hundred Phalange militiamen, under the command of Samir Gaegae, at the time party leader of the town of Bsharri and later leader of the LF, attacked Suleiman Frangieh's villa, killing his son Tony, along with Tony's wife and baby daughter and scores of others. Bashir claimed not to have given the orders, but he justified them "as an insurrection by 'farmers against injustice and feudalism'" (Traboulsi 2007: 209). The killings divided the Christian community and led to a major confrontation between the Phalange Party and Syria, resulting in the 100 Days War in the spring and summer of 1978, when Syrian forces bombarded East Beirut. Bashir emerged triumphant from this battle as the Syrians withdrew from their East Beirut positions, and soon after he was able to impose himself as the leader of the Christian community.[31]

Nabil reveres Bashir Gemayel, but as mentioned above, he is from Zgharta, the traditional stronghold of the Frangieh clan, and so he is against the Phalange attack on Tony Frangieh in the 1970s. He, thus, agrees with Jad about the mistakes Bashir made. The Ihdin Massacre, he says, "khassaretnā mnīḥ ka masīḥiye" (made us lose a lot as a Christian community), and "kānet ghalṭa min bashīr . . . kān mahwūs" (it was a mistake from Bashir . . . he was obsessed [with leading the Christians]), "wa-fara'etnā ka-masīḥiye beyn el-shmel wa-el-shar'iye" (and it divided us as Christians between the Northern region and East Beirut). As Nabil speaks and Jad agrees, I am struck by how much more consensus there is regarding Bashir's mistakes in dealing with the Christian community than there is around the circumstances of his collaboration with Israel. This is not to say that they deny the Israeli collaboration, but there is a strong belief that Bashir was going to turn against the Israelis. More important, this issue of collaboration is just not important enough to figure into our conversation at this time.

People who say that Bashir was planning on turning against the Israelis once he became president often dismiss Bashir's collaboration with Israel as unimportant. The same people who dislike, or hate, the SSNP for killing Bashir, also go on to say that it was the Israelis who were behind the assassination because he had begun to turn against them. They use as proof his call for a united Lebanon in all its "10452" km², a number that has turned into a famous slogan used till today. However, if the Israelis killed him, was it in collaboration with the SSNP, as we know that his killer, Habib al-Shartouni, was a member of that party?

When I have brought this up in the past, the inconsistency is usually explained, conspiratorially, by claiming that the war was dirty and the SSNP could have easily worked with the Israelis to this end. In this way, the SSNP are further demonized for their own collaboration, while Bashir's treason is washed away with the speculation that in his final days he was shifting and turning against Israel. All this is convenient; it produces enough noise so that a rational conversation around the Israel factor cannot be discussed without resorting to unsubstantiated speculative arguments and rumor. While Bashir can still be criticized for his inter-Christian politics, the move to distance his collaboration with Israel creates one more space for evading accountability in Lebanese national politics.

As we speak about the Ihdin Massacre, Nabil tells us that he knew someone who went up to Zgharta with the Kataeb Party to kill Tony Frangieh.

The historical details that inflect our present-day conversations, in this case completely diverting from the original discussion of elections, are not something that happened "out there" to an abstract nation or people. They are embedded in the personal memories of the people I love, and the people I encounter every day. Thus, we did not speak about whether or not, and when, the massacre happened; such historical knowledge and collective memory are implicit, as we all know about the event. Rather, what occurred was a flushing of a personal memory.

Nabil begins to spontaneously recount for us the way he experienced those days of the attacks. "The day we found out about the events in Ihdin," Nabil says, "we began to hear about and see all the zghartawiyye *(people from Zgharta) leave our neighborhood [of Hazmiye], and other parts of East Beirut, for West Beirut, the North or Syria."* He continues:

"We were afraid during this time. We were very afraid. I called my friend in the Kataeb, and my dad did the same, to see what can be done for us and other zghartawiyye. *You know, I had a lot of Kataeb friends, and they told us not to be afraid and to remain where we are. If you want to talk about fear, yes, we were afraid. You know, my dad had connections to the presidential palace; this is how close he was to the Frangieh family. And we were not sure how the Kataeb would react to this, even though we helped them a lot through those early years of war. We used to deliver food to the frontlines, for example, when the Kataeb got into a battle with the army in the neighborhood of Haret Hreik. So this looked good on my record with them.*

"Some zghartawiyye *stayed with us, mainly our neighbors, and we managed to get them out of town. I took them with my friend out of Beirut to the* madfūn *checkpoint. You know, this is the one that is close to Batroun. This was the border between East Beirut and the North during the war. So that no one would give them trouble, we dropped them off there and told them that "from this point on, don't worry, no one would bother you." The people we helped were various* zghartawiyye, *but one was the family of the right hand man of Tony Frangieh. So it was very dangerous.*

"When Tony's son, Suleiman Frangieh, came to power, he did the smart thing of embracing the LF members in the Zgharta district, and warned that no LF supporter would be harmed, nor would any person who was unconnected to the murder of his family. Because of this, many zghartawiyye *who had become LF during the years were able to return and visit, like my father's sister's kids (*wlād 'amtī*)."*

Nabil's stories kept flowing, the elections from the day before now barely on our minds as one memory led to the next. In these moments, it was as though floodgates were opened and my interlocutors wanted to relay all their memories in one session.

As Nabil and Jad speak about the LF and Bashir Gemayel's adventures against different factions of the Christian community, we stumble on the subject of the Tyous—a commando unit—because Jad knew them in their early days. "The Tyous got their name after an incident when they were fighting in downtown," Jad tells us. The group has mythic characteristics with different origin stories and Jad

*proceeds to explain to us his version: "They had an Armored Personnel Carrier
(APC; millāle in Arabic) that was hit during combat, and they were stubborn
(tayyasū) and refused to leave it behind. This is why they came to be called the
Tyous (the stubborn). Then, later on, they grew to take over command in the*
matḥaf *(museum district) at the Children's Hospital."*

*I probe about the timeframe of their formation, the incident with the APC,
and their growth, but this is all fuzzy in Jad's mind. He is more interested in
talking about his own experience with them and about five of the original Tyous
who had pulled the APC to safety. "They were a part of the Kataeb Party," he
continues. "One of them used to get up at night and mockingly give the call to
Muslim prayer mixed with curses and insults," he laughs. "The Syrians, who were
on the other side of the Museum district, waited for him one time when there was
a ceasefire. As he was crossing the road they shot him dead on the spot [long pause]."*

*"His brother, what was his name? Michel? I forget," he pauses. "He was clean-
ing his Kalashnikov and a bullet stuck in the chamber was released into his head.
They were* abadayāt *(strongmen) these guys [pause]. What can one say? They were
a real trouble to the Syrians," with this last sentence Jad holds a long pause as if to
reflect.*

"These were two out of the five, yes?" I ask.

*"Yes. I'm not sure what happened to the others. There was another that also
died, I believe. I think they all did. They all died in vain, not during their front-
line combat operations. These were the original guys, then others were added to the
group. My relations with the initial guys were really close."*

*"But relations between the Kataeb and Ahrar [the party to which he belonged]
were not good."*

*"Yes, but if you really want to go back to those times, you have to understand
that all those fighters who were on the frontlines fighting had no real problems with
each other. The problem was inland between the Kataeb and Ahrar, but on the
frontlines* (jabhāt), *the Ahrar of Sodeco, of Ain el-Remeneh, of the other frontlines
on the Damascus road, there were no problems* (mashākel) *between us and the
Kataeb. We were always together."*

*From here, the conversation takes different turns, but this prompts Nabil to
assert that although the Christian community paid a heavy price and there was
internal fighting with many mistakes, it was important for Bashir to do what he
did in trying to unite the Christian arms. The emergence of all these small groups,
or gangs, meant that the area was no longer safe. "In my opinion, this was the
right thing to do," he says in defense, "because before the unity of arms under the
Lebanese Forces, everyone had their own little [militia] shop open, and there were*

a lot of robberies. Bashir created an institution and an army, a structured and disciplined state with courts. And East Beirut started to prosper as a result of the increased safety."

"We're Full!" of the Past: Concluding Remarks

Eventually, after about a half hour of these back and forth narratives, competing as if someone would emerge the winner for having the most fascinating story, a moment of heavy silence overcomes the room. They have spoken about the people they saved, the people they saw die, the times they had to take cover, and the overall sense of watching people in their society kill each other. Teta has left the room now. I watch her depart energetically. She is full of life, a swimmer and an avid walker at the age of seventy nine, despite her experience of the war and the stories of her pain that I grew up on. Leila has been mostly silent throughout; Lara and Rola have chimed into the conversation from time to time with agreements and disagreements about different events and political positions, but mostly it has been Jad and Nabil who have spoken. The discussion has exhausted all of us, even me as listener and questioner. Nabil tells us that he is going to sleep, saying "shbi'nā" (We're full) and, in case we do not understand the irony in the statement, follows this with a smile, telling us "shbi'nā min el-'akl, wal-ḥakī el-siyāse wal-ḥarb" (we are full from the food and from all this talk of politics and war).

We all get up, and I can almost feel the air heavy and weighing down on the faces around me. A lunchtime discussion of current politics, like so many times before and after, could not be separated or severed from a memory of Lebanon's war. My relatives look somber, quiet, and lost in the wars of the past as we strain to move on with our day. The embodied past, seen in their looks, and the subdued mood I feel, make war's impact on current politics apparent.

The entire conversation illustrates how knowledge of the grammar of past wars—understanding and sharing the symbols, experiences, temporal markers, and history—allows one to talk about current politics with references to the past. Much of what has been written in this chapter was unspoken that afternoon. We assumed each other's knowledges, and this facilitated the seamless and unconscious transition between present and past. The references to the past also offered a non-confrontational way out of the otherwise contested present. While the present was unresolved, the past was set through the equation of *lā ghāleb, lā maghlūb* ("No Victor, No Vanquished"), where all were right and all were wrong, and everyone could take solace in their equal victimization. In this way, the war itself was wrong, the ultimate evil, but not necessarily any set of actors.

Still, frustration emerges because the same political actors that were involved in past wars continue to participate in present politics. This makes it easy to conclude a conversation as people sometimes do, saying that *killon mitl ba'don, kil el-massā'el mitshābkīn bi-ba'don,* or *mā raḥ yitghayar shī* (they are all the same; all the issues are interconnected; nothing will change), or, as Jad remarked earlier, *hek ḥayetnā* (this is our life). Lebanon's war, and the way it supposedly ended (by essentially continuing), facilitates such sentiments because it creates a link with a history that remains with us into the present and gives a feeling of continuity, a sense of intrinsic nature to the politics of today—that this is the way it is and will always be.[32] So it is very fitting that the conversation ended with silence after the discussion of the war and never reverted back to the elections or to the present and future political situation. In this way, the outcome of the present was embodied through the past and how this back and forth ultimately made us feel. Current politics remained extremely present, but only in the way it structured our initial entrance into our memory of Lebanon's war.

This conversation was not unique. I had so many like it during fieldwork and continue to do so at this present moment of writing. They vary with intensity and depth, but the weaving of a history of war into everyday life is so common, and is connected to war's presence as we anticipate future political violence. More recently, I sat with a friend at a café where we were discussing the architecture of the café and its surroundings, only to be told by my friend that his relative had passed away in the building next door during the 1982 Israeli invasion and siege of Beirut.

Our critique of the city and our surroundings took us into a forty-five-minute conversation whereby my friend recounted the personal story of how he was unable to see his relative before that person passed away, being stuck on opposing sides of the Green line. This memory triggered another and then yet another, all connected to the early 1980s and the period surrounding the Israeli invasion. The conversation was only interrupted when someone else joined us and pulled us out of the past. I sat there listening intently, but I couldn't help putting on my anthropological hat and thinking about how we had gotten here and why. And not every descent into the past is felt so somberly; very often it is accompanied by laughter and nostalgia of the good 'ole days.

It is this casual shift back and forth, the interconnection and coalescing between the present and past, but not any past, specifically a wartime past, that is illustrated in the conversation above. What kind of relations and emotions are produced through this fusing of past and present? What role do these spontaneous memories have in forming perceptions of the future, embedded as they are in daily encounters and speech? I explore such questions in the two parts of this book.

PART I

Anticipation

Chapter 3

"At the Gates of War":
Time, Space, and the Anticipation of
Political Violence

"*Sami, 'awlak raḥ yiṣīr fī ḥarb?*" (Sami, do you think there will be a war?)
Ahmed, a married man in his thirties, with two kids at the time of this writing, would sometimes ask me this question as I walked in to have coffee or
eat lunch at a café where he worked as a waiter in the Beirut neighborhood of
Hamra. I would spend several hours a day in cafés such as this one, especially
during the early days of fieldwork when I had no Internet at home, or during
Beirut's regular power outages when my apartment building did not have a
backup electric generator. This particular café was small and often quiet, so it
allowed me to meet Ahmed and develop friendly relations with him, as there
were usually no more than two or three other customers.

On days when Ahmed would approach me with the above question, he
would do this rhetorically after hearing the day's news. The question came
almost immediately after our greetings and he'd pass me a menu, and when
he was this blunt, it would usually be followed with a smile or giggle, as
though he were being playful rather than fearful. Sometimes I would try to
answer. At other times I would dismiss the question for what it was: a signal
to start a conversation and a way to bond between two people who did not
know each other very well—almost like asking about the weather. The question would allow me to ask him about his day, or I would engage with him in
a political analysis of the present. With Ahmed, the conversation would
sometimes move from current events to discussions of his future and whether
or not he should find work in Dubai before a war breaks out.[1] I could do little
to comfort him as we both entertained the idea of the inevitable beginning of

a war, its contours variably defined, and that it was a matter of when, not if, it began. Yet, anticipating war, verbally through his question and implicitly in discussions of his future plans, and turning the political situation into grounds for developing a social bond, seemed to be devices at Ahmed's disposal to establish some level of certainty amid the possibility of future political violence, a possibility that in turn was the cause of his uncertainty.

The constant anticipation of war runs deep within society in Lebanon, causing people like Ahmed to nonchalantly ask me the question above.[2] In this chapter, I will analyze the anticipation of war specifically during a time of sporadic bombings over several months in 2007, to think of the mundane locations of political violence, and how we come to live this political violence in and through ordinary time. I will explore the temporal dimensions of anticipating war in a zone of conflict, suggesting that we understand these practices as moving elusively in duration rather than confine them to and interpret them in a specific moment in time. The ethnographic encounters where this anticipation manifests itself intersubjectively in people's everyday lives works to elaborate on the relation between certainty and uncertainty that I observed above with Ahmed. The event of political violence is visible and implicated in the seemingly ordinary in a way that blurs the distinction between the event and the ordinary, and suggests the everyday as eventful.[3] I will address the ordinary not as an abstract notion, but as an experience I will explore ethnographically through a mother's advice to her child, a meeting among neighbors, and a traversal of the city.

Anticipation, in a general sense, is a deeply rooted phenomenon that guides our social behavior not just in regards to violence. It is a practice, as Jeganathan writes, that is not "confined to the verbal or the explicit domain of life," but encompasses "a range of ways of being, both subtle and sharp, muted and strong that are both spoken and unspoken, explicit and implicit" (1997: 185). The way we anticipate, and the meaning anticipation lends to social life, is constantly changing as people's feelings of anticipation connect dialectically with other people, situations, and objects around them. How we come to anticipate violence can then be described, but always only partially.

Tellingly, anticipation is a necessary condition of social interaction, and provides insight into how we imbue our history and our future with meaning (as in we live our lives constantly thinking of the future and what it might bring. We anticipate the developments in our work, in our relations with lovers, and the surprises each new day might produce). If we are always living in anticipation, it is specifically what is anticipated—in this case, forms of political violence—and how it is anticipated that make its discussion significant. There are different scenarios that breed multiple ways of anticipating violence, and a range of possibilities among people faced with similar circumstances. I suggest that this range, to a large degree, is determined by varying recollections and perceptions of the past, and by the very political interests and outlooks of the people involved, and these complicate attempts to confine processes of anticipation.

Specifically, the anticipation of war can be seen as an intersubjective moment; it is a way for people in Lebanon to relate to themselves, to others in society, and to the institutions around them. Under the pressure of social divisions, whether sectarian, political, or economic, this intersubjective space may offer alternatives for new forms of connection and relationality, and for meaning making in a diverse and seemingly divided national arena. The anticipation of war, then, becomes a way to think through regular mundane contexts of everyday life, and, more ambitiously, to think about new possibilities for social relations, connections, and solidarities, both in Lebanon and, perhaps more broadly, in states with protracted violent conflict.

Time and the Anticipation of War

It is a regular Saturday afternoon in mid-November 2007, a quiet day in my relative's home overlooking the city. I am in the TV room with Rola, whom we've met earlier, and her son Elie, who is a college student in engineering with no formal political affiliation. He is, however, strongly rooted in Christian identity politics.

As Elie and I are about to head out of the house in separate directions, a conversation begins between the three of us about the political situation and its ramifications, as the president's term is set to expire in a week and there is no replacement. That night I would write the following observations in my notes:

> Rola warns us before we go out to be careful and that this week is supposed to be bad. Then she laughs and says, "This week is every week." We giggle; a giggle that betrays uneasiness. Elie joins in and says, "We are always saying this, but who ever listens to the warnings? We end up doing what we want to do anyway. *Hek ḥayetnā* (This is our life)!" We all agree. Every week is the week the war is

supposed to begin or some conflict is supposed to explode. [(Fieldnotes, November 2007)

But war does not begin, and conflict only rarely explodes.

Rola's grave warnings about the imminence of war seemed to be expressed verbally and affectively through a gendered lens of caution and care,
embodying her role as a mother. The warnings, at that moment, were also
guided by her reading of the present situation and its politics. She was not
simply referencing some abstract phenomenon of political violence; she was
being informed by a past war that she had lived through, and that her son
and I, for the most part, had not experienced. The past, very clearly remembered, meant that Rola was, among other things, thinking of Green Lines
(ceasefire lines that divide cities or areas) and of killings at checkpoints based
on identity cards. It meant that she was thinking of religion inscribed in
neighborhoods to map her zones of safety. In this way, it also meant that she
was thinking of the East and West Beirut divisions of the 1970s and 1980s,
and experiencing anxiety about crossing from one side to the other. It was
this crossing over, as well as our staying late into the night—when battles are
perceived to take place—that she was implicitly warning us about.

People have a repertoire of learned practices that they may rely on in
different places and times, and here, one could observe in the slightest warning sentence to Elie and me, the way Rola was carrying her experiences from
decades ago to our present, making them habitual and essentially timeless. In
Lebanon, practices are transferred as society moves away from a period defined as war toward other moments defined in their relative opposition to this
war period (let's call these moments "not-war" to signify opposition rather
than absence, since opposition can signify both conflict and continuity).[4] The
two periods may be defined differently, but the lived experiences of people
may point more to a difference in intensity of war rather than to its absence.

Thinking of intensity as separating these periods might help to see how
the *ways of using* the space of "not-war" borrow from, and remain linked to,
the learned practices from the period of war before it. This borrowing and
transfer of past practices ensures that these periods of war and "not-war"
(commonly referred to as peacetime or postwar) interlope and merge, forming a continuity, but they do not reduce into each other; rather they overlap
and fuse in ways that often escape easy categorization, dichotomization, and
definition.[5] Thus, part of living in and interacting with the "not-war" period
is to occupy time with moments of anticipation and thoughts of the future

that are reflective of very real past events, and of the retold narratives of these events. Past practices end up working ambiguously as people try to rely on and remember the past for purposes of survival in the present. These past practices assist people in determining a level of certainty by informing their anticipation. However, they don't banish uncertainty.

Time, especially as related to the future and its determination by past war, is particularly important to this discussion. I think of time, in the Bergsonian sense, as duration (Bergson 1946), understood not just as a matter of living in and perceiving the present moment, but also as involving recollection and anticipation—the past and future—and about the way these moments endure rather than succeed each other (Caton 2014). An anticipation of violence can be felt as part of a duration that is constantly excavating past violence, so that what is otherwise thought of as an event in the past is never really part of the past, nor is it an event with a clear end or beginning. We see the past and present converge in Rola's warning—a warning informed by a previous bombing, as if that past bombing was still sending shock waves into the present; as if it had a social life of its own, by towering over our daily lives like a shadow or foreboding character, making appearances in newspaper articles, political speeches, and countless other sites. We also see the past collide with the present in how an old war determines Rola's warnings to her son and me, as we were traversing in and between the old divisions of Beirut, between its supposedly Christian East and Muslim West; categories that are no longer fixed and delineated in the way that they may have been in the past.[6]

One of the determinations of people who anticipate violence is to seek meaning and fixity in the world by attempting to predict and know the future; they are not always successful. It is much like trying to imagine what you will accomplish tomorrow: you might imagine the motions, but, as Bergson tells us, what you will think and feel in this future time "you can know nothing of today, because your state tomorrow will include all the life you will have lived up until that moment" (Bergson 1946: 19). One might imagine the "external shape" of an event, but trying to capture it in full will only lead one through a "duration" to the actual event, at which point there would "no longer be any question of foreseeing it" (19). As Bergson claims, duration is a place where things are revealed.

Anticipation, in general, can be a means to predetermining, or revealing, the outcome of an occurrence at some future time—in this way duration presupposes anticipation. Bergson suggests that with perception and witnessing, one can come to gain absolute knowledge by using one's factor of intuition, stretched over a specific period. Phenomenologists would argue that absolute knowledge is inconceivable and that at best, it is relative perception that one can hope to gain of a subject. Whether we agree with Bergson or not, we can safely say that through perception, and through what one has witnessed, we at least come to gain some knowledge. Since the whole point of the future is that it is unknowable in the present, people cannot comprehensively know the exact contours of the unknown. Yet, through anticipation people can act as though they know, for we might want to think of anticipation as bridging the anxious gap between perception and truthful or certain knowledge, between what people perceive in any given present and the certain knowledge of the future revealed in duration and the flow of time.

In general, people know beforehand that life is never fully predictable, yet they continue to attempt to gain complete knowledge of the future through processes of anticipation (that can manifest emotionally, mentally, bodily, or even materially in artifacts that might guarantee a future outcome).[7] These processes of anticipation are meant to deliver people to certain knowledge, and to what is then revealed in duration. However, the processes, despite their effort at certainty, are never in fact certain; therefore, they ensure knowledge remains relative rather than absolute. People in Lebanon, and perhaps more generally, are not located in the duration where things are revealed so much as they linger in processual states of anticipation that attempt to form continuity in what would otherwise feel like disruptions of the before and after; these disruptions, however, persist and do not magically disappear. This process of anticipation—the way people practice it in the present in order to alleviate anxieties about the future—and specifically, the knowledge produced by the anticipation of violence, can be thought of as a form of memory that generates meaning for people in the present, especially a political, social, collective, or communal meaning. Importantly, the anticipation of political violence can provide a useful technique to inject certainty into the uncertainty infused in daily life in Lebanon. The future moment of violence, partly excavated from the past, can then serve as an experience of certainty bounded with uncertainty, the two fused together and knit in time.

Yet the uncertainty that accompanies most anticipation ensures that no matter how prepared people try to be based on a past repertoire of learned practices, they will be presented with surprises that will reveal themselves, not necessarily as rupture (Taussig 1992), but as a continuation and extension of everyday life. For example, in Rola's imagination, the checkpoint is associated with certain practices, and fixes identities in specific ways. However, the notion of the checkpoint and its associations can also reveal themselves differently and multifariously. For example, an armed fighter at a checkpoint at the present moment may be searching for a mix of different identities in which the tactics Rola learned, based on past wartime experiences at checkpoints, may not be useful anymore. If she were to encounter this checkpoint, the newness may not present itself necessarily as rupture, but rather would be incorporated into the present that she would be forced to deal with.

This concept is further illustrated by events that took place on January 25, 2007, when fighting erupted between students at the Arab University of Beirut. We heard on TV that snipers entrenched themselves on rooftops, and that checkpoints were erected asking people for their identity cards and discriminating against them based on sectarian allegiances. But identity cards no longer have a person's religion marked on them, and the crisis was clearly based not on religion but on political grievances, revealing a disconnect between the purpose of the checkpoint and what the armed men were searching for. I learned in conversations later that people were supposedly wrongfully harmed, but I found that those around me saw the surprising episode folded into everyday life rather than as its rupture, partly because some version of it had been anticipated and some of it felt familiar from the past.

The January 2007 episode also highlights how the experiences of past wars, the way they are narrated, and the stories that enter our consciousness provide the basis for some of the techniques of war. In general, recollections of past wars, such as Rola's recollection of checkpoint practices, can enable techniques of future wars. If forgetting were so common and possible, then the technologies of war would not be so immediately remembered and executed. By technologies I do not mean the weapons themselves, but the way war is fought and lived everyday—the tactics, strategies, and maneuvers, such as those employed by fighters who are thinking in terms of past inter-city divisions or by civilians who know to hide in their bathrooms when a battle begins. Bodily and spatial techniques that are learned in the past are often transmitted and reused—as are discourses, which makes it easy in the case of Lebanon to revert to sectarian thinking. In this way, social traditions, as Mauss (2006) says, are carried forward through techniques. The anticipation of war, thus, becomes part of the social tradition due to ongoing and sustained political conflicts.[8]

Everyday Encounters of the Anticipation of War

The anticipation of war manifests in various encounters of everyday life as everywhere the talk of war seeps into daily conversations and decisions. One night, days before my encounter with Rola in early November 2007, I met with my neighbors who discussed whether to sell the building's electric generator or not, and whether to buy a new one. This conversation took significant importance because, as of yet, state-supplied electricity in the country does not reach people twenty-four hours a day, and while the area of Ras Beirut receives more electricity than most, it still sees three-hour daily cuts. Most residents are thus forced to purchase generator memberships with neighborhood electricity dealers, or to buy their own building generators. My neighbors were of various backgrounds, between Lebanese and Palestinian, Greek Orthodox, Sunni and Druze, and supporters of various parties across the political spectrum. Among their professions were those who were university professors, doctors, and UN staff, and they could be said to be middle- to upper-middle-class families.

In the midst of the conversation about generators, one neighbor said that there is no point in buying a new generator because a war is coming and there will in any case be no *mazūt* (diesel)—Israel's siege tactics of *ḥarb tammūz* (the July 2006 war) that made gas scarce informed this position. Another neighbor countered this, saying, "We need a generator because if there is a war then they might cut the electricity even more than the current three hours a day." She said that the *mazūt* prices would go up, but there would still be *mazūt*, and I agreed, speculating that in the coming war most likely there will not be a siege on the country like that in the summer of 2006, so we should still be able to get gas. The discussion ensued on the timeframe and possibilities for war, and was consumed by bursts of laughter as each gave an opinion. The conversation eventually transitioned to neighbors raising the issue that some were not paying their quarterly maintenance bills and there was no use buying a new generator if bills continued to go unpaid—neighbors who were not regularly paying were not present at this meeting. Such poor relations between neighbors when it concerns building maintenance and management are commonplace in many residences around the country. Those who were paying lived on lower floors and suggested that they could survive during the power outages. Mostly, this meant no access to the elevator, air-conditioning, or heater, as three hours without electricity were not enough to ruin refrigerated food. The meeting concluded with a decision to continue to research generator prices, but no action was taken until a year later when a new one was bought, following a full twelve months without backup electricity.

Just as the mundane afternoon with Rola and her son leads to talk of war, so does a nonpolitical meeting between neighbors to deal with residential matters. Such conversations often occur between bursts of giggles and laughter because people, whether the neighbors, Rola, or others I encountered, find their thoughts absurd. While the possibility of war is very real, and its anticipation is a recognized social fact, it still feels like an absurdity for the people concerned when talk of war and taking precautions against it seeps out of an unconscious and implicit realm into the consciousness of daily life; this absurdity often generates laughter. It is one thing to anticipate war, but as soon as it is discussed and becomes conscious, the anticipation turns into reality, a matter of fact, and one could explain this laughter as one way people react to the absurd notion of their anticipation being realized—it is the laughter of anxiety.[9] Thus, while anticipation of war denotes the possibility and potentiality for violence, speaking about violence can give the future an aura of being real, certain, and inevitable. Compared to this inevitability, one might think that the state of anticipation, where certainty meets uncertainty, can actually be a place of hope; hope against the expectation of violence, hope that the eventuality of what we anticipate will not be realized (Das 2007: 101).

Imbricated Formations of Political Violence and the Ordinary

In the summer of 2007, the war in the Palestinian refugee camp of Nahr al-Bared seemed distant to people in Beirut, and one could easily forget about the tragic developments in the camp. However, life at the Baddawi refugee camp, where most Palestinians went who fled the warzone of Nahr al-Bared, also gave way to mundane times when the war took a backseat.[10] One always forgets that the world lingers on even during the most brutal practices of humanity. An expression I heard from one refugee that, "We are bored, there is nothing to do," was a way to connect our lives despite the vast differences between boredom in the sanctuary of Beirut and that of the camp. In Baddawi, I saw people smoking *arguilleh* (water pipe) and having conversations that were not all about the political processes around them—this should not be surprising, but people who have not lived war, or other situations of protracted violence, are often somewhat astonished by the mundane in proximity to violence. In some moments, we drifted and spoke about our work, or what we did for a living, while other moments were spent in silence. I saw an old man taking an afternoon walk amid the crowd, boys just lingering around, playing, bored (Kelly 2008).

The mundane—and boredom—is not exclusive to the Palestinians in Lebanon. A similar phenomenon could be observed during the July 2006 war and other moments of violence in the country. In January 2007, during a riot that shut down the city and involved tire burning and rock throwing between different political factions, one could catch people in the streets in the midst of impending danger taking a proverbial time out. Waiting for something to happen, teenagers socialized and set up tables to play cards at makeshift checkpoints, much like their predecessors who were fighters during Lebanon's war (see Figure 4). All the while, the city and country were shut down and many feared for their lives. The acting out of the mundane and demon-

Figure 4. Street blockade during a riot in Beirut, January 23, 2007.

Photo Credit: Author.

stration of boredom (or even pleasure) could be seen as a type of political enactment or participation that displayed the teenagers' confidence. Through a relaxed posture, and by playing cards, the teenagers were showing their control and indicating that their opponent was defeated. Their posture seemed to serve a purpose of ridiculing, mocking, and even shaming their opponent, as if to say "the streets are our playground, what will you do about it?" From my position, this particular moment of a mundane activity (playing cards) circumscribed within extraordinary times, brought to the surface a feeling that our everyday lives had been hijacked by a political game between two rivals rather than by the existential battle each opponent made the conflict out to be.

Kelly tells us it is a common condition that situations of violence are never divorced from the mundane. He writes of the second Intifada in Palestine, where he explores "the meaning and implications of the ordinary and mundane in the midst of armed conflict" (2008: 353). He speaks of how "more time is spent watching TV, waiting for buses or preparing food, than it is shooting guns, hiding in basements or burning houses" (353). For Kelly, the "ordinary does not exist in opposition to violence, but is deeply implicated within it" (353; see also Das 2007). This is, indeed, what I have just shown in the previous example. However, I wish to take Kelly's argument farther, to claim that if the ordinary makes itself known within violence, then forms of violence also unfold within the ordinary. Seen in duration, the two states are always enduring, melding into each other, mutually imbricated and infused. One can be present in a violent conflict, acting out the ordinary, as Kelly rightly describes, and, within this ordinary moment, experience violence through the anticipation of hostility.

The mutual coexistence of forms of violence and the ordinary can be described through an ethnographic encounter.[11] In mid-June 2007, when the war in Nahr al-Bared was raging on, I was working with Dima, the architect and grassroots activist we've encountered in a previous chapter, to provide aid to refugees in the nearby Baddawi Palestinian refugee camp. I caught her in her apartment one day, distraught and expressing frustration in the midst of this war and the continual bombings of that summer. As we waited for friends, she communicated to me her fears in people's determination to continue their everyday lives. While Kelly tells us that ordinary life in Palestine is "an aspiration, a desire for a different kind of life" (365), for Dima—in Lebanon—it was part of the structures that perpetuated the descent into war:

When the civil war began in 1975 I was not around, I did not
see how it happened. But today, I feel I am watching how a war
happens, how a society goes to war. I am seeing how this happens
by making a society more complacent and making it accept things.
First, we accept political assassinations as a way to deal with our
problems. So they kill 10 people (civilians) to get to one politician, and we say "Haram the 10 people; *Allāh yirḥamun* (God have
Mercy on their souls), but the politician was smuggling weapons,
or deserved to go." And we make excuses for the death of civilians.
And slowly we are made to accept more deaths and killings to deal
with our problems . . . we lose a little of ourselves when we do this.
Soon a war will break out and retaliations will begin. I don't want
to be a part of this, I don't want to accept political assassinations
as a tool; I don't even want to become jaded to the point where I
dismiss it and just go on as if it is normal, as if it comes with the
title of being a politician in this country. Some people say justice
is being served when these people are being assassinated. But since
when was justice ever served by an anonymous entity (*kīf jiha ma-
jhūle bit-ḥa'e' el-'adāle?*). (Fieldnotes, June 2007)

Dima was struggling against becoming jaded and dismissing the assassinations as normal. Yet this was simply part of our long ongoing debates
about the moral implications, the meaning, and the role of our mundane actions in such times. The debates remained largely unresolved, and Dima, like
myself, continued about her days teaching, working, and frequenting local
coffee shops, as the war of Nahr al-Bared was ultimately far enough from
both our daily lives. The caveat remains, however, that forms of political violence would surreptitiously return in the way we experienced the ordinary
and what it made us think about, remember, and discuss.[12] In this process,
the ordinary in violence became suffused and imbricated with violence in the
ordinary so that violence would not appear as a rupture.

Sensing the Unsensed

The problem with a discussion around the anticipation of war is that it is
unseen and unsensed until it is identified—by being either voiced or consciously thought about. This led me to observe a contradiction that sur-

rounded the indiscriminate bombings in 2007. On one hand, people spoke about the bombings in a nonchalant manner. They would say things like "Not again!" or "Good, now we can go out because today's bombing went off already," or they would barely flinch and just go on about what they were doing in the moment. On the other hand, one would find far fewer people on the streets, like on the days after the assassination of former member of Parliament Walid Eido on June 13, 2007. People talked of how life goes on, but many tended to stay home, checking on a lonely family member or an aging grandmother, or going to the homes of friends and family to take comfort in sharing political and situational analysis. They acted as though they did not care and that life will go on, but for the few days after a bombing, this nonchalant attitude did not translate into people's behaviors in moving around the city.

In these moments, deserted rather than inhabited space becomes a trope to think through. De Certeau (1984) thought of place as being the consumption of space to produce something that is determined by "its ways of use." Thus, depending on how space is inhabited, we get a certain type of place. But what about deserted space? What kind of place is produced when the space is not being inhabited or used? Perhaps desertion itself, emptiness, the decision not to inhabit a space, is a type of consumption.

In the days during and after the indiscriminate and frequent bombings, mostly throughout 2007, Beirut residents determined the production of their city's space by deserting the city streets. People projected fear and tension onto places, and these places became inhabited by memories instead of by city dwellers, and by nostalgia of the hustle and bustle of what once was. "*di'āna Beyrūt*" (Pity Beirut, it is lost), people would say. Places were emptied, and emptiness began to take on its own meaning—of loss, of potential, of a dark anticipation for the next bomb. Through this meaning, a newly inhabited place was arising out of spaces of emptiness, and it was this, I suggest, that the rare passerby sensed rather than the emptiness per se.

City streets are often a reflection of the social world and can tell us much about society. Traversing the city streets of Beirut in those days after the various bombings, specifically in 2007, I found emptiness to be a grotesque allegory for political violence. In this emptiness, I saw the way fear played out; I saw the deterioration of social interaction; but I also saw how laughter and a spirit of carefreeness and cynicism one witnessed in the private spaces of people's homes could simultaneously exist alongside this emptiness. The hollowed streets, rather than exposing some profound sense of violence otherwise masked by people's laughter and cynicism, should be seen as a lens that, along with these other expressions, can reveal the contradictions, ambiguities, and negotiations people feel in such precarious times.

As I stood in the empty streets of Hamra on June 14, the day after Eido's assassination, which killed several other pedestrians, I thought of how this, alongside the private conversations mixed with laughter, was telling of what society is feeling and thinking. Thinking amid the desertedness, I could sense the fear, tension, and confusion. I could sense the want to emigrate, the anticipation of worse to come, and the preparation for war. I could sense all these things that I often missed in conversations with people when in their homes, where they would highlight or deemphasize the violence in an attempt to subvert it. More specifically, I could sense these things in what I heard people tell me, in Dima's expressions of frustration, Ahmed's talk of war, Rola's anxiety over her kids, people's repetition about their feelings of tension, and their decisions to stay home or where to park their car.

Two days after the Eido assassination, I was at Rola's home engaged in a political conversation with some relatives, jokingly commenting on how it was easier to maneuver through the barren streets that were now wider because security concerns made it so cars could not park on either side. Relatives laughed and agreed, after which someone responded by dismissing the bombings with a quote from Saint Paul on how "all things together work for good." I suggest that such conversations and interactions, filled with jokes and laughter, in the aftermath of bombings allow for a negotiation and ambiguous space to exist alongside the fear, tension, silence, solitude, and despair. In between the streets and those private spaces, one is perhaps able to listen to society telling us what it collectively feels.

But then, as time passes and the bombings become less frequent or appear to cease, space and time change, and revert to the way they were before the bombings. The streets are no longer empty. They become inhabited with people again, the highways are crowded at night, and through this habitation we see what is often thought to be social resilience. I try to think back to the steady, gradual shift to the way things were, but it is too gradual for even the anthropological lens. The barren and the inhabited merge into one, a continuous transition that appears as two states of affair only because we are unable to observe the continuous durational shift occurring within these states themselves (Bergson 1960: 3). The crowd incorporates the violent acts as part of daily life, and they become normalized. Certainty syncretizes with uncertainty, and people draw a sense of security from this and from forms of anticipation they know and have internalized. People start to go out more, though the anxiety seems to stay, but they begin to fear less as time goes by; and life, as they say, moves on.

While I was sensing things by being attentive to people's conversations and their experiences around the city (and country), in all these times and spaces of anticipation, it continued to intrigue me to think how people were themselves clearly sensing what was physically unsensed, namely, future forms of political violence and war, and how opinions and decisions were based on such senses. Jana, whom I had made friends with immediately after the July 2006 war, captures the nuances of these senses in a conversation we have one afternoon at a café in the neighborhood of Hamra called De Prague. She is a woman in her thirties, an artist, and not affiliated with any political party. She is invested in interpreting and making meaning of the war through her art, not being a passive victim to violence but rather negotiating its presences (see List of Characters for a further description).

As we sit on a semi-comfortable blue couch, sipping cappuccino, while Jana complains about the smoke, and I about my legs uncomfortably hitting against the low tabletops, Jana talks to me about how she feels we sense the war through our memories of a past war. She tells me she has dreams of this—not necessarily nightmares, just war-related dreams. She is not alone in having these dreams. I have heard this before. I interrupt her and ask how is it that we sense something that is not there? How do we sense something abstract? What does it mean to be constantly sensing a future war? Since it is mid-June 2007, and the war in Nahr al-Bared is still in flames, I tell her about how I notice Palestinians sensing an impending massacre. I tell her how I notice them anticipating yet another mass migration. I gather this from discussions with them, and which they base on the civil war, and on memories of massacres like in 1982, when Palestinians were massacred by the Lebanese right-wing Christian Phalange Party in Sabra and Chatilla. I remark that they fear this even though the conditions today are different.

Jana questions this difference and pushes me to see sameness and continuity between our present and past. "The civil war did not end," she says; "The story continues. When you watch documentaries of the war [like on Al-Jazeera TV], or think back to the war, the conclusion is that it is 'To be continued'; that the story was not over but that we are continuing with another chapter." Her point is that the players are the same, but just some years older, a function of the politics of "No Victor, No Vanquished" that has kept the wartime leaders in power and ensured that the causes of war remain.

If the faces and players are the same, Jana persists, that makes the Palestinians sense the future based on clear links to the past. She claims that the past is very much a present reality; it does not escape us and it is not merely a thread that connects us, but the very reality of the past that we are currently living. Even when there is no talk of war, she would sense it in what she read and watched on the news, or in seeing the same old faces of warlords in the media.

Not everyone thinks like Jana; the point is that people feel heightened anticipation and sense war because it speaks to an overall meaning making of the social world around them. This can lead one to consider the anticipation of war as an intersubjective moment. Through it, people in Lebanon form their relationships to their surrounding community—to the grocer or to representatives of political parties, for example. Through it, they also form a present that is based on entrenched past antagonisms—those that carry on from Lebanon's war—and that then guide them into a future that is stirred by uncertainty.

A Few More Reflections

People in Lebanon are constantly inundated by a discourse that claims a war is going to be waged soon, and like Ahmed at the beginning of this chapter, they often speculate and ask each other when the war might begin. They have certain imaginations of what this war will look like and who its actors will be, often that it is going to be an internal war or that Israel is going to attack, but rarely with defined contours for it. Whether they believe in the coming war or not, they cannot help thinking or wondering about it. The practices that are informed by this constant thinking of future war, by this anticipation of war, give another dimension to life in and around war that reveals the subtleties of this life, and its ability to take the war and its discourse and make it other than itself. In the midst of the physical perpetration of violence, practices of anticipation might be present in such mundane acts as playing cards in a shelter or listening to music or enjoying the company of friends, as these are circumscribed and inflected by ongoing armed conflict and assume meaning beyond the acts themselves. Between the physicality of war's violence and the period I have been concerned with, practices of anticipation might play out in a conversation with a waiter on moving to Dubai, a mother's warning to a child, or a neighbor's advice on housing matters. These cases highlight a different picture of people's lives in zones of conflict, despite war's enormous, spectacular, and expansionist power to produce itself in its timeless image of destruction, victimization, and suffering.

Time has been crucial to my argument, especially as an understanding of time as fluid, neither cyclical nor linear. Anticipation, I have claimed, works from a present to fold the past into the future. It is in this way, I maintain, that the anticipation of war acts as a form of memory, reminding people in Lebanon that the war is not over, and struggles for a better world continue.

The anticipation of war is a way to confront and use ordinary everyday life, fusing certainty with uncertainty, and informing the way we traverse the mundane, and the way we conceive intersubjective relationships within it. Thus, instead of walking along the Beirut corniche (seaside promenade), watching the sunset, and skipping on rocks; instead of going on a picnic, hanging out with friends at a café, or visiting the innocent lying sick in bed; instead of all these acts of everyday life being rather mundane, all it takes is a moment's reflection to see how these incidents can often become politically reconstituted and reused as acts of resistance, indifference, despair, hope, or survival. It is not war that is total or ever-present here. However, forms of political violence fluctuate in intensity and surely seep, at certain points in time, into the various activities, spaces, and moments of everyday life. One can observe this even in the workforce, where many businesspeople in Lebanon try to spread their risk by engaging in business overseas, and where people seek work in other countries to avoid the insecurity and instability that a potential war might bring.

One interlocutor, Bilal, a successful CEO of a technology firm and graduate of the AUB, told me, in a long conversation, of how the war years and the anticipation of war in general, governed his behavior; this is not indicative of how people in the workplace think and behave, but a representation of some of the views of a class of people. At the time we spoke, Bilal's company was engaged in a war disaster emergency plan akin to a natural disaster plan that might be in place in other countries. His view was that anticipation governs our life by forming our perceptions. "Once you anticipate the violence," he said in English, "you begin to react based on this and the anticipation determines everything." Even before any violence, we already foreclose the outcome. Many businesspeople, Bilal continued, have already factored the war into their behavior. War becomes built into work systems and business decisions both consciously (through disaster recovery) and subconsciously, thereby becoming a normal part of work.

Anticipation causes us to remember, and in the context of Lebanon it causes us to fold violence into aspects of daily life. Walking on the corniche one can see how the ordinary, always interacting with the surrounding context of the moment, becomes inflected with forms of violence through anticipation. It is this anticipation of political violence, however, that can act as a condition of possibility for change, or squandered, as it often is, into despair.

Often interlocutors are far more eloquent than researchers can ever be. I return to Jana, a friend with whom I have shared the most intimate and exciting of conversations and correspondences. Jana expressed an affinity with the everyday in an email to me after the Eido assassination. She was present at a beach club called Sporting at the same time as Eido when he was killed. She wrote to me two days later:

> I walked in [to the beach club], put on [the bottoms of] my swimsuit, and realized that I forgot the top part at home. I thought, I'll go home and get it and return . . . then decided to stay and swim in my shirt.
>
> I sat by fishermen who were carelessly throwing their fish on the ground next to me, and was watching two of the fish flipping and flopping like birds trying to fly, and I thought, what are they imagining as they die? And why don't I just get up and throw them back in the sea? I was thinking about death, about the last breath of the fish, and it took place, the explosion. (email communication, June 15, 2007)

Instances that are part of our everyday repertoire of practices—like sitting with fishermen—are in this way reused to make meaning out of acts of political violence and to put them in context. Observing fish in the process of dying is reproduced in connection with the death of a political figure and no longer just a simple day's act. The act of sitting with the fishermen, in this way, does not end there but continues to be reproduced to connect Jana to the bombing and its impact on her life. Her act is not merely an event but flexibly and fluidly exists in a Bergsonian durée that extends beyond sitting with fishermen and observing the death of marine life. The practices of anticipation deeply associated with war are informed by and exist in the passage of time. They are the ways Jana and others connect between a casual sitting with fishermen and a subsequent assassination. This connection is lost without her constant anticipation and without an understanding of political violence through its intensities. When violence is conceived of as simply an event, it is stripped from temporality and becomes depoliticized. Thus, practices of anticipation ensure the temporal and therefore political nature of violence.

Chapter 4

"This Is Our Life":
Experiencing the Intensification of
Political Violence

One night, during the July 2006 war between Israel and Hizballah, three of my relatives and I decided to go out for dinner in Brummana. Brummana is a town in the mountains of Lebanon overlooking the coast, predominantly Christian, and a summer vacation spot. My relatives had told me the restaurant we were going to had a beautiful view that overlooked the city and, with the war, customers could now also watch bombs being dropped on the southern suburbs; I was curious. When we arrived, it was around sunset at 7:30 p.m., and while eating, having a drink, and smoking *arguilleh*, we saw a few explosions in the distance and the city lit up. "Wow! It's nice!" my relative, George, giggled with excitement, only to turn to me and realize his choice of words. The reactions around the table were a hesitant, uncanny laughter that signified an inability to properly comprehend an amazing sight of destruction (it must have also had to do with my presence, both as an older figure and someone who disagreed with them). It had been a few weeks since the start of the war and the fear of being in the line of fire had faded, giving way to a voyeurism one could engage in from this distance without thinking of the dead.[1] Only in the moment after the beginnings of laughter do the dead return, and at the point they do is where laughter turns uncanny. I could not help think that George's reactions, and my silence, were all part of the disaster, and a way to sidestep our moral obligations.

To be clear, this scenario is neither unique nor new. One can find historical accounts of war voyeurism, whether it was people perched on rooftops in Boston to delight in the Battle of Bunker Hill before them (Corvisier and

Childs 1994: xxvi), or tourist excursions to watch the bombardment of Algiers by the French (Mitchell 1988: 57). The scenario of enjoying bombardment remains hard to come to terms with. Perhaps we are caught up in the exhibition of colors and we ignore the consequences. Beauty can be violent, after all, and the repulsive can be alluring.[2] Perhaps we related to the explosion as if it were on the news, and war, as Sontag shows, "was and still is the most irresistible—and picturesque—news" (Sontag 2003: 49). In a situation where one feels disempowered to change the course of a war, some feel the need to repress the moral questioning and empathy in order to make the present more manageable. A part of this is to confront reality as one might an image—with distance.

This outing, one of two of its kind that I partook in during that month of war, must be seen within a larger phenomenon where some people in Lebanon who were not from the South, Dahiyeh, nor Shi'a supporters of Hizballah, were spending their days at beach resorts in the North, or going out at night to restaurants, pubs, and even clubs, mainly in mountain regions like Faraya, where several nightclubs in Beirut relocated.[3] While present within the so-called theater of war, various forms of subjective energy meant that many of these people had a different relationship to this war and experienced it at another level of intensity.

After the July war, I began teaching a class on the anthropology of violence at the AUB. During the first session, this issue of people partying and going out during the war, without a care in the world, came up as a confusing space where students argued that at one point this was insensitive and perhaps immoral, but that people needed to continue with their lives in order to survive and to support the economy—a form of resilience. Seeing these acts as politically motivated tactics of anticipation is one way to move beyond this dichotomy to find meaning.

There are different ways and intensities of anticipating political violence. How one lives this anticipation is contingent on one's position in time with respect to the violence (one can think of this as during, before, after, or long after), on one's relationship to the perpetrators and victims of the violence, on one's spatial reference, on one's political and in many cases religious affiliations and identifications, and on generational and gender differences. In other words, it depends on the intensity of political violence and, on a subjective level, how and to what extent people feel and experience this through both individual and collective means of identification.

In this chapter, I want to argue that identity (such as class, sectarian, or

political affiliation), worldview (as in political and social ideology), and interests (social, political, and economic) contribute to people's experience with
the intensity of political violence, and, furthermore, are organically connected
to the way people experience the anticipation of political violence in everyday
life.[4] The anticipation of war becomes a way to think through state formation
and the formation of communities (national, sectarian, or otherwise), where
different practices of anticipation, taken together, are an allegory for how
people imagine their relation to the state and society as a national whole.[5] For
some it is an inclusionary practice, for others exclusionary and can be seen as
an evasion of moral responsibilities. These practices of anticipation, politically informed in some cases, produce a kind of cynicism, a cynical posture
vis-à-vis the state, politics and political change to be exact, that continues to
reinscribe and reproduce itself despite brief cracks that call for an outright
rejection of the current way of life, and thus a rejection of the idea that violence is on the horizon.[6]

To make these arguments, I draw on experiences from the July 2006
war, the May 2008 battles in Beirut, and the 2007 war on the Nahr al-Bared
Palestinian refugee camp. Dividing my observations along these events highlights that we cannot escape these periodizations. They may be experienced
differently, they may have ambiguous beginnings and ends, they may, as they
often do and as I have argued, meld with the ordinary, but people still bracket
these moments as events disturbing the functioning of everyday life. In cate-
gorizing these incidents as such, I am keeping the brackets people around me
use, since the incidents thus far, continue to be perceived and felt as events.

July 2006: War in the South and Dahiyeh

That evening in Brummana, with the explosion in the distance, was both
disturbing and revealing. I want to explore this episode in greater detail to
think through George's laughter, his subjectivity vis-à-vis my own, and what
it can say about how the intensity of political violence is felt and experienced.

My relative, George, in his early twenties, is not politically involved but
leans slightly toward the politics of the LF, which is politically opposed to
Hizballah. The LF was perceived to be supportive of Israel's mission to eradicate Hizballah's armed presence in the country by any means, and WikiLeaks
documents now give more credence to what was only a perception at the
time. While George was opposed to Israel's war that summer, he nevertheless

apologized for its actions by putting the blame on Hizballah, reiterating the position that if Hizballah had not captured Israeli soldiers and had disarmed, then there would be no war. For George, and my other relatives, this was not the first time going out. For them, going out to see their friends, to party in clubs in the mountain district of Brummana and have a good time, seemed a normal thing to do given that they were not in immediate danger.[7] In George's case, there was an irreconcilable "sour feeling," he tells me in an email several years later, "that people are dying and we are out having fun. Not to the extent of wanting to help out in some way because I didn't agree with how it started and didn't feel obliged enough to do something about it. Politically, I think I wanted Hizballah to lose but not get wiped out, deep inside I was happy when they got back some town or fired a rocket at the Israeli Navy bombing our cities!" There were many like George that summer, his friends at least, who felt indifferent or powerless and thought to make the best of their situation, or were secretly hoping Israel would defeat Hizballah and rid people of this party's politics. Publicly, at the time, I often heard the outings defended as a form of resilience, a motivation to keep the economy moving, or as another form of resistance known as *sumūd* or perseverance.[8]

From my perspective, the difference in the way we each reacted to the anticipation of political violence, namely Israeli airstrikes, is very meaningful. George's actions were ambivalent, at best politically informed rather than politically determined, and his choice of actions can largely be explained as an ongoing process of internal negotiation that questioned how one was to get on with life during bombings and a situation of war. In this way, going out, or clubbing, was an act that could have a range of meaning, from complicity with the idea of eliminating Hizballah, to a more neutral, even positive notion of maintaining an impression of a strong society willing and able to endure. To say that George did not anticipate political violence would be to disregard his entire context and environment, his political conversations and arguments about the war, his engagement in speculation about where the bombs we heard were falling, and his debates over Israel's real targets. Although his actions were a result of ongoing internal negotiations, much of his reasoning for going out less than normal was based more on security reasons—fear that it was not safe—rather than empathy with the victims. The episode can call into question empathy as providing the limits of recognition and where one places boundaries of communal identification and solidarity.

This form of anticipation, where a person feels less vulnerable, considers that the risk of violence is higher elsewhere, and does not believe him- or herself to be the target of violence, is a very important zone of possibility within the anticipation of political violence. It is a zone where certainty blurs with uncertainty to produce, in this case, a kind of ambivalence. The certainty, and feeling of safety, does not deny the presence of violence. Rather, certainty is generated within a context of anticipating violence as a result of one's connection to the geographic location (Lebanon), to history (past experiences of violence), or to the demographic target of violence (the Shi'a in the July 2006 war). Such historical, geographic, or demographic connections to a target of physical violence, force those who are not the target to imagine a relationship precisely through a lack of violence or through their own safety—violence is still present in this case because we might ask ourselves, "safety from what," if not a violence that is happening to the other. In other words, rather than absent or present, political violence has levels of intensity. One's subjective energy, informed by geography, history (or even memory in this case), and demography, leads to a (de)intensification of political violence.

To put this in perspective, when people in Lebanon were going out in July 2006, it was in the context of expecting they would be safe from Israel's airstrikes—they were not in the South or Dahiyeh, their past experience was that Israel did not generally bomb their areas (or even when it did, the bombings were perceived as strategic targets like bridges or military installations), and they were likely not Shi'a or Hizballah members. This is remarkably different from an Italian or Egyptian going out in Rome or Cairo during the same period. The latter, unlike those in Lebanon, would not have considered their relation to the July war when going to the market or to a nightclub.[9] Potential violence to the self and to the other are places to locate violence's anticipation, but each has its own repertoire of practices that become informed by politics. The encounter above with my family is one such example of this type of anticipation of political violence. This account also suggests that people, like myself, often find themselves experiencing periods of instability alongside their kin networks or even, for many, within their specifically sectarian communities or surrounded by politically likeminded people.

George's anticipation seems to be derived from his feeling that he would not suffer any consequences from the airstrikes. "We're going out because nothing will happen here," he would say. Several times he even came back closer to or past midnight. The airstrikes and warfare, in these moments, were not absent, they were simply elsewhere. The immediate future was safe enough to engage in nighttime entertainment. That he still anticipated bombings was made possible, however, because of a discourse around him that all of Lebanon was under attack and that he belonged to the same entity Hizballah operatives and supporters belonged to—the same Lebanese nation. His refusal of this discourse and his inability to connect to Hizballah or see any common ground did not matter; he was still embedded in the zone of Israel's violence.

George's relation to (or dissociation from) the target of violence seemed to reinforce the idea that his imagination of the future would be based on anticipation of his safety from this violence. To put it another way, George anticipated violence through an imagination that he would not be the target; in either case, a relation to violence was still wholeheartedly present. And it is this negotiation of one's safety within a conflict that produces the ambivalent moment where certainty presents itself within the uncertain future. It also produces the emotions, identities, and overall subjectivities that circulate to make possible the varying subjective intensities of political violence and its future expectations. These intensities are a way for people to form affective communities, communities that share a sense of emotional connection and understanding vis-à-vis an experience. In this case, an affective community forms as people feel together that they are not targets, not threatened, and share an experience of dealing with war in specific technical ways—going to the beach, to a party, staying home, engaging in relief efforts, fleeing the country, or in our case going to a restaurant. The way each person lives the intensity of conflict will help explain how they might position themselves.

My own anticipation that night was quite different. Of course, as the author of these words I have the privilege to give both George's acts and mine meaning. Serving as ethnographer and interlocutor, my analysis risks placing myself on a moral high ground, as the critical and reflexive academic. Rather than avoid my feelings altogether, I would rely on the explanations of other interlocutors as to why my feelings of and reactions to the anticipation of Israel's violence were different. In conversations with friends—arguably as acculturated to this environment as George—I would come to learn from them that the difference in how we anticipated violence during the July 2006 war might have been because I was more convinced about the right of Lebanese to maintain a resistance against Israel, whereas George was not, or at least he was not convinced of this specific resistance movement. This difference in politico-ideological positioning has many possible origins, one of which is our differing kin solidarities. While I lived my entire life abroad and my adult life away from parents and relatives, George came of age in his parents' home. Although he often disagreed with his parents on internal politics and voting, he was probably still influenced by his family surroundings. His family did not support Hizballah or any non-state-initiated resistance against Israel, and this may have had an impact on his views given his daily proximity to them. My relation to a sectarian, political, or familial community was (and is) weak. This, coupled with my convictions about resistance, might have made me prioritize feelings of connectedness with those who were being targeted over family or sectarian political loyalties. This political disposition could be the source of my discomfort in going out, and of my preference to spend the rest of the war active in relief work.

My solidarity with the resistance in part stemmed from solidarity with victims who had lost their homes, their lives, and their kids,[10] and in part from a calculation of anticipation whereby I felt that the violence in the South and Dahiyeh could spread to the rest of the country. When George and I went out that night, our imaginations of the future came from different places: his was of safety and mine of potential harm. These vantage points are politically informed and serve different interests. People's refusal (including my own) to anticipate violence targeting their bodies or surroundings, and instead to think of themselves as safe, occurs, I argue, from within an environment of varying threats and anticipations of violence that allows them to construct themselves in opposition to the targeted group, thereby also contributing to a Lebanese narrative of state formation.

Although anticipation is future oriented, it also reflects anxieties and fears of what has come to pass. In this sense, how people anticipate, and the intensity of this anticipation, would at least depend on recollections of past violence and the way this past was experienced, on their current political positions and interests, and on the way they identify with different segments and groups in society. The last point implies that people may also anticipate violence in similar ways as part of sects or religious groups, though the fact that political allegiances shift often enough means that one cannot reduce behaviors of anticipation to these sectarian or religious affiliations. George, I, and another relative of ours who fought the Palestinians and Muslims during Lebanon's war, each anticipated the violence in 2006 differently despite our being Christian (and with some overlap in terms of our sects). One's affiliation to the beliefs of a certain political party might, on the other hand, be a better indication of how one will perceive and feel about different forms of violence and thus anticipate the future—George is closer to the LF, my other relative to the Marada, and therefore more supportive of Hizballah's positions, while I am lost in the Lebanese political landscape for my affinity to the Arab "left," which is itself undetermined and politically disoriented. People across the board, no matter their political or sectarian persuasion, will often feel the violence and uncertainty of the future; it touches everyone. However, what is feared, how change will proceed, who will be at most risk, these questions are determined differently across groups and become contested sites for political debate and for conceptualizing the formation of state-society relations.

Sab'a 'ayyār (May 7): War in the City

The month of May 2008 presents another example of how those who felt the anticipation of violence and safety were constructing themselves in relation to the group targeted by political violence. On May 7, 2008, fighting broke out in the streets of Beirut, with significant battles taking place in my neighborhood of Hamra.[11] On that day, the March 8 coalition came rolling through the streets of the city, accompanied with heavy firearms, to put an end to the dominance of its rivals in the March 14 camp. The March 8 political parties that took part in the fighting were Hizballah, Amal, and the SSNP, while from the March 14 coalition it was Al-Mustaqbal and the PSP—the Christian factions were not openly involved. According to Hassan Nasrallah, Hizballah's general secretary, who declared the war in a televised speech on May 8, one day after the fighting began, this battle was a result of the March 14-led government passing two resolutions that dealt with the removal of the head of airport security, an ally of Hizballah, and the dismantling of Hizballah's telecommunications system—an analog communications system they use to communicate between their resistance fighters. The stated aims of this battle were to reverse these two government decisions. The March 14 coalition claimed this, however, as proof that Hizballah had turned its weapons on Lebanese, thereby no longer being a pure resistance.[12]

I heard Nasrallah's speech on May 8 at around 4:30 p.m., at a café I often frequented. There was hardly anyone there, and as soon as the speech was over the café owners decided to shut down, as they were told the number of armed men was increasing in the streets. I left with four friends, Rasheed, Dima, Marwan, and Anna.[13]

The café closed and we started to walk out of the shopping center in which it was located. I remember I was walking down the stairs, almost at

the bottom and close to the street, when the shooting began. It sounded like
it was coming from around the corner. Dima was already in the street; I saw
her duck, turn around, and stop for a split second only to continue walking. I
screamed for her to come back but she kept walking. Rasheed was still at the
top of the stairs taking his time, and I ran up to tell him to start running
because some of us had already left and they were shooting in the streets. We
stepped into the streets; I didn't know why we were doing that any more; all
I knew was that Dima, Marwan, and Anna were already out there and I felt I
had to follow. I wasn't thinking of myself. That's a lie. I was thinking of myself, but I don't think I saw myself as a single unit anymore; I was part of
them, and they walked.

A man with a Kalashnikov and a green army vest ran out of a building
and started shooting in a direction away from us. When I think back now, I
feel it must have been in the air. There were at least six or seven other men
in the alleyway. At the cross street above us an SUV stopped and men were
getting in. More heavy rounds of gunfire! We started to run, unaware of the
directions of the bullets. We got to the intersection of Hamra and *shāreʿ el-
skarbināt* (Shoes Street), and from there we ran down to Makdisi Street,
turned the corner, and found a brief respite to breathe. I looked at my friends
and we started laughing.

"Is this it?" asked Anna, as if disappointed. "Yes, yes, what do you want?"
I responded. And we kept running. Rasheed looked at me and I screamed:
"So much for there not being a war? What do you call this?" We laughed,
perhaps absurdly, perhaps in excitement, and unable to believe we were running away from shooting in the streets so close to us. I ran as fast as my legs
could take me, and as I ran, I remember so clearly thinking that it wasn't me
running. I felt as though I was no longer an ethnographer but a video journalist, and my eyes were the video journalist's camera lens bopping up and
down, as though my feet were not mine and this was all on TV. I felt this was
not my reality, or couldn't believe it was. I was an observer, watching my own
life from a distance, but, really, I wasn't. One could hardly be analytical in
such moments, and it was only much later, when writing these words, that I
could think of this role I assumed myself to take. It was almost as if the footage of war that I had seen throughout my life was influencing how I was
meant to witness myself. [14] Ethnographers have also been the target of violence and the subject of escape from it, but in that moment it was the video
journalist, or perhaps more accurately, the actual camera lens producing the
mainstream raw footage of war, that I seemed to transfer my emotions onto,

and it was as if that camera fulfilled my desire to be its lens and to see through it. The moment lasted for a split second before I was jolted back to reality, feeling the chill sweat on my face and the sounds of whoever else was on the street that day. We finally reached Dima's place a few blocks away, where we would spend that night and the next while the fighting continued in our streets.

What happened to us on May 8, 2008, can be seen in the context of the ambivalent space produced between the uncertain future of war we antici-pated, and the cocoon of certainty in our own life that we tried to maintain to secure the continuation of a meaningful life. Certainty and uncertainty cannot be understood here as dichotomous, but as syncretic and fused states occurring simultaneously. This also calls into question practices of anticipa-tion that may not always be successful. The last place my friends and I had considered fighting would breakout was in the supposedly cosmopolitan neighborhood of Hamra.[15] Like my friends, there were others I had bumped into earlier that day, at "Score Supermarket," who were out-of-town under-graduate students stocking up on junk food, less because of the insecurity they felt, and more because schools and universities were going to be closed, and they took it as an opportunity to hang out together at home. I joked with one of the foreign students I knew from the Lebanese American University (LAU), "*Shū* (what), you are stocking up on food?"

"No, just some munchies. My friends are going to hang out at my place since there is nothing else to do," she had responded. We laughed and neither of us was thinking of the events as a direct threat to us. I would later hear that her parents forced her to leave the country with the help of her embassy after fighting under her building got so bad that there was a dead body lying in her street.

My good friend Rasheed had told me to come to his café to watch Nas-rallah's speech together as a way to pass the time. Even as late as minutes into the speech, Rasheed would tell us that an all-out war would not take place, so far as this meant (in part) militias taking control of the city and using heavy artillery over protracted periods of time. While in hindsight this was techni-cally true, in those first days after fighting broke out, no one could be certain anymore, and in the moment of street battles with semi-heavy weaponry one had no time, nor did anyone care, to distinguish between nuances of a war and a battle, or the social scientific definitions of war; hence my rhetorical com-ment earlier while running, when I questioned his conclusions.

We were aware that there was an SSNP and Future Movement party presence in the area—two rival groups in the current political landscape. I had even warned Rasheed a few days earlier that we were living in a little bubble that was not as big as some of my friends thought—it extended west from the beginning of Hamra Street to Caracas Street, and north to include the AUB (Figure 5). Stepping outside this area, one felt in another world where a war was brewing. Thus, in this "bubble" we had believed ourselves to be safe. It was perhaps the model that we wanted the country to represent, and in it we felt safer because we were not the targets of a standoff, increasingly, and at least in rhetoric, between Sunni and Shi'a, represented by the Future Movement and Hizballah, respectively. What we had not realized was that our politics, being independent of the major political divisions—even though Rasheed, for example, is Sunni—had played a part in defining the way we anticipated violence and therefore behaved. On the other hand, the SSNP (its members being from different sectarian backgrounds) and the Sunni Future Movement had been on higher alert, planning for when the moment arose, and waiting for orders because the Hamra area was a key strategic

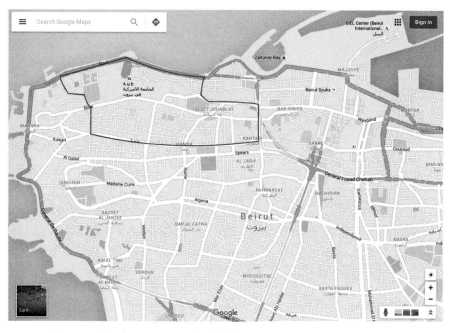

Figure 5. Google Maps image highlighting the bubble where we felt safe.

Credit: Author.

location for both parties who would stand to lose a lot if it fell to the hands of their opponent.[16] For the SSNP, this was particularly important because Hamra was the last bastion of strong SSNP presence in Beirut and a necessary stronghold. Our anticipation, or imagination of the future, was based partly on a specific recollection of the past, where Hamra, during the wars in the 1970s and 1980s, was generally not a place of heavy battles and, for the most part, escaped major clashes.[17]

What I find from observing the anticipation of political violence over time with some of the friends mentioned above is that the intensity of anticipation can begin to transform as our relationship to the physical violence develops. When people sense the physical violence to be moving closer in proximity, or when it actually transpires in surrounding vicinities, a cartography of violence begins to form in people's minds. Through a collection of news reports, estimations of where sounds of battle are coming from, and word of mouth, people begin to get a sense, sometimes wrongly, of where bombings or armed confrontations are going to strike and where it would be safe.[18] As physical violence emerges that does not target one's body, one's experience with this violence and all the subjective energy that goes into such experiences is deintensified. One may begin to feel the anticipation of violence less in terms of violence to the self and more as a function of one's own safety. This type of certainty of being safe comes about from the repeated anticipation of violence, as well as a better understanding of how and where violence is operating. In a sense, certainty is here carved out from within a general situation of uncertainty (uncertain times and experiences), showing that certainty and uncertainty are not mutually exclusive, as people might tend to think of them.[19]

This is clearly seen in the way the battles in May played out. In the months prior, Dima had anticipated violence to the point of questioning whether she would leave the country, and how she would manage if people were fighting in Beirut. Yet, when the fighting began on May 7, this did not stop her from going out the next day, May 8, to watch Nasrallah's televised speech. She had carved a space where fighting, though near, seemed to be elsewhere. Similarly, Rasheed had also expressed an expectation that some type of battle would occur and that this was a threat to our life; however, when the fighting began, until it physically reached our street, he had begun to feel safe, insisting that we could hang out outside our homes.

The morning after we had been caught in the streets as gunfire rained on us, we woke and turned on the news to learn what was going on outside, and what we could and could not do with our day. Soon after, Dima received a message on her phone from a Lebanese bank, Société Générale de Banque au Liban (SGBL). It read: "Dear Client, apart from Hamra, Mazraa, Verdun, Barbir, Sadat, Bliss, Khalde, and Mar Elias, all ATMs and other SGBL branches are open to help you with your needs." She read this out loud and we laughed. The message read like a map of the conflict spots. All these areas were in what was formerly known as West Beirut, and they were the areas where some of the main confrontations of the previous day and night took place. For people not in these areas, it was a warning that these places were off limits. For those of us in Hamra, we left the house briefly to stock up on groceries. The message was also a confirmation that in other parts of the country, in places like Jounieh, Zahle, and elsewhere, in towns in the South, North, and Metn (Mount Lebanon), business and life were operating, more or less, as usual. The message was perhaps a marketing scheme, a way for the bank to instill confidence in its clients, but it can also be seen, in a wider sense, to stand for the way people live these violent confrontations, and the way they lead their lives as they anticipate violence. Those who devised this message must have understood the power of anticipation, how people in the country will define their spaces in relation to the ongoing battles, and how all this would give shape to perceptions of safety. They intended to give an extra layer of assurance to their clients—no matter their political affiliations—that business continued as usual, and that safety could be found amid the battles. And indeed, business did continue, as my own traversal in the country in those days will show. In the next two sections, I place myself during the events of May 2008 in two different parts of the city and country—both, however, predominantly Christian—and with interlocutors in varying situations to illustrate how political and sectarian affiliations impact people's experiences with political violence.

Leaving Home and Traversing the City

On May 10, the fighting had subsided in Hamra and many shops had re-opened. Although some were cleaning glass from their store front, the material damages were not as great as my interlocutors and I had expected considering all the explosions and shooting we heard. Fighters with the SSNP who participated in these battles would later tell me, over coffee, that most of the shooting and rocket fire was aimed at the sky and used to scare the other side. Around mid-morning, my relative, Jad, called and began to tell me that what I was seeing and experiencing, the normalcy and people in the streets, was what people experienced during Lebanon's war. He explained that during that war, one side would gain control but would not be able to hold onto that position long enough and a new battle would start and change the facts on the ground. After a battle, people would walk out, open their shops, and life would return to normal for a few days until a new battle flared. So what I was experiencing, he said on the phone as I walked down Makdisi Street, was not so different from life during Lebanon's war (or "the war" as he put it, and by which he mostly meant 1975–77), and this was what scared him most.

As I spoke to different people that morning, no one was convinced that there was any real victory. It seemed too quick, too clean, and too easy. They feared either an underground resistance to the March 8 factions, although no one took this proposition too seriously, or, as they framed it, that groups in the Palestinian camps and militants in places like the North would start Al-Qaeda style bombings. They were all speculating and looking back, doing so with creative imagination based on their readings of past wars in Lebanon (for example, the Nahr al-Bared war the year before), but also of the way wars in other countries in the region had transpired—namely, the influence of Al-Qaeda in Iraq.[20]

That day, for lunch, I drove to Jad's house. I had refused to leave Hamra the last two days, despite the urging of relatives who wanted me to leave to their home in the Metn region. I was not alone experiencing this pressure from family. Several of my interlocutors were also asked by family members to stay with them in safer parts of the country. A friend's grandmother was at home alone, and he took the first chance of safe passage to check on her. Others I knew less intimately had similar stories. Some parents of Lebanese and foreign children called from overseas and pleaded with their children to leave the country; many listened to these pleas and left by taxi, and, in the case of many Jordanian students, on buses provided by the embassy.

My refusal to join my family was partly out of fear that, as a man, I might be mistaken for an armed combatant, and thus not have been able to get out of "East Beirut," as new cartographies of violence re-created the old divides of East and West Beirut. The other part was my feeling that to be anywhere but home was terrifying. During Lebanon's war, my family would often refuse to leave their apartment to go to the shelter in their building because they wanted to remain home. Similarly, in July 2006, people in the South refused to leave their home in many cases, and felt safe at home even though this could mean certain death. To leave home was to "court danger."[21]

A Kuwaiti-Lebanese friend in Beirut asked me once why people leave a war. She tells me she wouldn't do it, "My house is my home. I've been here for 11 years." Like Allen Feldman (1991), I see home as being a sanctuary in Lebanon. The one thing I hear from everyone, my parents, family, and friends, is not to go out, to try and stay at home as much as possible, and not to move around. It is dangerous to be in the streets, or to be driving in a car, or to be in a restaurant or other public place—this is where people are targeted. Nor is this notion of the home as sanctuary significantly altered when people learn that one of the victims of the Ashrafieh bombing, in May 2007, was in her house when the blast from across the street killed her. Home is still perceived as the safest place, and home with family, relatives, and friends safest of all. As opposed to the streets, home offers a measure of certainty, and more so if one has access to television, radio, or Internet to pinpoint the location of armed conflict from news reports.

On my way out of Hamra that day to see relatives, I could see the old civil war borders spring up almost spontaneously, even though the battle lines were in no way divided between East and West Beirut. Driving across town that afternoon was itself tricky as some roads were closed and others still risky. The Fouad Chehab Bridge, the main artery into Ashrafieh from Hamra, was shut down with burning tires and I had to take the beach road from the Phoenicia Hotel.

When I crossed into Ashrafieh and drove to Dikweineh, the traffic and bustle on the streets were not remarkably less than most other Saturdays, but it was a significant change from the areas experiencing battles. I felt the changing mood in the social activity on the streets consciously solidify and make present the invisible divides of the city. I wondered how I might have felt and thought if I had been on this side of the city the last two nights.

I arrived at Jad's house at 2 p.m. and he had invited some friends for lunch, serving his specialty: homemade tacos and fajitas that he had learned to make while in the United States for college. Upon arriving, the family laughed and wished me well, "ḥamdella ʿal-salāme." The mood was very different, even though I was only a fifteen-minute drive from home. They were planning a lunch with friends, and a ten-year-old relative of mine was playing downstairs in the surrounds of their apartment building. Still, I felt they were tense in the way they spoke about the political situation. However, by now, knowing where the fighting was taking place and where it would likely occur in the near future, the feeling of an intensification of violence had dissipated and they felt relatively safe. Added to this was the fact that their political side, March 8, had clearly won this round of battle, and equally, the fact that they were neither Sunni nor Shiʻa, invested neither in the existence of Hizballah (they are Aoun supporters) nor in the Future Movement (the two main rivals in this battle). Together, these placed the battles at a distance, and my relatives took on a different bodily relation to the fighting from those I encountered in Hamra in the early days after the fighting. The anticipation of violence was very real and felt, but it was no longer anticipated as an immediate threat to their own physical existence or survival—it was not a matter of life and death. Rather, it was a general anticipation of war affecting the social world around them that was ultimately creating a disturbance to their own social life and threatening the ways they would practice their daily life. They could, of course, be wrong, as my friends and I were a couple of days earlier—after all, even, or especially, in times of precarity, life can be more precarious than we imagine it to be.

Later that evening I would go to Jounieh to hang out with Basil and Zuzu, the two interlocutors encountered at the beginning of this book. In the mountains and in Choueifat there were still reports of heavy fighting as we sat in a restaurant listening to live Arabic music while people danced. This situation was not much different from what is said about Lebanon's war, and about the country's reputation at that time, where people partied while fighting was terrorizing another part of the city or country. I often get the feeling that people are conscious of this past when they repeat it, and that they do so with pride in such a reputation. I suggest, however, that contrary to being seen as a contradiction, going out at such times can be understood as a decision people took based on their sense of self and identity—it was in many ways associated with a particular sense of being Lebanese—and on their relationship to violence's anticipation at a given moment and the perceived risks this may or may not entail, as we saw with George earlier.

It is not a hedonism, dancing on the graves, or lack of empathy that governs their behavior—or at least these are not the only explanations— rather, it is foremost an assessment of how one feels the intensity of violence, how one relates to the overall context of violence, and how one perceives one's relationship to those being targeted. This relation to the target directly relates to the way one envisions a national identity, for it is the weak feeling of solidarity between communities that causes people in one area not to feel their own body, and their own national community, as being harmed. In the example of Zuzu and Basil, both were able to compartmentalize the conflict and confine it to an imagined West Beirut because, despite being March 14 supporters, they identified with their sect above and beyond the wider political coalition, and the Christians were not, for the most part, involved in these battles. Being from neighborhoods that are not religiously mixed would have also made it more difficult for Zuzu and Basil to feel any affiliation with the factions in their coalition representing Muslims, and those involved in the battles. Empathies might have run along different lines for those living in mixed neighborhoods, like Hamra or Mar Elias, where people interacted with different sects and had different socialities.

The longer armed conflict is physically present as a threat, the more people become normalized to it and begin, as much as possible, to return to patterns of life as if this violence were absent. A relative tells me of a time during the war when he and his father were sitting on their balcony overlooking Beirut, drinking whiskey, and watching bombs fall in what seemed like a distant neighborhood in the city. He tells me that he got up to refill their glasses and when he entered into the kitchen, he found that it was damaged from an explosion that had hit the back of their house. Until I had witnessed people nonchalantly watching the bombs fall over Dahiyeh during the July 2006 war, and experienced sitting with my friends and watching TV as a battle waged in our streets in May 2008—at one point a rocket hit the building behind our apartment—I always found my relative's story to have a hint of exaggeration. The reality seems to be that one quickly normalizes a situation in order to manage the passage of time. The event and the normal ordinary everyday meld together. Like certainty and uncertainty, feelings of normality and violence can be folded into each other, confusing these states of experience, and collapsing objective and subjective forms of violence.

Violence, the war, becomes something one lives with and in spite of. Some might argue that people tire from thinking about the pain of others and this causes them to get on with and enjoy their own lives. This position would hold if it were not for the selectivity by which people choose who falls within the community deserving of thought and care for their pain, and who does not.[22] Thus, one cannot exclude the possibility that this attitude of getting on and enjoying life is also an evasion of moral responsibility in wartime. In either case, I suggest that it is weak bonds of solidarity across communities often religiously, politically, and regionally defined, coupled with high threats to one's own affective community, that causes people to behave the way they do, and that presents an obstacle for them to feel the pain of others.

Negotiating Present and Future Conflict

As we sat at the pub that night, Zuzu told me he had spent the last three days at the Kataeb Party headquarters armed and ready to fight. It was only after the threat to his political party had subsided that he was ready to socialize outside headquarters and enjoy a night out. Over the course of my fieldwork, he had maintained that the war was behind him, that he now had a family to be responsible for, and that he would not fight if a war broke out again. But in May, when the time came, he rearmed himself, turning once again from citizen to fighter. Zuzu, however, did not see this as joining the war front. He believed this was a defensive posture just in case the other side attacked, and he would correct me on more than one occasion when I reminded him of those days in May and how he was prepared for battle. "No, Sami, this was to defend ourselves, but if you mean by war that I would attack, no, I would not do that anymore."[23] So participating in war, I was to understand, only took place when a person was attacking. In this case, Zuzu tells me that there was no way the Kataeb could let the 'awmiye (SSNP) attack and not do anything about it. He says, "Anyone but not the 'awmiye. Hizballah, Amal, the Communists, but not the 'awmiye." One sees again the present manifestation of the Kataeb-SSNP hatred related to the assassination of the Kataeb leader and President-elect Bashir Gemayel in 1982 (see Chapter 2).

Weeks after, Zuzu's wife, Aida,[24] would scold him in front of me and his kids when he laughed at a comment Basil made about hoping the war would return. I had gone to Zuzu's house outside Beirut for a Sunday barbeque lunch. This was an area of the country that saw little to no fighting during Lebanon's war, but Zuzu had not moved into this house till the mid-1990s after getting married. Zuzu's family apartment was in a three-story building, the façade of which had not been painted, and the roof still had not been tiled, as though another floor was to be built later. The apartment had two bedrooms, a living and dining room, two bathrooms, and a kitchen. We sat on one of their long and narrow balconies that overlooked the mountains and part of the Mediterranean. The balcony pointed eastward, and for most of the afternoon it did not get direct sunlight. Instead, a perfect, cool spring breeze lingered that almost put me to sleep after lunch.

I sat down with Basil and his wife, Josiane, while Zuzu started up the barbeque and Aida prepared tabouleh, hummus, fries, and a few other dishes, like beef stroganoff. We drank whiskey and nibbled on fresh *lauz* (almonds) while waiting for lunch. Among the varying conversations that afternoon,

Basil began to brag about how he wished the days of war would return because they were great; Zuzu agreed. At this point, Aida started lecturing
them about fighting. "*Mā it-dabbaḥū shabābkon? Mā bi-kafī? Mā it-dabaḥ
ikhwetak? Izā riḥtū bi-kūn fidā al-waṭan?*" (Didn't your guys get butchered?
Didn't your brothers get butchered? If you go would it be as a sacrifice for the
nation?) Zuzu responded: "*Akīd, izā riḥit bikūn fidā al-waṭan!*" (Of course, if
I go, it would be a sacrifice for the nation!).

   Both Basil and Zuzu tried to convince Aida that there was no army and
so they needed to take things into their own hands. Aida was adamant about
her position that carrying weapons was irresponsible. This exchange was
clearly not what I had imagined from speaking to Zuzu weeks earlier. Back
then, he assured me that his wife knew and was fine with his decisions because it was for a greater good. Yet, Aida seemed to draw on the irony of
nationalism and losing bodies for that sake. In this posture she tried to expose the paradox of sacrifice for the nation. She appeared to me conflicted
but ultimately unable to influence her husband's conviction that he was
needed to defend his people (narrowly and loosely defined as Christians).

   That night when we were out after the May battles, Basil had expressed
the same sentiment about wishing Lebanon's war would return. "*Kānet iyēm
ḥilwe*" (Those were the good days), he said. Zuzu had conveyed this as well,
and when I asked him about it he pondered for a moment and then claimed
that it was mainly because those days brought more freedom. He was young
and hung around with the "boys" all day, and did not have to go to school.
Things were more affordable during the war as well, and he didn't have to
worry about his next meal. Zuzu and Basil were also not married, and it is
equally likely that this was an expression of nostalgia for their single days and
for their youth.

   Basil told me he would love it if Hizballah would enter the Christian
areas because he wanted to fight them even if in the end he were to lose.[25]
Part of this is an obvious flexing of muscle and revolves around maintaining
dignity, but another part concerns a very real anticipation that one day he and
his community will be attacked (this stems from a belief and fear that Hizballah wants to take over the country). This anticipation of violence to be
instigated by a clearly stronger opponent, having not occurred yet, allows
people like Basil to posture himself as the brave patriarch who is ready to
protect his community. He says all this with *ḥamas* (fervor), that Gilsenan
explains, is "a fierce readiness to defend" oneself or one's community, and is a
"vital element of honour" (1996: 160). So far as Hizballah has not attacked

them, Basil is able to carry his honor as a protector, and his hopes for war can be seen as an imagination of a future with dignity that resembles his recollection of a strong, brave, and heroic Christian past, which stood its ground throughout the entire war in the 1970s and 1980s. This hope is a way to posture himself as dignified while waiting for a possible attack. Basil finishes his expression of bravado telling me he would butcher the Aounists—or FPM— as well as Hizballah because they are allies. "*Bnīk ikhton 'alla hizb-allah taba'on*" (I would fuck their [the Aounists] sisters and their Hizballah) he concludes aggressively.

At the end of that night, on May 10, I drove back to Hamra from Jounieh. The streets were quiet and deserted, much as they were during *harb tammūz*. I left close to midnight because I felt uneasy about returning to my neighborhood, where I expected checkpoints to be erected despite the army's injunction that no armed men should be visible in the streets. With the government paralyzed and being the target of all the week's fighting, the army was in control and taking its commands from its general, Michel Suleiman. As I crossed over the still invisible lines demarcating East and West Beirut, I began to feel tenser. I passed the Phoenicia Hotel, tracing the same route I had taken earlier that day, and took a left at the Gamal Abdel Nasser statue to see in front of me armed men sitting on the side of the road. When they saw my car approaching, they stood up and moved toward a barrel they had placed on the side of the street as a makeshift checkpoint. I stopped, felt myself tense rather than nervous, lowered my window, thanked them for their work, "*ya'tīkon el-'afye*," and they sent me on my way. Being a man, alone in my car at night, did not help allay my fears. Nor did the fact that I had just been fraternizing with members of the Kataeb party and LF, their enemies. However, not being a member of any political party was the reason I found myself out so late in the first place, whereas others were home, and still others, feeling more implicated and connected to a specific politics, namely, the politics of March 14, did not traverse certain neighborhoods for a long time after that May. In this way, identity politics played a role in how people anticipated violence, where and when they expected violence to present itself, and who would be its potential targets.

Nahr al-Bared: War Elsewhere

Practices of anticipation were also governed by identity politics a year earlier, in the summer of 2007, during the war between the Lebanese army and the militant group, Fateh al-Islam, in the Palestinian refugee camp of Nahr al-Bared. Unlike *sab'a 'ayyār* or *ḥarb tammūz*, the war on Nahr al-Bared was much longer, and was accompanied by a series of bombings nationwide, but aside from these bombings, it was mostly seen as contained within the Palestinian camps.[26] In order to understand how the politics of this conflict influenced people's practices of the anticipation of violence, it will be useful to first discuss briefly how society in Lebanon defines itself vis-à-vis the Palestinians.

In 1948, with the creation of Israel, Palestinians dispossessed of their land made their way to the newly surrounding countries like Jordan, Syria, and Lebanon. The way they were treated in each country differed. In Lebanon, and from the beginning, they were seen as a potential threat to the demographic composition that was the basis of the Lebanese political system.[27] Except for a few Christian Palestinians, most were not given citizenship or civic rights, and their conditions worsened as a result of their exclusion from political and economic life. It was primarily during the rule of President Fouad Chehab, starting in 1958 and through the 1960s, that the Palestinian population was considered deviant and was the subject of surveillance and repression by the Deuxième Bureau (military intelligence). In November 1969, the Lebanese army and Arafat signed the Cairo Agreement (see Appendix 1), which allowed the PLO to stage missions against Israel from Lebanon. Arafat subsequently made Lebanon a base for the PLO after the liberation movement was defeated and forced out of Jordan in 1970. In Lebanon, the PLO was allowed to arm itself unimpeded by the Lebanese army and government. The Lebanese Christian political forces were against Palestinian armament, and after years of minor incidents and confrontations, the Palestinian and Christian factions finally turned to sustained armed conflict in 1975, thus providing a catalyst for Lebanon's war. The PLO in Lebanon was defeated in 1982 with Israel's wide-scale invasion of Lebanon and siege of Beirut. At that point, the PLO and Arafat were escorted out of Lebanon to Tunisia, where they stayed in exile till the Oslo Accords brought Arafat back to the West Bank in the 1990s.

The Palestinian refugees of Lebanon are for the most part seen as the "other," either to be relocated outside the country in whatever way possible, or whose right of return is enshrined and must be fought for in order to re-settle them back in Palestine. Few see them as part of the community in Lebanon, and those that do accept them are more inclined to do so from a distance. A minority of Lebanese advocate for Palestinian refugees' civil rights and their right to resist. It is within the backdrop of all this history that the war on Nahr al-Bared united many Lebanese across political persuasions. They could finally stand behind the army against an enemy and prove their patriotism through this stance.

People I interacted with, family and friends, over the months of the war were upset and afraid, but not because of the destruction to the camp or the attack on the lives of the Palestinian people and their uprooting from Nahr al-Bared to the Baddawi refugee camp. Instead, they were upset and afraid for their own lives and anticipated the spread of the fighting to other places in Lebanon. The indiscriminate car bombings in and around Beirut that in-creased in the first weeks of the war did more to heighten the fear of war than the actual fighting in the camp. Few made the connection between the Lebanese army's bombing of the camp and Israel's bombing of the South the year before. Shortly after the fighting began, I published an article online taking a clear position and drawing attention to this point, and to a petition being circulated that highlighted the blind patriotism and religious symbol-ism being used. I wrote:

> A few days ago I woke in the morning to find the following email petition in my inbox asking for my support and signature:
> Our Army is our pride—Petition
> · Our support goes to the Lebanese Army, our soldiers, our na-tional pride
> · We send our condolences to the families and the martyrs
> · Always proud, always in our hearts, always in our prayers! God Bless YOU and your families for the sacrifices you make each and every day
> · We bow in respect in front of their courage and devotion—We are a witness to the strength, honour, wisdom and patriotism of the Leb-anese Armed Forces as well as its glorious history and magnificent skills and tremendous heroic sacrifices it gave our beloved Lebanon.
>
> Support our army and our soldiers for all the sacrifices they are making. They are the guarantee to our salvation.

I continued to write that in the context of people calling out for the army to "finish us from the Palestinians once and for all" (a phrase I heard repeated many times), this "salvation":

> that we are to be guaranteed of by our support of the army in this petition is a salvation from the Palestinians. In our habitual, almost instinctive resort to religious imagery, this petition claims the army as Jesus Christ[28] and the Palestinians as all things evil.
>
> Have those who signed the petition and who have celebrated the Lebanese army in the streets not drawn any connections between the army they are so fond of and their Zionist neighbors? In the first three days of the recent events involving the Lebanese army and Fateh al-Islam in the Nahr al-Bared camp, the Lebanese army committed what would amount to war crimes in a similar fashion to that of the Israeli army in Gaza and in Lebanon last summer, firing on a civilian population indiscriminately. When the Israelis do this, we scream at the injustice, but when the Lebanese army does it we applaud them. These are double standards. ("Cheering to the Beats of the Palestinians' Misery," Electronic Lebanon, May 25, 2007)

These views were met with much anger from acquaintances and others who wrote to me in response to the article. People assumed the refugees sheltered the Islamic group Fateh al-Islam, which the army was fighting, and then questioned why the Palestinians would do this—never mind that many of these same people were also directly and vocally calling for the army to "finish us from the Palestinians." They did not seem to consider the idea that destroying the camp was a form of collective punishment, or whether they would accept this same treatment if it were their own neighborhood in Beirut being bombed in this way. What mattered more was probably a fear of Palestinians based on past experiences from Lebanon's war, when the army was no match for the PLO in Lebanon. These sentiments, particularly the fear, had a powerful impact on the way people then went about their daily lives and how they anticipated violence.

That summer went ahead, the tourists came, though some stayed away, and people went on with their daily lives. In Beirut, the fighting in the North seemed as though in a distant land. Although I was involved in humanitarian relief work to the Palestinian refugees in the North, and spent part of my time organizing political events in protest against the war, I also went out at night with friends visiting from out of town. One night, at a rooftop nightclub situated near the Beirut port with a view out to sea and to the North, I caught myself thinking of the violence in the distance. Maha, a friend of Palestinian origin who worked in an advertising firm, perhaps noticing my solemn stare in the midst of flickering lights and uplifting beats, asked me about my thoughts. This led to a quick exchange in which I mentioned the Nahr al-Bared camp, and she became dismissive on the grounds that the army had to do what it was doing, that we needed to get on with our lives, and that there was nothing much we could do in any case. Maha's position revealed some despair and hopelessness in the situation, but she also seemed to excuse the collective punishment meted out against Palestinian refugees in this case. While I cannot say with certainty that her position was against refugees, the episode did lead me to reflect on the question of the ethics of proximity.

Was I concerned because the war was down the coast within my national borders? Or perhaps it was because I felt politically or socially close to the suffering refugees? At what point would it be ethical for me to party without any consideration for the suffering of others? Would it be when the fighting is in Syria? In France? Or in Iraq? Was the difference in empathy toward this community between Maha and me any indication of how we imagined our collective community? Did it betray class interests on her part to dismiss these refugees? The questions and their responses are necessarily political. They strike at the root of the politics of recognition within the country, and to the limits of our obligation to others and the way this obligation is defined in everyday discourse. The limits of our recognition of and obligation to others is, in a sense, a reflection of the limit of the nation as a community. When people disregard Palestinians, or when they disregard the Shiʻa, or when people in one neighborhood disregard people in another neighborhood or region, all this sets limits on what the nation as community ultimately translates to in everyday practices that involve care, empathy, and obligation to the other, and whether to rescue the other and mourn them.

About a week after the fighting started, along with Rasheed, Dima, and other friends, I attended a concert held by the famous Lebanese musician and playwright Ziad Rahbani. Unlike during the incident at the club, the audience here was clearly and explicitly sympathetic to the plight of the Palestinians being attacked in the camps not more than an hour away by car. We were constantly reminded of war during the concert. At one point, Rahbani opened up a song by saying that it was first written and performed in 1975, a time that was tense and led to Lebanon's war. People laughed at the irony and similarity with the present. During the concert, I wrote in my notes that "I see the stage as a sinking ship with the country burning around us." The next day, in the papers, Ounsi al-Haj, a renowned poet and writer who was at the concert, wrote that the concert reminded him of the sinking Titanic (*Al-Akhbar*, June 2, 2007). Our mutual anticipation of the country's fall, so intensely felt at this time, was politically constituted as part of our intimate relation to the site of the perpetration of violence—Nahr al-Bared—and our politics of identification. For others, the war was a time of fear, but also a time to rejoice. For those who rejoiced, the Lebanese army was standing against the Palestinians for the first time. This position was founded on recollections of past threats as far back as 1973, when, these people believe, the army should have dealt a blow to the Palestinians in Lebanon. And this position is conditioned on the perception of Palestinian power and status as unchanged from the 1970s.

Of course, the war was also an ambivalent time, one of negotiation, reflection, and ambiguity of positions. Rather than go out while remaining conflicted, as I did many times, others sealed the ethical question by ignoring it altogether. I would like to suggest that this was not denial, evasion, or escape. Rather, it was more akin to a feeling of disempowerment. The war would go on whether they questioned it, protested it, or felt miserable about it. It was perhaps more consistent to go on with everyday life, which would go on in any case, without concern for those who cannot be helped.[29]

Cynical Reactions

I have been arguing that the way people relate to various communities can be an indication of how they anticipate political violence. Forms of identification, bonds of solidarity, worldviews, and people's political, economic and social interests can all determine how people experience violence and its anticipation. What might appear as contradictions—people going out while others are bombed, or people ignoring a war while others die—can be explained through practices of the anticipation of violence that are politically constituted. Rather than contradictions, these experiences can be a lens through which to understand Lebanese narratives of state and communal formation. Thus, national identification, or Lebaneseness, if it were ever possible to locate it, has its limits where empathy for certain victims stops. In other words, if a Kataeb Party member cannot relate with the pain of a Hizballah supporter being bombed in July 2006, it calls into question the limits of this person's community (or ingroup) rather than the limits of their humanity.[30] Through the ethnographic experiences I recounted in this chapter, my intention has been to show the ways in which these limits of community are negotiated within an environment of anticipating political violence.

Looking back on the various episodes in this chapter, the July 2006 war, the summer of 2007, and the battles of May 7, 2008, and thinking back to all my interlocutors, cynicism is one frame of thought that seems to govern people's reactions as they anticipate political violence. Whether it was George and his friends who were ambivalent about going out in July 2006, my friends and I at the café in May 2008 who accepted our little zone of safety within the deteriorating politics in the city, Zuzu and Basil who dismissed small battles as barely being worth any mention, or my friend at the nightclub in 2007 who expressed a similar ambivalence to George, all these people seemed to have a similar understanding that "this is our life" (*hek ḥayetnā*), that the alternatives are few and far in between, and that everyday survival must continue.

People knew that the situation was not normal, that their ordinary was not as ordinary as they would like to believe, and that the event was now. Yet, they continued to engage the world as if they did not know this, as if the situation were normal, and as if the event had past and the ordinary were now.[31] Navaro-Yashin (2002) tells us that the cynical posture is one in which we indeed know how things are, but act as if we do not in order to, among other things, survive and manage everyday life. Sure enough, this is the sentiment one hears time and again, whether it was from my students at the AUB after the July 2006 war, my friend who nudged me to dance the night away as the Nahr al-Bared camp was being shelled, or people I saw who went to work every day, and even started new businesses in times of heightened anticipation of violence or during outright battles. People wanted to survive, and they saw very few alternatives ahead of them, which in turn motivated the way they lived their lives in the possible wake of political violence.

The idea here is that the anticipation of violence is intersubjective, it acts to fuse certainty within uncertainty, it leads us to see violence and the ordinary as bounded, and it is informed by people's identifications, political and otherwise. It allows us to see the limits of communal solidarity, and produces cynicism in people's daily lives. Next, I will turn to the way the anticipation of war can be mobilized and even manipulated by different forces in society.

Chapter 5

Enframing the Anticipation of War

"Hinne 'am bi-namū el-ḥarb" (They are stoking the war). I heard my interlocutors say this quite frequently, laying blame on political actors and the media for contributing to the growth, sustenance, circulation, and development— or economy—of the anticipation of war, even though these actors might have felt similar or perhaps more pronounced forms of anticipation. My interlocutors would say this in frustration in reaction to a political talk show or a politician's public statements. In this chapter, I explore this line of reasoning and claim that social and political actors (politicians, media, military, and others) are involved in producing, promoting, and distributing objects and practices that contribute to the anticipation of war. The anticipation, more than just a feeling, intensifies and develops into a shared experience through the circulation of these various objects and practices (like checkpoints and talk shows).[1] One can imagine that people would not be left to feel uncertain about the future or to anticipate war without a contest emerging over how to influence, capitalize on, and ultimately enframe this future. By enframe, I mean the attempt by social and political actors to order and contain the anticipation of war (or the future more generally) through the circulation of a specific set of practices (such as speculation and prediction), objects (such as billboards and checkpoints), representations (such as in media and art), and discourses (such as political speeches).[2] My interest in this chapter is to think about how the repertoire of practices, objects, representations, and discourses of the anticipation of political violence come to shape, inform, and affect people's actions and experiences in the world (Kochan 2010: 583). And how, together, they produce a narrative that can shape the meaning of war and peace.

The process of enframing occurs at all levels, but it is especially visible among sociopolitical agents located in key places of influence and power: political parties, paramilitary factions, sectarian institutions, foreign states, local government, media, the business sector, academia, art world, and national government. Their maneuvers at the macro level seep into everyday life and enframe ways of thinking about the future. How is uncertainty enframed, managed, and circulated in everyday life? And how does the future come to be instrumentalized for specific ends?

As we have seen, the period after the end of Lebanon's war was not absent of armed conflict, bombings, and other forms of political violence. It can be said that an economy has emerged to capitalize and gain from this climate of uncertainty—just as war economies develop to capitalize in wartime.[3] Pietruska argues, in the American context, that as people in the United States were confronted with "uncertainty and indeterminacy" about their future, "prediction became an increasingly ubiquitous scientific, economic, and cultural practice, and forecasts, whether accurate or not, offered illusions of control over one's future to citizens of a rapidly modernizing America" (1995: 1). An economy grew to offer consumers and producers certainty in this increasingly unpredictable world. Similarly, an economy has emerged in Lebanon that is taking advantage of people's general sense of anticipation of war.

Elites have a certain relationship to the future that is important to consider when thinking of the circulation in society of different practices and objects. Dunmire writes, "The prospect of an open and uncertain future is viewed by those in power as a threat to their status" (2013: 26). By attempting to know and control the future, politicians present themselves as though they know what the future holds. Dunmire continues, "Dominant political and social actors, consequently, seek to contain the uncertainty inherent in such moments through policies and actions designed to shape the future in ways that will maintain the status quo" (27). My intention is to highlight some of the ways sociopolitical agents in Lebanon come to control and commodify the future to maintain their power or advance an economic agenda. I suggest that their forecasting, predictions, speculations, security strategies, and overall decision-making play a role in influencing people's self-perception of the future. This is not to say that the future is not precarious or may not actually bring about war, but that this feeling of future war is rationalized and reinforced, and remains a predominant concern because of the practices of various sociopolitical actors who, through various means, can materialize for people the war they are imagining.

Fortunetellers are not the only ones who try to tell the future, or give us

a handle on our future and provide some certainty about it. People are doing
this all the time, and in this chapter I look at some of their objects and practices, and explain how they are oriented toward the future. From checkpoints
to commemorations, from advertisements to political speeches, from talk
shows to political posters, they all try to predict the future, prevent a specific
future from happening, or frame the future. Valsiner writes that people have
a "fascination with future visions [as] a psychological means for coping with
the uncertainty that exists precisely because of the inevitable disappearance of
the present to the past, leaving the person always facing the future" (1993:
14). Since the future is always uncertain, to some extent, it is possible for
fortunetellers, but also for powerful sociopolitical actors, to capitalize on reconstructing people's "present-time ambiguous feelings about their uncertain
futures" (14). The ambiguity present in the nature and meaning of violence,
and the precarity imposed by a conflict zone, turn this uncertain relation to
the future from implicit to explicit—to the point that people can become
certain about uncertainty.

Political Rhetoric: Influencing Perceptions of the Future

During the years of my fieldwork, politicians oscillated in their speeches and
statements between warning that war would come and reassuring people that
it wouldn't. For Riskedahl, such rhetoric "can be strategically used to accomplish particular social goals. Specifically, they may be used to reorient the
Lebanese audience to a different understanding of current political events by
drawing emotive connections to past events" (2007: 308). The rhetoric of
politicians saying that war is unlikely was especially interesting. The question
"which war?" was not always clear, but it could take the form of, for example,
member of Parliament Ghazi Aridi claiming that "civil war" would not occur,
but perhaps "more dangerous problems" could (*An-Nahar*, February 21,
2008), or simply that there would be "no war" as Grand Ayatollah Moham-
mad Fadlallah once suggested (*Al-Akhbar*, November 13, 2007), both of them
responding to the constant circulation of rumors that war was on the horizon.[4] One expects that if the situation were calm, one would not hear a politician talk about how there will be no war, for this would be a foregone
conclusion.

In June 2007, my Arabic tutor expressed the increased frequency of such
language—that there would be no war—and felt this had the opposite effect

of signaling uncertainty and danger to come. Politicians could use this type of caution to suggest they had some certainty about the future and people should not worry. One effect was to set these politicians up as gatekeepers of the future. It also allowed them to define what war was and wasn't. To claim that there would not be a war in the future implied the country was currently not experiencing any war. This was an assumption that brought with it implications for thinking about everyday life as well as policy.

Yet, often, these statements and speeches also warned of war, and would come in the form of politicians cautioning an abstract "us"—standing in for Lebanese society—not to continue in the same path or direction lest civil peace (al-silm al-ahlī) be broken, a civil discord (fitna) erupt, a crisis ('azma) worsen, or a war begin. One example is when a politician, Jumblatt, announced one day to his supporters on television that "if they [perhaps Hizballah, Syria and/or March 8] want chaos, we welcome the chaos; if they want war, we welcome their war" (New TV/Al-Jadeed, February 10, 2008); another is when Hassan Nasrallah cautioned Israel on February 14, 2008, after the assassination of a senior Hizballah leader, Imad Mughniyah, that "if they wanted an open war then let it be an open war."[5] Such discourse offered by these agents—the same agents in control of the means of violence (and, in many cases, the media)—works to keep violence on people's minds and can serve to influence (even manipulate) social perceptions of the future. Since past rhetoric of violence is viewed causatively as having led to acts of violence, the feeling goes, present rhetoric can lead to future acts of violence (Riskedahl 2007: 315).

If these political agents can have an impact on the levels and ways of anticipation, then perhaps they could frame issues of security and stability, and be more prepared for future outcomes, thus potentially deflecting violence and making it less likely to occur—and becoming "key figures in maintaining peace" (315). My Arabic tutor was alluding to the idea that political leaders in Lebanon could use various channels to maintain a level of fear and anticipation of the coming war, so that people continue to feel that these leaders are necessary for a sense of communal security within a constantly unstable state headed for violence.

One of the repercussions of these political statements that played on varying levels of threat is that through them, the Zu'ama (communal leaders), for example, Hassan Nasrallah, Samir Gaegae, or Saed Hariri, seemed to ensure that anticipation trumps any process of seeking judgment or accountability, which, in turn, made sure that the status quo of their power sharing remained. There could be, after all, no victor and no vanquished. The war, always a possibility, means that one must tread carefully in calling for accountability, lest civil peace (*al-silm al-ahlī*) be put in danger, incidentally by the very players who warn of that impending danger should their political consensus be compromised.[6]

Media and Advertising: Commoditizing the Anticipation of War

If politicians can influence levels of anticipation, the media does not shy away from its role either. The political situation is kept on people's minds through a host of televised programs, including, of course, the news, which offers daily images and accounts of armed political violence.[7] Some programs employ political analysis to speculate about the future, others use humor to make light of a dark situation.[8] Kraidy writes that public culture in general, but reality shows in particular, are "a magnet for contentious politics," and contenders use its space "to advance their agendas by attempting to redraw the boundaries of Arab public discourse" (Kraidy 2006). In these programs, whether reality shows or otherwise, future uncertainty—of identity, nation, and political situation—becomes a topic in the present, and often, the programs become a "symbolic field of battle" that viewers can use to imagine the contours of the next physical conflict (Khatib 2007: 36).

During my research, there were popular talk shows like *kalām al-nās* (*People's Talk*—or the talk on the street), and *al-ʾusbūʿ fī sāʿa* (*The Week in an Hour*), and comedy shows that focused on social and political issues like *irbit tin-ḥal* (*Soon to Be Resolved*), and *bas māt wattan* (a play on words meaning "smiles of a nation" and "when a nation died"). Local stations would also often switch from regular programming to live news coverage when there was a protest or bombing. Television shows—including the news—are important because they have the ability to frame politics, and mobilize and influence the public (Khatib 2007).

There was frequent interruption of regular programming during my fieldwork, and political analysts and politicians would be invited to provide analysis at these times. For example, the March 8 sit-in that began in December 2006, as well as daylong strikes in January 2007, turned local channels into almost twenty-four-hour news and political talk show programming, so did the July 2006 war. Assassinations would have the same impact, and programming would be interrupted for days to cover the aftermath, the funeral procession, and the political fallout. I watched the news and many of these talk shows on a fairly regular basis, often in the company of friends or family, some of whom are interlocutors in this book. These programs would lead to our own analysis and debate, and it was not uncommon to stop listening to the television in favor of our own conversations or to talk (or shout) over the program, speculating about the future and interpreting the past.[9] For example, my relatives turned on the TV and let the news run all morning the day of the assassination of Major General François Al-Hajj—regular shows were interrupted that day. And when one relative walked into the house after narrowly escaping the explosion (his car was partly damaged), we expressed our relief—*ḥamdela 'al salāme, katter kheyr Allāh* (Thank God for your safety, may God increase good fortune)—and then went back and forth between, on one hand, watching the news, the images of the explosion, and the immediate political analysis, and on the other hand arguing over speculations about who was the perpetrator and what this might mean for the future.

During the events of May 7, 2008, even though the fighting in the Hamra neighborhood was taking place outside our window, I remember how my friends and I watched the news to understand and locate the conflict in the present, but also to speculate about its trajectory in the short-term future. We could hear the sounds of gunfire and rocket-propelled grenades (RPG-7, locally known as B-7), but we were unsure how far or near they were, or which political parties were fighting each other. "Turn on the TV," Dima would say, knowing that all local channels were focused on the current situation. We would watch briefly to try to confirm what was taking place outside and to try and gain some understanding of the overall political situation, which we could not ascertain from merely hearing the sounds of battle or looking out the window.[10]

After the Hariri assassination in 2005, "television assumed a central political role" (Kraidy 2010; also Khatib 2007). Future TV[11] programming became exclusively focused on the political situation, and it ran a diagonal black band on its logo and a digital counter marking the days since the assassination. The logo remained even after Future TV returned to regular programming many months later. Kraidy provides another example, telling the story of how the Lebanese Broadcasting Corporation (LBC) reality show *Star Academy* brought the tensions between Lebanon and Syria to the stage in those early days after the Hariri assassination when a Syrian was voted off the show, even though the Lebanese contestant was last in the public vote and should have been voted off (2010: 171). The contestants had been affected by political events. Using their primetime visibility, they brought this to the viewers. The real political tensions are reflected on TV, but when they do so they provide further reminders to the public of the intense precariousness of the political situation.[12]

The popularity of television psychics in the last decade is another indication of how the Lebanese media have commoditized the general insecurity of the future that is prevalent among people. Psychics such as Michel Hayek, Mike Feghali, and recently Leila Abdel Latif, usually appear on New Year's Eve (and other times during the year) to comment on what the next year has to offer politically and predict major events to come (social issues are also spoken about to a lesser degree, but these are often ignored when people re-tell the highlights).[13] These predictions and superstition can serve "to circumvent the veil of uncertainty and anxiety" (Torgler 2007: 719).

Hayek had this to say in one of his predictions from 2007: "the Palace of Justice will be shaken twice. . . . An army site in Lebanon will face gunned (or armed) assault . . . Attack on two clergymen from different sects . . . Worrying signs seen toward the musical Al-Rahbani family."[14] Some of these and his other predictions listed did come true, which only gave him more visibility and legitimacy.

There are other actors in the sphere of media, taken more broadly, who have a role in the narrative of war, such as graphic design and advertising firms. We can see, for example, Beirut-based offices of global advertising firms play their own role in managing anticipation. Local franchises of international companies, like Häagen-Dazs and Johnnie Walker, are other actors, and engage in similar ways with the purpose of attracting consumers, thus commodifying anticipation.[15] In the first image (Figure 6), future uncertainty filled with war is taken as the basis to warn citizens to do more for their country; the designer calls on people to mobilize to prevent further suffering. Designers of this image are attuned to the reality of armed conflict—perhaps referencing the Nahr al-Bared war given its timing—and to the symbolic power of threats of future war in Lebanon, as well as to a Lebanese general sense of patriotism. They build on already existing frames of war but further entrench and reinforce it visually.

In the latter two images, more is going on as the advertising agencies, by representing past conflict, end up politicizing people's visual public sphere. In the first commercial (Figure 7), which appeared a few weeks after the May

Figure 6. Small text reads: "Save it before none is left."

Figure 7. Häagen-Dazs commercial in downtown Beirut, June 2008.

Photo Credit: Author

2008 battles and the signing of the Doha Agreement that ended the armed
confrontations, Häagen-Dazs builds on recent political affairs. This advertising campaign appeals to the customer's sense of relief and satisfaction of a
conflict that is, at least temporarily, over and past, and to the sweet short-
term sensation that comes with political agreement. The campaign exagger-
ates this agreement by framing it as reconciliation to make its own product
that much more appealing. Yet, for the onlooker, the advertisement is more
than all this; it serves to insert politics into a mundane moment of people
strolling, shopping, and relaxing in downtown Beirut (or other places where
one could spot this ad). Upon seeing this ad, one might be pushed to discuss
the political situation, and to speculate whether the agreement would hold or
the parties would return to armed conflict given that real issues have not been

resolved. Indeed, this is exactly what happened as I sat with friends in downtown Beirut, enjoying the summer at the end of June 2008. A friend spotted this picture; we laughed and began to talk about the absurdity of the advertisement and how smart it was. I then took out my phone to capture the image, and we turned our conversation to analyzing the Doha Agreement (see Appendix 2), whether it would hold, and to assess the overall political situation.

In the second commercial (Figure 8), the traditional Johnnie Walker looks unperturbed as he walks across a destroyed bridge. This scene appeared right after the 2006 war in which Israel had destroyed around eighty bridges.

Figure 8. Johnnie Walker billboard, July 2006.

Credit: Leo Burnett Worldwide, Inc.

I initially did not give the ad much attention until several people mentioned
it as a brilliant image, and referenced it in discussions to argue about Lebanon's resilience. While this advertisement was certainly meant to appeal to
notions of Lebanese resilience and make people think of hope and strength
in moving on and rebuilding, it also ensured, similar to the previous example,
that both past war and its possibility for recurring would be injected into the
spaces of everyday life and one's everyday traversal through the city.

These practices by powerful actors, who also live within the same atmosphere of the anticipation of war, cannot be taken lightly—no matter how
creative or genius the actual marketing strategies are. They become part of a
repertoire of practices that impose the war, knowingly or not, into people's
consciousness and push them to counter with their own politically informed
practices of anticipation so that they can deal with the political and social
institutions around them.

These different actors coalesce on society, if not steering or managing
social perceptions of the future, then certainly playing a part in keeping certain forms of anticipation in people's consciousness. Byblos Bank offers one
example (see Figure 9). They marketed a no-fee credit card for military officials during the war on Nahr al-Bared as the bank's way of showing its patriotic support, and building on the idea that it is local and invested in the
community's future.[16] One way this can be read, however, is with clear irony
of exploitation, as military personnel, especially foot soldiers, are among the
poorest in the country and a credit card, even with no fee, would contribute
to creating a new spending pattern involving credit, thus plunging this relatively poor constituency farther into debt. Whether it is companies that can
capitalize on present wars and precarious futures to sell their products and
appear to relate to the patriotism of the people, or politicians whose actions
appear to ignite the masses by playing on their levels of anticipation, the future becomes a place from which to vie for and maintain the status quo of
power.

Political party public relations consume much of the billboard space in
the country traditionally reserved for consumer advertising. Hizballah's are
far less subtle, sometimes displaying images of war and weapons that make
the association clear and immediate. For a long time, various versions of cel-
ebratory posters of the victory in the 2006 war almost entirely monopolized
the billboards on the airport road that runs adjacent to a Hizballah-dominated
municipality. Pictures that commemorate martyrs are another way motifs of
war and its threat remain embedded in people's consciousness.

Figure 9. Byblos Bank no-fee credit card for military officials during the war of Nahr el-bared. Ad reads: The card of honor, a compensation/promise for your sacrifice.

Photo Credit: Author.

The March 14 coalition is often more subtle and better at concealing references to war and threats to communal existence. Two examples below come from the time of the 2009 parliamentary elections. In the first, member of Parliament Nayla Tueni is pictured under the slogan "In Defense of Lebanon the Great" (Figure 10). However, in this case, it is obvious that she proposes to defend the nation from a war with Hizballah, and the implication is that the nation is under threat (from Hizballah or Syria) and her election victory would save Lebanon. In the second picture, member of Parliament Nadim Gemayel is seen on a red banner with a caption that reads: "We remain steadfast today and tomorrow" (Figure 11). This slogan raises the specter of threat against the Christian community, which, it is said, must remain steadfast from the possibility of extinction from this land. Gemayel's victory would ensure Christian existence into the future in the face of a possible war with Hizballah, or other enemies.

The subtlety was reversed in an "I Love Life" marketing campaign that inundated people in Lebanon in 2007 (Figure 12). The March 14 coalition had come up with "I Love Life" billboards, implying that those in the March 8 coalition subscribed to a culture of death and did not care for life. Months later, the March 8 opposition responded ingeniously with their own subtle marketing, adopting some of the same slogans such as, "I Love Life" and "We Want to Live," followed by words in graffiti font such as "with dignity," "undictated," and other qualifiers to suggest that there was more to life than life itself.

Another example of media that uses the precarious situation of future war is in the form of banners that hang above streets and are put up by neighborhood groups; these are prevalent around the country. These banners are often made from cloth with a basic design, and can have political or religious messages (they can also be used for purely commercial purposes). In the example of Figure 13, Zira'a neighborhood youth (*shabāb al-zirā'a*) hung a banner in the Mina district near Tripoli.[17] The banner reads "We will not surrender to terrorism. The international tribunal is coming, coming." The slogan reminds onlookers of the context of bombings and assassinations plaguing the country at this time. It leaves open who the terrorist party is, but the implication to anyone with local knowledge is clear that it is Hizballah or Syria, given that it is hung in a predominantly Sunni area near Tripoli with significant March 14 support. The suggestion that the tribunal is coming is meant to reassure the people that the country will persevere, whatever

Figure 10. Banner of parliamentary candidate Nayla Tueni, daughter of assassinated MP Gebran Tueni, hangs from a building in Beirut, May 2009. The slogan reads, "In defense of Lebanon the great," a phrase used by her late father.

Photo Credit: Deen Sharp. Ashrafieh, Beirut. April 2009.

the costs, and that they should remain hopeful as the future is optimistic. Despite the anonymity, onlookers understand that the banner is raised with the approval, overt or tacit, of the March 14 coalition. These are not independent civil society actors like the ones I will discuss in a later section; these are groups with heavy political backing that use popular local tactics, such as these banners, to appeal to people about a specific political agenda that should prevail.

Figure 11. Banner of parliamentary candidate Nadim Gemayel, son of assassinated former president Bashir Gemayel, with slogan: We remain steadfast today and tomorrow. May 2009.

Photo Credit: Deen Sharp. Ashrafieh, Beirut. April 2009.

Figure 12. "We want to live . . . in Lebanon."

Photo Credit: Samar Maakaron.

This tactic of hanging banners in streets is common across the entire political spectrum, and the only identifiable markers as to which groups these banners belong to are the message, the location, and sometimes the signature color (the group in this case had signed off in the Future Movement's sky blue color, which could indicate ties to this movement). The banner allows a passerby to generalize, "visually materialize," and identify the neighborhood: how it would align in a future war, what kind of tensions exist, who its enemies are.[18] For example, in the south of the country it is virtually impossible to find March 14 banners. The banner serves to reduce an area to one color, to define lines of solidarity, and to direct the passerby, as well as the neighborhood resident, to imagine the future through a specific prism.[19]

Figure 13. Banner in Mina, "We will not surrender to terrorism. International
tribunal is coming, coming."

Photo Credit: Author.

The Checkpoint: Performing the Anticipation of War

The checkpoint, or *ḥājez*,[20] is a crucial part of the overall narrative of political
violence. Lebanese and Syrian military checkpoints, militia checkpoints,
neighborhood checkpoints, permanent and flying checkpoints, and security
zones (*murabaʿ amnī*) are some of the different types of checkpoints people
in Lebanon have been subjected to over the years.[21] There are checkpoints on
highways, around a bend on mountain roads, and in tight neighborhood
streets; there are security checks at malls, universities, and specific neighborhoods housing politicians. Checkpoints may operate in slightly different
ways, and have slightly varying connotations for people, but in general, and
taken together, they are another place to think about the ways both the constant presence and, more important, the possibilities of political conflict en-
croach into daily life. The anticipation of political violence is structured

through the performative space of the checkpoint, where the movement of bodies negotiates and aligns with people's imaginations, perceptions, and emotions about the future. Through these performative processes at checkpoints, where subjects are made, the anticipation of political violence is also given material form.

Checkpoints and military installations have been constant fixtures in the lives of people in Lebanon for at least the last forty years.[22] In a sense, people have grown accustomed to them, and it might take foreign travelers (or even Lebanese coming from abroad) to express their anxieties at seeing the military presence before people are reminded of how these checkpoints have invaded their everyday lives. Pradeep Jeganathan (2004) has identified the checkpoint as a border point that has a double effect of enforcing security and, more important for him, raising the level of anticipation whereby the soldier manning the checkpoint feels insecure when a car approaches—always anticipating the terrorist—and the passenger in the car is reminded of a future possibility of violence when she or he sees the checkpoint, thereby making the passenger feel insecure. This is all the more so when a random (or flying) checkpoint (ḥājez ṭayyār) suddenly appears, thus suggesting an escalated security concern. At some level, one can think of this checkpoint as a target site for violence, or as a border that separates what is supposedly safe from an area that could be a possible target. It also serves as a gate to identify the possibility of certain types of flow of people, weapons, or other materials deemed illegal. In all cases, it serves as another reminder: a reminder of a past war, of future political violence, of ongoing political subversions, or of the ineffective state that needs a crude form of constant military presence to discipline and control the public and make the public think it is protecting its future. These checkpoints do not only delimit geographies or manage flows, but, as spaces where the anticipation of political violence is performed, they also play a role in framing the imaginings of future violence.

The naturalization of checkpoints in everyday life does not negate the uncertainty of being pulled over to show identity papers or have one's car searched. Like many people in Lebanon, I have heard the infamous words, ʿal-yamīn (to the right), and I have been asked to get out of the car for further inspection, with the always looming possibility and dread that more might transpire than a simple search. This is more or less standard, and people have experienced far worse. While often, people around me who occupied privileged spaces would not view checkpoints as spaces of anxiety and would not think twice about the inconvenience of military checkpoints before leaving the house, a heightened anticipation of conflict or an intensification of political violence would change all this. I have, on many occasions, been personally cautioned by family to be careful because of extra checkpoints. On the other hand, at certain times, especially among nationalists, these Lebanese military checkpoints have been a source of pride, and some people are relieved to see the army asserting its presence—this sentiment was especially noticeable during the Nahr al-Bared war in 2007, when people felt this was a necessary added security as the army was fighting a war against a militant group, or more recently after bombings in 2013, in reference to Lebanese army and Hizballah checkpoints on the outskirts of Dahiyeh to keep people safe.

The checkpoint takes on many meanings, and it can appear far more normal for some than others. As a Lebanese citizen, with a PhD and a particularly privileged class background, I do not live in fear of this site, and I take its presence and any treatment I may get from soldiers as routine. Yet, for some, like Palestinians, this site is more intrusive and fear producing, as Palestinians are refugees that are seen as potential political destabilizers (or, more bluntly, as possible terrorists).

In summer 2007 I had been going back and forth between Beirut and the North during the war on Nahr al-Bared. A group of us were providing relief work to Palestinian refugees displaced from Nahr al-Bared to the Baddawi camp and were engaging in political mobilization against the way the army was dealing with the crisis.

Early at the start of the conflict, I drove north with Ussama, a Palestinian male friend and graphic designer in his late twenties, not thinking twice that two men in a car might be considered suspicious. Checkpoints had not yet gotten as strict as they would the next month, and stories about Palestinians being stopped had only recently begun to surface. Ussama and I arrived at *ḥajez al-madfūn* ("Checkpoint of the Buried") near the town of Batroun. I drove up slowly and cautiously. The *madfūn* checkpoint, like many permanent ones, has a developed infrastructure so that the driver can see the colored cement blocks and barriers from over one hundred meters away, and the soldier sits in a cement booth.[23] Other checkpoints that are erected on the fly, or manned by political parties, as in the battles of May 7, 2008, could be put together with gasoline barrels, old tires, or rocks. This particular checkpoint also has road signs well in advance telling drivers to slow down. There is a shaded area to the side of the road where those chosen for further inspection stop to be searched. Indeed, we were chosen, and Ussama and I pulled over to the right and parked under the steel canopy. A soldier, half bored, half annoyed to have to bother with us, walked up to my window—the driver side—and asked each of us for our ID. Upon finding out Ussama was carrying a Palestinian identity card, they told us to get out of our car, and took him for questioning. Ussama remained calm, and I was told to follow him up the steps on the side of the road that led to the military barracks on the hill above us. The sergeant in command came out and began to ask my friend questions while I waited some distance behind. The entire episode did not last more than five to ten minutes, as fellow activists who had been following us, and who had social capital as professors at the AUB, stopped and spoke to the sergeant, who eventually sent us on our way without serious questioning.

Similar, more serious incidents take place in the country all the time. Workers, the poor, Palestinians, and people driving older model cars are more likely to get stopped, women and couples (especially visibly rich ones) less likely. In fact, on a number of occasions, middle- to upper-class women I knew expressed surprise on the rare occasion when they were stopped and wondered about the reasons for this, and if they were singled out because the soldier wanted to flirt. They anticipated the checkpoint differently. There were times, especially during the war years of the 1980s and immediately after in the early 1990s, when the checkpoints (particularly Syrian military ones) were a source of fear and women of all classes were cautioned against going out alone at night for worry of being accosted, sexually attacked, or killed at checkpoints. During my fieldwork, however, the checkpoint as a border, to middle-class and more privileged women, was less a concern, perhaps signifying that this place marked class far more than it ever marked gender. One interlocutor explained it in banal terms as a relic of the past whose purpose she often questioned. To her, some of the permanent checkpoints, like *ḥājez al-madfūn*, had become part of the landscape. They were almost akin to a tollbooth—with the metaphor being quite exact at certain times in the past when people would find themselves paying militia fighters and Syrian soldiers to pass without harassment. Still, the checkpoint was about the control of women, too. Not only in that men feared women crossing them, and thus, limited women's movement, but also in that women capitalized on the (mistaken) knowledge that political violence was the realm of men, and used this to smuggle arms, people, and goods through checkpoints. In this way, women were just as central to the machinations of political violence and to the maintenance and breakdown of security.

Throughout the summer of 2007, the visibility of checkpoints in my notes grew and I began to register their presence. But checkpoints were not only something my interlocutors and I approached by car, they also began to affect our lives in more intrusive ways. When leaving the city for relief work in the North, we would have to think twice and make sure women or Lebanese were in the car with Palestinians to ensure they would not be stopped. Checkpoints near Nahr al-Bared became a site of protest. For those who were supportive of the army, these checkpoints were a point of pride and a necessity in the architecture of security needed for the state to be strong, secure, and sovereign.

The ḥājez is a space where people perform for the state and where the state itself is performed. A person might begin by positioning him- or, rarely, herself as a friend of the state, and if things escalate, the person might embody impending personal violence by acting afraid or, alternatively, remaining resistant and firm. Whether one anticipates political violence on a national scale or on their personal body, the checkpoint is a space where one has to manage the anxieties of future violence. It is, after all, a place that constitutes authority and, knowing this, people expect power to manifest itself there in possibly violent ways.

Many choose to show deference to the soldiers' authority in such moments of anxiety, and might even deliberately greet them by calling on a shared community with the soldier through such phrases as ya'tīk el-'afye yā wattan (literally, "may God give you health, my state," but generally a sign of thanks for one's services)—I greeted militia members at a checkpoint in a similar way in Chapter 4. This is the case even though most know the soldier has very little authority and may joke privately about the weakness of the military—which is seen as unable to fight an external enemy, like Israel,[24] and some argue it is purely for domestic use to quell any internal dissent.

Still, it seemed that most of the time, and for many people around me, the checkpoint was just another part of the road. A surprise random checkpoint might raise questions or produce a sense of frustration, mainly for slowing traffic, but this is folded into a sense of the expected and into the idea that, hayda libnān ("this is Lebanon"). The ḥājez, as both ordinary and as producing the fleeting thought of danger to come, frames the anticipation of violence as something normal and naturalized into everyday social life, but at the same time, as sustaining anxiety and fear. The ḥājez is one location where this anticipation is structured materially in a physical space, produced symbolically through competing meanings and practices of checkpoints, and embodied through people's performative tactics in such encounters.

Civil Society Representations: Mobilizing Uncertainty

While politicians are talking about the future, political parties are trying to manipulate people's perceptions of the future for political loyalty, various media are capitalizing on perceptions of the future, and checkpoints attempt to make us think the state is protecting the future, the future begins to dialectically influence the present. In this way, the anticipation of war becomes something to respond to and to have a conversation with. Civil society groups and actors play a part in building the narrative of war's anticipation. All around town, this future war, rarely defined, can be seen in material formations in which civil society groups most likely feel they are pushing the general population to mobilize and act against war before it is too late.[25]

In Figure 14, an NGO named *muqāwimūn* (Resisters) decorated a bus with a banner that read, "The bus is waiting around the corner." This was done on the occasion of commemorating the anniversary of Lebanon's war. Parked in downtown Beirut, this bus, with the banner and Lebanese flag,

Figure 14. NGO *muqāwimūn* (Resisters) banner in commemoration of Lebanon's war, warning that "the bus [war] is waiting around the corner." *L'Orient-Le Jour*, April 13, 2011. Copyright *L'Orient-Le Jour*.

creates a direct association to Lebanon's war for any onlooker. But the NGO activists are not content with reminding people of past war, they are forward-looking, playing on heightened senses of anticipation, and predicting the future around the corner.[26] The slogan suggests that the activists are certain about the uncertainty of the future, and that they know, if the situation remains as it is, that the war is waiting for people nearby. People's anxieties are reconfirmed and reproduced, and perhaps this is the intent of the activists, who hope to mobilize onlookers to react and act.

Graffiti artists form another element in the interplay of narratives that together enframe the anticipation of war and mark it on the city's walls. Whereas the city's buildings remain marked from the destruction of the 1975–1990 war, graffiti artists can provide additional imprints to bring the future into the present for those who traverse the city. During my fieldwork, I was not interested in street art per se, and did not collect images from that period. I began to notice intricate designs, murals, and paintings more and more in the last four years. Thus, I include a sample of three artworks that could be found in the city in 2013–2014.[27]

I conducted an interview with Ali Rafei (February 24, 2014), the artist whose work is represented in Figure 15. He explained his motivation for this image as having two parts. First, it is an expression of his personal feelings of the situation in Lebanon. The image is meant to suggest how cheap life is, and when the bombs begin to go off then your life is really up to chance; it is "not in your hands." When I asked Rasheed, the engineer and activist we've encountered before, about this over email, he agreed, and interpreted it as life being left to "chance and statistics," and that you could die by chance when the bombs go off. Second, it is directed at the viewer, where Rafei wants people "to reflect on themselves, and to ask 'what am I going to do? Am I going to leave my life to fate and chance, or do something about it?'" Rafei wants to deliver a message. His intention is not to force people to do something, but he hopes that if they already have ideas, such an image might trigger the seeds of action. Crucially, Rafei is able to mobilize what has come to be a sticky association between Lebanon (represented here by the cedar tree and the colors of the Lebanese flag) and war or political violence (represented by bombs), in order to make people question what they want to do about their future. Rafei is here taking the future and holding it up to people's mirrors for them to see. We are, thus, reminded about the certain uncertainty to come.

In Figure 16, the artist seems to be motivated by similar ideas as the "bus" activists. It is as if the artist is expressing frustration with the city by

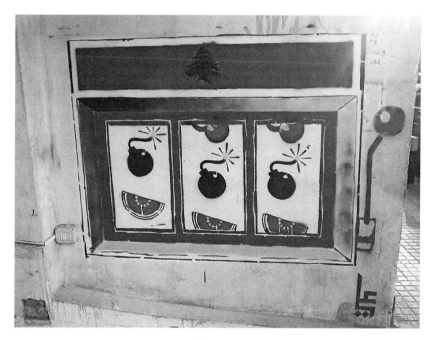

Figure 15.

Artist and Photo Credit: Ali Rafei.

saying, "One April 13 is enough"—this is said to be the day Lebanon's 1975–1990 war began. In doing so, onlookers are reminded of both the past and the future as they walk about in their everyday life. The artist may want to jolt people, but what are people to do? Their own frustrations and anxieties are intensified as markers of future war appear all around them with greater intensity. Like the bullet holes and war torn buildings that hark to war past, these objects remind us of the future and take part in processes of framing (see also Figure 17).[28]

I asked George about his impressions of such graffiti and other political slogans and signs. He told me that he tends "to look at the nice positive ones that don't remind [him] of the situation," and that these war related ones "don't stir up any emotion." George felt that the news and radio stations were already "doing a good enough job to always remind us" what people are living through. On a larger scale, my argument is, in fact, that these street images and art, alongside news and radio, are part of the narrative to constantly remind us of war, when actually, one could ask if it is not enough that the real

Figure 16. "One April 13" (in reference to the start of the Lebanon's war).

Photo Credit: Amar Shabandar. Source: http://www.lebanesewalls.com/.

bombings and death already remind us of the war to come. The images in the streets seemed to be something George claimed he was able to ignore and disregard—he resisted their meaning when they were of a political nature, and tied his ability to resist them (his word was "ignore") to remaining positive and happy living in Lebanon. One might be stirred to question, as Sontag (2003) does, whether an image could ever be used to get people to actively mobilize against war.

From public space to public bathrooms, it is difficult to escape the ways in which future war frames the present. In one example (Figure 18), someone writes a survey on a bathroom door of a café in Hamra. The person asks: "When do we think the next war will come? This week? This summer?" On the next line they write, "When will we supply Picon and Smeds cheese in the bomb shelter?" These are a reference to easily accessible and popular brands of cheese spread used during Lebanon's war, again bringing past and future into the felt present. One person responds that the war has already begun; another says, in English, that it will begin "today!" Finally, another responds with "When will we stop the

Figure 17. "The region is unstable" (literally: in the devil's palm).

Figure 18. Bathroom door, café in Hamra. The writing asks "When do we think the next war will come? This week? This summer?" "When will we supply Picon and Smeds cheese in the bomb shelter?" "When will we stop the idiocy?"

Photo credit: Author.

idiocy," perhaps referring to the idiocy of scaring people with such questions, or maybe to the idiocy of the political system. These and other examples may be seen as attempts to make light of a dark and heavy situation. Yet, such scribbles turn into a dialectic of war past, present, and future, and create a conversation among strangers. In this way, the narrative of war's anticipation travels from one person to another, intensifies, and develops into a shared experience.[29]

Ritual and Commemoration:
Reproducing the Future from the Past

Rituals and commemorations are other ways by which practices of anticipation come to be structured. They are practices that help people deal with threat and vulnerability by establishing and reinscribing community. Two emblematic commemorative practices that I want to discuss are the memorial event around the massacre of Sabra and Chatilla, and the Bashir Gemayel commemoration. These two examples of the way an anticipation of violence gets inscribed in commemorative practices are significant for their importance to society in Lebanon. As part of this discussion I also want to show how a willingness to sacrifice for the nation is bound up with, and feeds into, anticipation. But first, let me provide some background on the two events.

On September 14, 1982, president-elect Bashir Gemayel was assassinated in a Phalange Party office in Ashrafieh. Sheikh Bashir, as he was commonly known, was one of two sons of Pierre Gemayel, founder of the Phalange Party. He had risen to power and united the major Christian factions under the LF in an effort to unite the Christians in arms (*tawḥīd al-bunduqiya*). His success made him the most revered Christian leader, and he was perceived by many, even by some non-Christian constituents, as the only one able to end the war and unite Lebanon. His detractors saw his close alliance with Israel as an anti-nationalist and treasonous position—the LF were being trained by the Israelis in Israel—that could not possibly make him a candidate to lead the country, and he was assassinated by Habib al-Shartouni, a member of the SSNP. The assassination was seen as a huge blow to the Christian community and it is considered to be the point their dreams for Lebanon fell apart. In the years after, and up till the present, Bashir Gemayel became like a saint for his followers as the savior of Lebanon (Haugbolle 2010), and his message was seen as the true one to follow for there to be peace. It is in this light that the commemoration of Bashir Gemayel's assassination takes on significant meaning.

Two days after Sheikh Bashir's assassination, Lebanese militiamen from the Kataeb Party entered the camps of Sabra and Chatilla, under the cover and supervision of the Israeli army—who were responsible for the camp as it was under their control—and massacred over fifteen hundred people.[30] The assassination was used as a pretext for the massacre after the Christian forces blamed the Palestinians for Gemayel's death, even though it was revealed very shortly after that the SSNP, not the Palestinians, were involved in the plot.[31] The massacre took on international significance, coming as it did after the withdrawal of the PLO from Lebanon under international supervision, and with international guarantees for the safety of the Palestinian refugee population left behind. Foreign observers and volunteers were also present to witness the full extent of the massacre and to document it, which gave this event more attention than other previous massacres. In the following years, the Sabra and Chatilla massacre came to be one of the single most defining moments of Lebanon's war, of Israel's responsibility in the war, and of the brutality of some of the Christian armed factions. That 1982 was the year of Israel's invasion placed these events within what many already see as a watershed moment in Lebanon's war. My interlocutors often referred to the war in terms of before and after 1982, saying, for example, that the real sectarian war began after 1982. One interlocutor, a former fighter with the Communist Party, even broke down fear as operating differently before and after this date.

Just as supporters of Bashir Gemayel hold commemorations on September 14 every year, the Palestinian community holds a remembrance for the victims of Sabra and Chatilla every year on September 16. In 2008 I attended the Sabra and Chatilla remembrance event with Rasheed after having observed the commemoration of Gemayel's assassination two days earlier with other informants.

For me, the contrast of the two events was very disturbing. On one end, at the Gemayel commemoration, there were thousands of people (arguably all Christian) in celebration and out in public to show the strength of the party and its commitment to Bashir Gemayel's path and ideology of a strong nationalist Lebanon. Around me were people who probably cared little about the massacre, and even if some did, there was no time to reflect or remember such events. Worse still, the massacres were committed in the name of this community and it was quite likely that some perpetrators were among those in the crowd.

On the other end, the Chatilla remembrance did not rally more than two hundred people, among them international activists. In a small memorial park on the outskirts of Beirut, it was somber and made to feel marginal. To make matters worse, in an almost comedic scene, the official presentation and speeches began with the Lebanese national anthem, and if we take the massacre to be one committed by Lebanese against Palestinians, it was as if the perpetrators were presiding over the victim's memory and enframing the victim's past. A few minor Lebanese and Palestinian political figures stood on the podium and spoke empty words about Palestinian victory that sounded cynical given the occasion. They talked about sacrifice and the martyrdom of the victims as not going to waste, and that it would bring Palestinians closer to return; they also praised Hizballah for defending the cause. The victims, standing on the side, were never acknowledged or allowed to speak. The small crowd sat around, talking to each other, complaining about the heat, and uninterested in what they had already heard many times before. I heard some complain about why they were even present, as if forced to be there by an obligation to the dead. Ironically, the highlight was a foreign speaker, who followed empty words with an initiative to give school children laptops and then proceeded to hand them out to ecstatic children.

The two events present different relations to time. The Gemayel commemoration is like a masquerade after a sacrifice, turning an assassination and a tragic death into a celebration of life, and giving meaning to the sacrifice through a renewal of Gemayel's path. This was powerfully represented in the religiously loaded slogan, *bashīr ḥay fīnā* (Bashir is alive in us). I am reminded here of Abdellah Hammoudi as he alerts us to the "anticipation of history . . . that is set in motion by sacrifice," because a joyous feast in the future follows the ritual of sacrifice and is legitimized by the sacrifice (1993: 139). So Bashir's sacrifice sets in motion a commemoration that anticipates a past of glory, and does so by also calling forth future sacrifice for the nation. What is being anticipated is the possibility to reclaim the past glory, and the nation, through struggle. Thus, violence is reconstituted through commemoration and its entanglement with sacrifice. One can observe this among the crowd in the commemorative practice itself, but also by witnessing those away from the scene, politically opposed, and threatened by the commemoration's nationalist renewal.

The remembrance of Sabra and Chatilla presents an entirely different relationship to anticipation. In similar ways, the officials at the event tried to turn the sacrifice into an occasion for "a joyous feast" in the sense of flipping the tragedy into a moment of victory, proclaiming the strength of the community and the nearing return of the Palestinians to their homeland. However, the attempts by these officials were a failure, and this was evident in the disinterested looks of the crowd and the frustration of the victims as Rasheed, I, and others spoke to them after the event. In this case, the commemoration was neither an entanglement nor a continuation of the sacrifice (there was no masquerade). Rather, the commemoration turned into the sacrifice itself; it reinforced the past as present. The situation of victims having remained unchanged and in a constant state of waiting—to return, to gain civil rights, to be compensated—ensured the act of yearly remembrance was for them a practice of daily life.

In such ways, and when the context of past wars remains unresolved, the anticipation of violence is continuously reproduced through these rituals, and through people's relationship to the state. These two rituals of commemoration are especially significant because the events they mark and reference are still employed today as defining moments of Lebanon's war. People, for example, reference them in conversations about the 1975–1990 war to speak to the war's brutality, in the case of Sabra and Chatilla, or to refer to the time when hope was lost, in the case of the Christians with respect to the Gemayel assassination. In Chapter 2, I recounted how mention of the Gemayel assassination worked to steer the conversation to the past, and to continue to allow people to hold grievances against the SSNP that organized his assassination. Nabil and others, when thinking about the need for a strong president, mentioned the Gemayel assassination; "Bashir could have brought the Lebanese together, *di'āno* (it's such a loss)," I would hear Nabil say. Thus, for the communities affected and far beyond, these commemorations and memorials, and the events they reference, play a structuring role at particular moments to think about the expectations of future political violence, when and why it will occur, and the forms it will take.

Resolving the Past?

At some point, the flames of anticipation become so overpowering, like waiting impatiently for an absent lover (Barakat 1995: 23), that we see something take shape other than fear or feeling safe. We see something other than a desire to act ordinary or to conquer the violence; and certainly other than a will to survive. At such a point, when the anticipation becomes so intense, one can hear in the whispers between friends and family a curious emotion surface: "Let the war come already so we might end our problems!" (*khali el-ḥarb tiji ḥattā ni-khlas ba'a!*).

And when violence does rear its head and becomes visible at some point, when it intensifies and there is an attack of sorts, here we can observe the antagonisms of people's relation to the state and the communities around them. Some will rejoice in the initial euphoria of change that the violence so crudely promises, as we could see in the cases in 2006–2009 (and beyond) where members of March 14 supported Israel's war on Hizballah, many people in Lebanon supported the war on Nahr al-Bared, and many embraced the need for the May 2008 battles. They will call for a *ḥasem* (to resolve or resolution). A word often used in the context of the Nahr al-Bared war, but also more broadly in referring to how to deal with almost any political contest in the country. The Lebanese army needed to *yiḥsum* (resolve) the conflict in the camp, one would often hear during the 2007 summer months; this was the banner under which the army maintained its war and why many were happy to see it take a stand at the site of a Palestinian camp. Without *ḥasem*, or the power to create the conditions of a final resolution, to be out of the throes of a politics of "No Victor, No Vanquished," people seem to believe there is no way to control the country, either totally or through some form of power sharing. The word in itself does not carry more weight than its English equivalent, but in the Lebanese context, the absence of resolutions to conflicts—civil and uncivil—makes the invocation of *ḥasem* not a mere resolve to be taken lightly, but accompanied with a whole repertoire of actions. The pursuit for resolution, *ḥasem*, can drive the country to war; the lack of a *ḥasem* leaves people in a continuous struggle to battle over their differences. So long as the state does not step in to declare a resolution, there is a constant seeking of a *ḥasem* and with it the constant feeling of a potential for violence. We see, then, how language—the language of *ḥasem*—can become a site, or a strategy, for constituting anticipation (Das 2007).

People will call for a *ḥasem* so that the country will move forward and so they may no longer live in anticipation; some will even jump at the opportunity to carry arms to play a part in this change. This rejoicing, it must be said, is a political act, and in some respects an act against the politics of *lā ghāleb, lā maghlūb*. Those who do not rejoice also engage in a politically constituted act of not doing so because they see no strategic benefit. In the final showdown, in this final break where anticipation gives way to physical violence, we come to see that the concern is not, and has never been, about violence. Rather, what lies beneath the anticipation of political violence is simply a question of change (of the status quo partly represented by the above politics) and what type of change lies on the horizon. It is this story, one centrally about change, which underlies the narrative that is told and retold through the objects and material representations that were explored in this chapter. Overarching power dynamics that see elite political and social forces framing the future and how people come to think about it influences this story of change. Dunmire writes that "rather than narratives of genuine possibility and potentiality, contemporary life is defined by 'institutionalized master story lines' which serve to limit understandings, experiences, and relationships" (2013: 41). One can see this in Lebanon, where instead of narratives opening up futures and being open to all to participate, they are increasingly allocated asymmetrically—only some narratives count.

What was surveyed in these pages is only part of the overall narrative by which the anticipation of war comes to be enframed in people's lives. Other aspects of this narrative include theater plays, music, and crucially, land speculators, businesspeople, and corruption schemes (Leenders 2012). I have already discussed, briefly, some examples of ritual and commemorative practices, and what we will see in the next chapter is the way other local practices of memory work and production also play a role in this overall narrative. I turn now to Part II of this book, and to a focus on the politics of recollection and the way the past influences the present.

PART II

Recollection

Chapter 6

Active Forgetting and the Memory of War in Everyday Life

The technology of silence
The rituals, etiquette

the blurring of terms
silence not absence

of words or music or even
raw sounds

Silence can be a plan
rigorously executed

the blueprint of a life

It is a presence
it has a history a form

Do not confuse it
with any kind of absence
                    —Adrienne Rich, *Cartographies of Silence* (1978: 17)

I am driving around in my car while running a few errands with Jihad. Jihad is in his forties, unmarried, tall, and tanned, with light brown hair. He is a handsome man with a rough beard and dark piercing eyes. Jihad fought with the Communist Party in the 1980s, mainly in operations against the Israelis, although he did take part in several internal battles. Today, he is a political activist who uses his animations to tell his stories, and belongs to a circle of my friends.

We are in the Tareeq el-Jdeedeh neighborhood of Beirut near his apartment; we really should be at the beach. It is hot, the summer humidity is upon us, the streets are more or less jammed with cars, and some people are honking as they try to maneuver through the narrow street we are on. Jihad and I are having a conversation about war as I drive. He tells me: "After the war, you don't want to see your comrades for awhile because they are a reflection of your memory [*mrāye lal-zākira*; literally a mirror for your memory] and you want to forget and just live peacefully." Jihad and I had come to know each other during *ḥarb tammūz*, and would see each other every so often over the next few years during activist meetings and social gatherings. He was a good friend of other interlocutors in earlier chapters, like Dima and Rasheed, and together we organized nonviolent political actions and would frequent some of the same coffee shops.

This moment of opening up, of talking about his days in battle did not come easily. I had sat down with Jihad at a café in Hamra when we first met two years before—on a tip from a friend who said Jihad had fought and would be willing to speak. At that time, he refused to open up, remaining ambiguous and superficial, and I would find out now that it was because of his own coming-to-terms that he did not want to share experiences and play witness for my research. The above comment about mirrors and reflections of memory was made while driving down a street in which Jihad had been involved in a major battle in the 1980s; this street had recently become a Sunni-Shi'a fault line witnessing several violent outbursts in the years of my fieldwork. Jihad's comment was not an isolated affair; it existed within a repertoire of conversations and experiences I had been observing throughout my fieldwork, and which are crucial to understanding the structuring force of the ongoing anticipation of war.

Importantly, I draw on Jihad's instruction that he "want[s] to forget and just live peacefully" to introduce the concept of *tanāsī,* or active forgetting, which Nietzsche (1989) connects to the human capacity to feel happiness, and which disconnects us from history. I suggest that this was and continues to be a practice that occurs in Lebanon, and more accurately describes the collective process of memory work.

Jihad's comment also calls on me to argue against a mainstream narrative that says post-conflict societies are often afflicted by amnesia, and here I join other scholars who have weighed in on this in different contexts (Sorabji 2006; Aguilar 2002).[1] The notion of a state-sponsored amnesia after Lebanon's war was and continues to be a salient characterization of postwar society in Lebanon, despite some social scientists writing against this in the context of Lebanon (Hanssen and Genberg 2001; Haugbolle 2010; Larkin 2012; Nikro 2012).[2]

Many NGOs, cultural workers, and architects in Lebanon are concerned with sites of memory such as commemorative sites, libraries, books, buildings, and other sites where memory can reside. The task ahead of people in Lebanon, it is said, is to build these sites and ensure that the war will not be forgotten so that it is not repeated. There is a popular saying for this, *tindhakar mā tin'ād* (remember but don't repeat). The assumption is that memory, in terms of *lieux de mémoire* (or sites of memory), will heal the wounds of society and open a way forward from war and destruction.[3] These sites of memory, as a way to remember, are therefore assumed to be a positive social quality, and "postwar" human rights discourses depend on them. I offer a critical turn away from them by highlighting, through ethnographic moments, the importance of everyday, spontaneous lived memory,[4] and how remembrance of past war in everyday conversations and experiences intensifies the feelings of possibility of future war.

In contradistinction to *lieux de mémoire*, stressed by various NGOs, artists, and other individuals, I stress the long presence of forms of memory related to the everyday lives and practices of people that have been capable of bringing together multiplicities of tactics and interpretations and of opening up options of remembering and forgetting.[5] Instead of thinking in terms of memory that is absent or erased, I consider memory's visibilities, and I think of how certain moments and spaces can intensify lived memory and influence subjective energies. This kind of memory, I argue, is not a therapy, but nor is it a rupture or some kind of violence. This memory is a way of life, and it enables the anticipation of war as the past is brought to weigh on the future.

Challenging Forms of Memory

Jihad's expression of wanting to forget struck me as unusual, even inaccurate, when I first heard it, so I decided to challenge him on this point. I told him that in my experience with other ex-fighters, I noticed that there wasn't a deep desire to forget, or the type of amnesia that is commonly attributed to Lebanese society at large. It seemed to me that it was not a question of ex-fighters wanting or not wanting to forget. Rather, I had observed that ex-fighters were quick to open up in situations where they could trust their interlocutors. So, for example, in family gatherings, relatives would share their experiences, or, on other occasions, I would listen as formerly armed militiamen, my interlocutors, would recollect with each other certain war-time events. In fact, the most common phrase I heard throughout my research with those who identified themselves as former fighters was: "Ah, the war, those were the good old days" (*Kānet el-ḥarb iyēm ḥilwe*)—the phrase was perhaps a result of comparing the old days to the disappointing present.[6] This left me with the indication that it was not to be forgotten. War stories would come in the form of a passing comment, a narrating of a brief account, or recollecting a funny wartime moment, and they would often come unsolicited and at unexpected times. These countless incidents, where former fighters had no problems remembering the war or meeting up with other fellow fighters from their brigade, were reason for me to doubt Jihad's comment. Jihad was implying that ex-fighters wanted to stay away from each other so as to forget because this was the only way they could live after the war.

After mentioning my observations, Jihad explained that it was not a simple memory of the past that he had wanted to forget. The forgetting that he and others were engaged in was associated more closely with forgetting past ideals one held, and with the type of person one was during the war, and the type of person one turned into, or was forced to become after the war. For example, after the signing of the 1989 Taif Agreement that ended the war, people tried to forget past ideals they held in order to pursue and live with the jobs they were forced to take. These comments pushed me to think of different types of memory, even within what is known as episodic memory—memory that entails remembering past events—which is what concerns me most here. Saadi Nikro explains these types as a distinction between memory and remembrance, writing that

> it is necessary to distinguish memory from remembrance, so that [memory] is not a mere exercise in remembering (as in a putting-back-together) or representing the past, but more importantly a recovery of the past as a site of contentious debate and dialogical

contact. Where remembrance relies on a strict epistemology of reference and representation, the work of memory develops within a
dialogical play of past and present, so that neither can ever be fixed
and exhaustively accounted for. (Nikro 1999)

Jihad seemed to be talking to me about memory rather than remembrance. Events were remembered, but the struggle he and his battle friends
had after the war was how to make sense of the "dialogical play of past and
present" in order to carve out a space of meaning in their everyday lives. Seeing his old battle friends was part of this dialogical play, but he seemed to say
that in the early years after the war, he and his friends preferred to disengage
from this specific play among all the others they inevitably took part in.

Importantly, there is agency in this type of remembering that is structured by social arrangements (Olick and Robbins 1998: 109). Agency is an
important piece because without it we make absent Jihad's very personal expressions, as well as the narratives he produces, which play a part in collective
memory work.[7] Gilsenan stresses this relation of how collective memory is
constituted through narratives. In the region of Akkar, Lebanon, he tells of
how "Men spoke, retold, represented and mimetically re-performed situations of conflict, of face-to-face challenges, of sequences of wounding or
murder and revenge, of personal or collective action" (1992: 86). Through
this retelling and re-presenting, a form of social memory around violence was
produced. By extension, Jihad's earlier expression and narrative communi-
cates a wider common sentiment, not only because our conversation began in
front of two other people, or that he was not confiding anything in me that
he had not already discussed in intimate gatherings, but because they were
expressions retold from within a broader social context. Jihad was active in
producing a collective memory through his public expressions of memory as
seen in his act of expressing the past in conversation with me, and through
his cultural work and the narratives this work produced.

Jihad was suggesting that he tried to forget the type of memory related
to personal experience. And that this form of memory could be forgotten if
there is no contact with those people with whom one has had a shared experience in the past (Halbwachs 1992: 24). While this could happen, and while
memory in general tends to move toward oblivion (Ricoeur 2004), the experience of Lebanon's war, being shared by an entire society, albeit in different
ways, ensures that collective forgetting becomes a near impossibility because
of the very persistence of contact between people and across groups. There is

always a dialogic play between personal and collective, and between past and present, no matter how hard one tries to consciously avoid it. The very conscious avoidance is part of this play.

When Jihad sees his comrade (*rafīq*[8]), what takes place? He tells me that he would see his comrade and remember a past event, or perhaps a way of life, how he and his comrade used to think, the values that they held, who they used to be and what they stood for. Upon remembering this, at least in the years right after the war, Jihad tells me that he would feel a sense of heaviness, and even shame—a shame of putting aside party ideals, of having to compromise with Lebanese capitalism, and of being unable to keep up the fight for their mutual causes with the same intensity. However, this shame is very much an emotion in the present, one that stems from how he judges himself and his comrades, and from the choices he has had to make as an artist trying to make a living while using art to resist. It is this memory, one that places the past in the present, that people in Lebanon have tried to evade, but they did this unsuccessfully precisely because contact with people in society is always futile to avoid, and because the intensification of political violence, through forms of remembrance, remained a constant possibility in the minds of the people.[9]

Active Forgetting: Contextualizing Memory and Amnesia

Jihad's story reminds me of Abidin Kusno's (2003) interpretation of a short essay by Indonesian writer, Seno Gumira Ajidarma, titled *Jakarta 2039*, where a father on his deathbed tells his daughter of gang rapes he committed in the Jakarta riots of May 1998. Upon her discovery, the girl asks how he could have done such a thing, to which her father responds:

> I don't know. Everyone was insane. Everyone did it. We felt that we were being led. None of us know how this happened. We have never talked about it. I have never wanted to meet those men again. When we met, we have never talked about it. We do not want to remember it. (Kusno 2003: 173)

But he did remember it, whether it was spoken about and remembered out loud or not, just as Jihad did. One observes in both cases a conscious effort to forget. In Arabic, the word *tanāsī*, from *nasā* (to forget), generally translates to choosing to forget, to the subject's active engagement in forgetting, or conscious forgetting, which implies an undercurrent of remembrance and an agency in forgetting. This concept more seriously captures what was occurring in Lebanon in the so-called "postwar" years. *Tanāsī* is the opposite of anamnesis, where the subject tries consciously to remember. And if one listens carefully, one can sometimes hear people in Lebanon say, in relation to a TV program or cultural event about the war, that they have had enough and have (actively) forgotten the war (*tnāsaynā el-ḥarb*), rather than use the construction *nasaynā el-ḥarb* (we have forgotten the war).

The consciousness and agency embedded in the process of *tanāsī* more accurately reflects the type of forgetting a collective can partake in.[10] Kansteiner tells us that "the threshold between the individual and the collective is often crossed without any adjustments in method; collectives are said to remember, to forget, and to repress the past; but this is done without any awareness that such language is at best metaphorical and at worst misleading about the phenomenon under study" (2002: 185). While it might be metaphorical or misleading to claim that a collective forgets, or that it can undergo any forgetting in a unified way, there might be an implicit agreement to try consciously and actively to forget. But this remains part of a dialogic experience that is conditioned on remembering, and it makes the concept of collective amnesia rhetorically empty at best.

My conversation with Jihad led me back to my field notes in search of what was being said concerning recollections of the past, and I soon began to question more seriously the notion of amnesia and the general consensus of a state-sponsored amnesia that many felt existed after Lebanon's war.[11] Haugbolle (2010) has provided the most comprehensive summary and analysis of memory work in Lebanon to date. Echoing Kansteiner (2002), he speaks out against "misrepresenting the past by producing metaphors" and "facile deductions" through terminology like amnesia and trauma (2010: 9). For Haugbolle, "collective amnesia almost became a cliché of public debate" (102), but he accepts the notion of a state-sponsored amnesia because it became somewhat of a social fact that social actors responded to. He eloquently captures the memory work of the period, saying that in Lebanon there were

> memory makers, people of the creative class who became occupied
> with questions of how to memorialise the war through social and
> artistic activities, and produced books, testimonies, films, articles,
> graffiti and architecture through which the war was remembered.

On the other hand, Lebanon's political groups produced a different type of memory culture based on hagiographic frameworks for understanding the past that were used to underpin and legitimise their political identity. (2010: 8)

The claim Haugbolle makes is that these actors acted in response to, or as resistance to, a state-sponsored amnesia that was manifested through an amnesty law, the often repeated "let bygones be bygones," and an "absence of state-sponsored attempts to establish what happened in the Lebanese Civil War" (4). But this actually does not amount to amnesia. The amnesty law was not meant to enforce a "culture of amnesia," it was meant to bring political parties to the diplomatic table, to unite the country, and to promote a culture of tolerance and reconciliation between political parties, rather than between individual victims. Effectively, the state did not sponsor amnesia, but forced people, through its tentacles—such as the media and political factions—to believe the war was over and to interpret their present as postwar.

Rather than any state-enforced amnesia or remembering, there was an abrogation of responsibility on the part of the state, which left a narrative of the war open to interpretation. In fact, if the state enforced anything, it was to lead the way to multivocal expressions of memory. Instead of sponsoring amnesia, which perhaps only a strong, controlling state could do, the state opened the way for interpretation and expression that resulted in the intensification of an everyday lived memory of war as if its time did not stop in the past. The state neither was able to make the population totally forget, nor had the will to call for remembering the war in the past without constantly regenerating its future possibility from within the present. The entire official amnesia argument further comes apart if we question which actors were promoting it within the state. On the contrary, ministers and politicians were speaking about the war to the press continually after the war and through the 1990s, and rather than relegating the war to the past, politicians, cultural workers, and the media constantly reminded people that war was around the corner.[12] People in Lebanon were not living in a time after war, where they had become more peaceful so long as they remembered it was past. Instead, they were constantly reminded that they were living in a time in between. War around the corner in a future time, and war past, made the present unstable, precarious, and contested.

The amnesia debate played out in various sites that included the cultural sphere (Haugbolle 2010; Westmoreland 2008), and in debates over the reconstruction of downtown Beirut, where it was also said that the war was being erased (Sawalha 2010; S. Makdissi 2006; Hanssen and Genberg 2001; Nagel 2002). However, to a large extent the reconstruction of downtown kept the war in the limelight. Upon seeing downtown, in the 1990s and today, one is reminded of the war and what it destroyed as one looks at the empty city and the "Disneyland"-style buildings. While the architects might have intended to absent the war from the city, cities have a way of subverting their planners (de Certeau 1984). If the war was missing or disappearing in its physical representation (as brick and concrete), it was present and intensified in how one spoke of downtown and represented it both in speech and through various forms of cultural production.[13] One could rarely speak of the new city in construction without referencing the war it was trying to render invisible. The very debates about memory and reconstruction led to an amplification of memory (Hanssen and Genberg 2001).

The process of the reconstruction of Beirut's central district, the way Lebanese approach life, their penchant for "good times," and their nighttime partying, have all been given as symptoms of amnesia, when they should be seen as living examples of *tanāsī*, and as efforts to cover up or suppress the possibilities of clashing memories. And what if we observe the work of memory as always already about the work of power—the way power functions, sets conditions, manages and controls through memory?[14] The process of *tanāsī*, as having agency, can then also be seen as a work of power. And could this be where the real tension and discomfort of memory work lies: not in its descent to oblivion, but in its ever-easy cooptation in the service of an oppressive power rather than as resistance to it?

Hourani (2008) disagrees with the amnesia thesis as well. He seems to think, and I agree, that there is a "structural power to silence" people in society, from political opponents to historians to filmmakers, which "advocates of the amnesia thesis mistake for a state-enforced or popular will to forget" (2008: 303). Hourani writes that "The repeated representation of a war [in films] in which the rich and powerful seemingly played no part is a constant reminder to the viewer of the power of the wealthy to escape criticism and to evade responsibility" (303). This representation, or lack thereof, becomes a power in itself, which is the power to silence, often mistaken for forgetting. Such moments of silence, and others like it where memory of war is said to be absent, should not be used as a claim that people in Lebanon have forgotten. This would be a simplistic interpretation of the silence that people exhibited in public, and often even in private, over the years. Silence does not denote forgetting, nor absence, rather it is a refusal to engage in open acts of interpretation and reflexivity;[15] it can be an inherently political act (of forgetting), and, as in the silence before the storm, it can signal danger—the danger of a future war.

Memory as Lived Experience

For people in Lebanon, the past persists and threatens to continuously fold into the present, so forgetting the past war can be an escape from the present and a move forward to the future.[16] One finds that the past is lived, and memory preserved, through a process of active conscious forgetting captured through the action of *tanāsī*.[17] People tell stories, they have political discussions that inevitably have to recall the past to situate the present, they hold events related to the wars, they discuss it in the media, they hold seminars on the topic, they write books, they produce art, but in the midst of this, these same actors say they want to forget, and *"mā bidnā nit-zakar"* (we don't want to remember). In turn, the discourse centers on how society is amnesiac. In an ironic twist, memory is actively sent to oblivion only to be retrieved.[18] How, after all, can people forget something, the remnants of which are felt and lived every day on the ground?

Rather than forget, people adopt strategies to remember certain experiences at specific moments, and perhaps it is more accurate to think of people as engaged in archiving the war rather than suppressing or forgetting it.[19] In many ways, however, they were unable to do even this because one cannot archive daily present life. The war, continuing to be lived even after people were told it was over, made archiving difficult, if not impossible. The very continuity between war and the period after, the so-called postwar, has made memory a continuously lived moment, one that is not seized by history.[20]

In Lebanon, those who were fighting to confront history and to establish *lieux de mémoire* in the form of commemorations or national monuments, such as UMAM Documentation and Research,[21] as well as other organizations and individuals, were assuming a notion of memory that was seized by history.[22] In other words, confronting history is to confront memory—the two were one and the same.

On the other hand, many people were actually still living aspects of the war, effectively turning their entire social space into sites of memory, where the war was constantly reinscribed in public space. This was true for the different communities in Lebanon that saw traces of war in their lives every day, whether through Israel's occupation, internal threats, or the reconstruction of the city, which brought with it new sets of tensions and reminders that the war continued by other means.

So there is a spontaneous memory; history has not yet seized memory and the jury is not out on which of the two will dominate. The line for where memory becomes history continues to be lived and is not yet fixed (Haugbolle 2010; Khalili 2007). In the meantime, people create their own sites of memory, not as archival work, but as a lived spontaneity in their traversals within the country, in their gestures and conversations with each other, in their habits and with their bodies. The spontaneous feeling of anticipation of war is one such way that people live their memories; it makes the quest for memory not simply a search for history, but part of daily life, part of their subjective energy, in which war memory continues to be lived as anticipation in present and future time.

Memory as lived experience can be seen in the way people and the state relate to such things as cultural productions and commemorations, to give just two examples. Works about the war were not absent from cultural space,[23] and these productions give us an idea of what people choose to remember. It is this choice that has been criticized by those who call for greater attention to wartime memory. That the state censored certain works on memory is an indication not that it was sponsoring amnesia, but rather, that the narrative it wanted to tell was not in line with that of the censored works. This was a battle not over remembering or forgetting, but about different forms of remembrance.

The state did allow various types of commemoration, for example, but these forms of memory were not simply about the past—they were also about the present and the future. Dates such as September 14 to commemorate the assassination of Bashir Gemayel; September 16, in remembrance of the victims of Sabra and Chatilla; August 31, to remember the disappearance of Musa Sadr; and others are considered not only as historic events, but as persisting into the present and framing the future as open wounds. Others, such as May 25, liberation day from Israel, are reminders that Lebanese must continue to fight for their sovereignty. None of these dates were ever censored as they could have been. Communities could organize their own events, turning places like the Beirut district of Ashrafieh, the refugee camp, or the southern suburbs of Beirut into places of ritual remembrance. Memory was inscribed into the streets, speeches were given, and promises of redemption or protection of the community were often made. These commemorations were not simply a record of an objective past; rather, they were ways to gather the community to show unity in the face of a past that continued to threaten people every day.[24]

Memory Work as Production and Consumption

In the anticipation of war, we see memory get produced and consumed in a specific way. Importantly, memory is produced in part through the very process of its consumption.[25] What this implies is that remembering the war, and choosing to forget it, are processes that involve different political and social actors always competing and interfering with each other in the process of producing memory. There can hardly be a remembered incident without an accompanying way to use or employ that remembrance (for the future, for example); likewise, with forgetting and its uses. Forgetting leads to useful ways of being in the world based on what people find to be significant for their lives (Borneman 1992). And even erasure, whenever that may be the case, is a type of production that society interacts with through a relationship of lack.

I see the dual-directional hyphen between production↔consumption to be where the work of memory takes place, and in the forces (politicians, cultural workers, media, and other people) pulling between the two to be where power is manifested. My contention, as we will see in the next chapter, is that society in Lebanon is deeply engaged in this hyphenated space, and it is this that keeps memory alive in a spontaneous space in the purview of daily life.

The constant anticipation and recollection of war plays a key role by forcing memory of the war to be part of consumer patterns. For example, people might claim that they go out and spend in order to forget, and may point to this as a denial of the past. Yet this "going out" and "spending" is often loaded with feelings of anticipation that make people talk, in some sequence, of war, then politics, and then the past. And if they do not speak of this, then they are often challenged by others, if not while "going out" then at some moment in time before or after, where "going out," partying, or spending becomes enveloped in discussions of remembering and forgetting past war. This can make consumerist patterns politically laden and intertwined in memory politics even if intended as an act of denial.

Certainly one must be careful not to assume these scenarios for the entire population, and I do not mean to claim that memories of the war are an inevitable part of all discussions or consumption patterns. But when observing the active scene at high-end beach clubs, night clubs, and other social places, or noticing the active real estate market, or seeing business (large and small) open up, it was not uncommon to hear people around me express a rhetorical sentiment along these lines: *bit-ʾūl hal balad dākhel bi-ḥarb?* (Would you say this country is entering into a war?) or *bit-ʾūl fī ḥarb bi-hal balad?* (Would you say there is a war in this country?). The sentiment can open the way for a discussion of war around the corner and can lead to recollections of past war. Through the consumption of what others are doing and saying about the past, memory (remembering and forgetting) gets produced. All this relies on dialogic relations and on people reading each other and consuming the "dialogical play of past and present" in order to (re)produce a form of memory. This reading is a continuous process in society. And while I do not subscribe to the simple statement that individual memories create the sum that is collective memory, I do see collective memory as a *reading* of individual memories. This reading is an interpretive play of the everyday practices of ordinary persons on one hand, and the practices of the state—loosely defined as government, media, or other political elite and powerful social actors—on the other. In this way, memory is not simply about archives, commemorations, and other *lieux de mémoire*, nor is it just located in places or people—or their practices as such—but in hermeneutic practices of the everyday more specifically. Memory, always present, is made visible and produced through the way others *read* practices rather than through the practices themselves. Inasmuch as these readings are similar, we can say that a collective memory emerges.

Kansteiner writes that groups "only have a chance to shape the national memory if they command the means to express their vision, and if their vision meets with compatible social or political objectives and inclinations among other important social groups, for instance, political elites or parties" (2002: 187). In other words, memory work is about hegemony and who controls the means by which to produce ideology—the process, not memory, is hegemonic. And like any hegemonic force it must defend itself in order to maintain its control. Rather than think of the work of memory in terms of denial and amnesia, we might want to remember Gramsci, and to think of the processes being played out as one involving the dominant social order trying to assert hegemonic control over history and truth. At the same time, various segments of society vie for this control and try to align their interests to better position themselves in case the social order weakens, and in case new spaces form to allow these new forces hegemonic control in producing an alternative history.[26]

Thinking of Ways Forward

Two weeks before leaving the field to go back to the United States,[27] I went to an exhibition organized by UMAM that was a photo gallery of war memorials, titled "The 'War' Through Its Memorials." I had not given the exhibition much thought as I made my way to the "hangar" where UMAM often held events. The hangar is an extension to the villa that houses the organization and its archives; the whole space, comprising a two-story villa and garden with an attached warehouse, has the feel of a quiet little oasis in the midst of the overcrowded and bustling area of Dahiyeh that surrounds it.

I made my way around the hangar, observing picture after picture of war memorials from different regions of Lebanon. As I did this, I could not help but feel shocked, mainly for believing in what people usually say about the lack of civil war memorials in the country. I counted twenty-eight memorials! But who is counting? The staff later told me that these are not all of them and they have collected more, but twenty-eight is good enough for anyone to realize that, for a country of approximately four million, there is a fetish with remembering, a kind of "hypertrophy of memory" (Huyssen 2003: 3). Most of the memorials commemorated soldiers and fighters, but there were also a few in memory of civilians. For me, this episode spoke to the coexistence of lived memory with *lieux de mémoire*.

As I looked at memorial after memorial, I wondered how we could still scream that there is collective amnesia, that there is no collective memory, and that we need war memorials. In all this screaming to remember, it seems people in Lebanon forget. But they forget the memorials, not the war itself. It is as though we may have really found a kind of oblivion here: that in calling for a work of memory, we forget, and deny, the memorials commemorating the experiences of different groups, thus undeniably advocating an erasure of histories, competing truths, and finally, memories. Instead of these memorials, civil society calls for one, all-unifying, national memorial that will capture fifteen years of war in one still structure. And would this structure capture the blood, gore, and guts spilled by the victims? War memorials are meant to be "quiet, still, reverential and tasteful," and they have the capacity to aid in ennobling the next war in this stillness and quietness (Hedges 2009). They do not "evoke the raging battles, nor the fear of the men, nothing of what would actually restore some of the past realistically lived by the soldiers," Marc Augé writes (2004: 87). Only the lived experiences, the stories my Teta continues to tell me while holding back tears, and the moments experienced with ex-fighters as they recall the past can hope to capture such effects, and even then only partly.

The past exists, not as absolute knowledge, but as a construct that each person builds differently in relation to the present. For example, the relatives of the disappeared were unable to let go of the past, constructed as it was through the spirits and memories of missing relatives. Such an immovable past was a construct of its agents, yet, in many ways, it was unconsciously reproduced and out of the actor's control. Agents like the state and communal groups, or civil society groups and the families of the disappeared, try to fight to force their narrative of the past. The Lebanese state did this; Solidiere, the real estate development company tasked with rebuilding downtown Beirut, did this in the way it chose to rebuild; civil society, in calling for a memorial day or statue, did this. The debates around memory were intertwined with critiques of state-sponsored amnesia. This was a process of production and consumption that continues into the present in the way people in Lebanon talk about the war, the past, and themselves. This type of memory may or may not lead to reconciliation, as memory workers would often like, but memory in itself may not be where reconciliation is to be found anyway. And reconciliation itself may not even be desired, especially not if it comes at the expense of postponing justice (Meister 2012).

Mahmoud Darwish, in his seminal wartime poem of 1982 Beirut, argued for a "memory for forgetfulness" (also the title of his poem). Saadi Nikro eloquently interprets Darwish, writing that

> Memory, Darwish says and yet does not say, is not about remembering and preserving a particular past ("the past" represented by the symbol), for that would only consist of another form of forgetfulness. Memory must become a site or scene of thought, inquiry, and dialogue—a polyphonic, aural terrain of emerging voices. (Nikro 1999)

I read this project of a "memory for forgetfulness" as a calling for greater reflexivity. This reflexivity calls on us to read the other and feel the other's pain as a project of restoring justice, rather than reconciling the powerful and keeping old structures of power intact. This project is not simply about understanding and remembering the causes of the war while forgetting the traumas (Traboulsi 2011). For my impression is that people do understand and remember the causes, they simply disagree on what these causes are. To understand the causes requires not simply to interpret the past by remembering it, but to interpret and be reflexive about the interpretations themselves. In other words, people must be asked to reflect on and interpret their memories and the dialogical experiences of their community's past in order to generate a meaning out of this past: to understand not just the causes, but the outcomes and the meanings this has engendered *for others*.

Such a project requires a greater commitment to reflexively scrutinize one's self and one's positions. Yet, reflexively thinking of the self and the past is a task, I would venture to say, that few societies do so well. My argument has been that people in Lebanon experience a livable memory of war, one that is always present but made visible in their everyday lives through triggers that are embedded in conversations, bodily practices, and encounters, but also in architecture, landscape, the media, and cultural productions. This calls for a confrontation with power in its more malicious forms rather than a concentration on war memory, and by extension, *lieux de mémoire*, as a remedy to social problems. My concern in analyzing memory work has been to think of how society in Lebanon might restructure social struggles to be more effective in directing their confrontations, especially in a place that refuses to hold the political system accountable.

In the end, Ziyad, a close friend of mine I met during fieldwork and a mutual friend of Jihad's, in his early fifties with graying hair, seems to have said it best as he responded to my explaining to him the purpose of this chapter. "My friend," he said in Arabic, "in Lebanon no one has forgotten. And if there was somewhere someone who did forget, then he is either a madman or a *miḥtāl* (sly person). In all cases, this system perpetually works to produce in us a memory for killing." Indeed, there is an element of slyness—a trick, a lie—in pretending to forget. And there is a sense of pretense in *tanāsī* or active forgetting, which is the most present form of forgetting among people. Yet, perhaps it is in Ziyad's last clause that we can think of a way forward. Ziyad asks us to think of the system, to confront it and not memory, and to confront the political and social roots of disagreement. I pondered over this for a long time, and thought of my friend, a political party member who is also involved in independent political work and who has participated in the war at various levels. Carrying thoughts of memory as an always engaged hermeneutic practice, I turn next to ethnographic encounters to critique the idea of remembering in order not to repeat the past (*tindhakar mā tin'ād*).

Chapter 7

Ambiguities of War's Remembrance: Two Episodes

In this chapter, building on the previous one, I will elaborate on the ways in which lived memory of the war is made visible and intensifies in people's conversations and encounters, and how this works as a strategy for dealing with everyday life. I will also look at how the constant anticipation of political violence ensures that Lebanon's war is a continuous living memory. To do this, I will recount two moments with interlocutors that draw attention to the ambiguities present in processes of memory work, and speak of the role of active forgetting (*tanāsī*) in producing collective forms of memory.

In the first encounter, memory manifests dialogically through what Hammoudi (2009) calls "communicative configurations," which occur between my interlocutor and me, and in our surrounding community. In the second, ambiguities of memory work appear with my interlocutor as we walk through the city streets in downtown Beirut. Here, a politics of "No Victor, No Vanquished" is revealed in the way a person remembers the past. In this episode, I suggest that people are never really certain whether they remember or forget, or when they are doing each, and they often contradict themselves as they try to make sense of and verbalize their past. The two encounters show the ways remembering and forgetting are processes highly influenced by intersubjective experiences in society, but despite this, personal experiences offer a window into understanding collective social moods and motivations. These encounters allow us to rethink the politics of memory in a precarious place where people are constantly feeling a threat of war, and to conceptualize anew the idea of memory in its infinite multiplicity rather than thinking of a need or necessity for a master national narrative.

Daily Embodiments of the Past

If people are constantly remembering the war and there has been no amnesia as some feared there would be, then how do these memories get triggered? And how do people negotiate their memories within a context that continues to reinscribe the politics of Lebanon's past conflict both in the present and future?

One regular day in April 2008, Nabil and I sat in his TV room. Nabil is a relative we've encountered previously in this book. He is Maronite and someone who took part in armed fighting in the early years of Lebanon's war. He sat with his laptop open in front of him, papers scattered around the table, and the TV turned to the day's news. The room we were in, like many balconies in recent years around the country, used to be an open, outdoor space and, in this case, part of the garden, but Nabil and his wife decided to enclose it with glass windows to gain space in their house. From the room, one could see Beirut and the Mediterranean Sea; it is a remarkable view despite the haphazard construction that has turned Beirut's skyline into concrete chaos, and despite the urban sprawl that has left the mountain range between his house and the city littered with random buildings of different sizes and shapes.[1]

We were listening to the news when Nabil began to tell me about a program on LBC (Lebanese Broadcasting Corporation) that dealt with the civil war and had aired as part of the commemorations during the week of April 13, 2008. "Oh, did you watch it," I asked. "No, I changed the channel," he replied, following it with "*la-'an bit-zakernā bil-ḥarb* (because it reminds us of the war)."

When Nabil made his comment about forgetting the war, I was surprised. I knew Nabil better than this. How many times had we argued about current politics that led us to recalling the past and to him explaining the causes of the war or drifting into a story of one of his experiences? Still, at the time I let it go.

Later, as I searched my field notes for such encounters, I was struck by the connection between Nabil's above statements and a conversation with him only a few hours later at a relative's house where we were invited for a barbeque. Nabil and I joked around while pouring our drinks—I my usual vodka tonic, and he a whisky, or maybe, I cannot remember clearly now, it was a glass of vodka with kumquat that someone in my family had concocted some time ago. I had noticed and commented on the unshaven look Nabil had going for him that day. "Nice beard," I said. "Yes, I want to look like your people (*jamāʿtak*)," implying the Shiʿa. It is a comment I was used to because it stems from arguing tirelessly in conversations against family, where my politics are perceived to be sympathetic to the Shiʿa community as well as other non-Christian communities. I often treated these remarks with a dismissive chuckle, preferring to let it go and be non-confrontational, or shot back, but careful to never lose the smile that ensured civility. Many times I felt, both in the moment and later, that our politics could one day overpower our familial relations and push us away from each other. I dreaded these thoughts, but there was a time during research that I felt Nabil and I were drifting, pulled apart by seemingly irreconcilable political positions; his comment came in the midst of this.

Several possibilities existed for the unconscious behaviors taking place between us that day. Nabil's comment was a joke, and I treated it as such, but I knew—and I believe he must have as well—that it masked a deeper political emotion of animosity that, if unchecked and pushed to its limits, could create fissures in our relations (G. Hage 2009). On the other hand, one can reason that the whole encounter was a kind of game; a taunt or a tit-for-tat performance that we engaged in because our solid relational bond could survive this pressure. Would Nabil make similar comments ("I want to look like *your people*"), or take such positions with people of similar political inclinations to me but with whom he does not share an unbreakable bond? The question remains open, but it casts ambiguity and doubt on the incident and on the way people position themselves and use political ideas and beliefs strategically to relate to each other.

I was able to deflect the deeper implications of Nabil's comment by recalling an incident that happened two days earlier, in the freshman class I was teaching at AUB. It so happened that in class one student assumed I was Shiʿa specifically because of my beard. In response, Nabil laughed. His next move was to find common ground by suggesting that Christians grew their beards too during the war. "*Skaut*," he said (which literally means to shut up, but in this context was a playful way of saying, But on a serious note now!). "Look at how we [Christians] were during the war," he continued excitedly, "with our beards down to here," and he placed his hands around his face, close to his upper chest to express length. He continued by reproducing a memory from Lebanon's war: "There was a time when I was first going out with [my wife] and had to cross the Green Line. There were two checkpoints. The first was manned by the Tyus[2] and the second by Numur el-Ahrar.[3] I was stopped at both checkpoints. At the first checkpoint, they let me go because of my Christian name. At the second one [also manned by Christians], the guy started to curse me and I could not but stand up to him. We ended up getting into a gun battle," at this point Nabil's voice began to get louder from excitement. "We began shooting at each other! I hid behind my car, and the whole stand off lasted for quite some time!" He followed with, "But no one got hurt in the end . . ."

"What happened to the car?" I asked. "The car was screwed [giggles]. And then, what would you expect? I got to [my wife's] house and what does she ask me: Why are you late? [laughing hysterically] Can you believe it? [laughing continuously]. We then called people and got *wāsṭa* [connections] so that this doesn't occur again." There was a pause, and then he continued with a tone of sadness and pain, "So many people were lost in this manner during the war. Ahrar killing Kataeb, Kataeb killing Ahrar, even Kataeb killing Kataeb."

tin-dhakar mā tin-ʿād (Remember so as not to repeat)[4] is a slogan used each year in relation to April 13, the remembrance day of Lebanon's war. The slogan was developed by a group of associations working on remembering the war, primarily the organization Mémoire pour l'Avenir (Memory for the future) (Barclay 2007). It targets Lebanese society in an effort to make people remember the terrible acts of war and the open wounds they are supposedly forgetting. The idea behind it is that it is necessary to remember war in the past in order not to repeat it in the present or future. The slogan came as a response to the perceived idea that the state wanted to forget the war and create an overall amnesia. But Nabil did not want, or perhaps he did not need, TV shows to remind him of the war so that he does not repeat it. All it took was a very mundane trigger, such as my beard, and a comment from a student earlier that week to stir memories and for him to conclude by denouncing the senselessness he believed the war to have generated.

While civil society that week seemed busy trying to make society remember by bringing people to events to speak about the past, others like Nabil and many who lived the war were busy remembering as they tried to forget (*tanāsū*).[5] I suggest, furthermore, that Nabil's story of a specific incident during the war years is never wholly detached from a larger social process of remembering war's significance and framing its historical moments. While it is a personal conversation held in the presence of intimate others, it is also one that finds an echo around the country.

This incident is especially interesting because, of all the people I encountered, Nabil spoke the least of his past. His children told me on a number of
occasions that he had not spoken to them about his experiences in the war.
Only recently, as they got older, did they begin to hear things, but never in
detail. They knew he was caught and abused by the Syrians, but not why,
how, and the ways he was tortured. I always wondered if Nabil's stories to me
were conveniently timed when his children were not around, though if it was
I never picked up on it, nor did I pick up on it with others I spoke to. Perhaps
this careful game of negotiation between storytelling and secrecy was one my
interlocutors learned to play almost naturally, so that my anthropological
senses could not pick up on it. Nabil was not the first to tell me that he did
not speak in front of his children, nor were his kids the first to tell me their
parents did not talk to them about the personal and painful stories of war
(such as fighting or being tortured). Yet the stories were told to me at the
most unexpected times, often around others, and even when their children
were in the room but supposedly engaged in other activities—this latter situation always made me think there was a part of them that wanted their
children to know, but without the guilt of being the ones to do the telling, as
though their parents' war stories would corrupt the children or perhaps
change the way their children perceive them.

Memory is often transmitted from one generation to another so that the
receiving generation might remember events even if not present at the time
itself (Borneman 1992). Contrary to the idea that parents did not talk to their
children about the war, often dismissing them with terms like *Allāh la-yi-
farjīk* (May God not show you), or *aktar min hek mā tis-'alū* (More than this
don't ask), or by summing it up with the phrase *tin-dhakar bas mā tin-'ād*,
the younger generation is still able to put together narratives of the past
based on different sources.[6] This reconstruction of the past depends, of
course, on whether the young individuals care to know, to ask, or to be attentive. Subjective energy and the interpretation of narratives are what give
memory both power and presence, but ignoring the memory does not mean
it is absent, just invisible. The two most overt sources from which the young
might formulate narratives of the past are from programs in the media, and
even more powerfully, from survivors and perpetrators of the war who might
not speak in front of their own children, but who have no issues speaking to
other children and other persons from younger generations.[7] Nabil and others find themselves negotiating when, how, and what to remember, and the
experiences and lessons of past conflict continue to circulate and to be

remembered, especially since an intensification of political violence is projected for the future.

Negotiating Memories in Motion

I heard the phrase *tin-dhakar ta-mā tin-ʿād* often in my conversations with
ex-fighters. I want to draw out one way this phrase is mobilized and some of
the ambiguity embedded in memory work. I also aim to show how the victim
status that results from a politics of "No Victor, No Vanquished" can manifest in the way someone like Zuzu, the former militia fighter we've encountered earlier, remembers, perceives, and talks about the past.

Not too long after my encounter with Jihad, I finally managed to get
Zuzu to tour parts of downtown Beirut with me to recount the war while we
traversed the same streets where he fought years before. The reasons for this
"tour" were not so much because I felt memories would be jostled within a
place—though this was true—but I had come to realize that in motion,
while walking or driving, a different knowledge could be exposed from that
of the confined space of a seated conversation. The process of reaching a destination with my interlocutors, or even meandering aimlessly with them, this
process that we might call a moving-together, produced a level of solidarity
that was revealing. This moving-together was further enhanced because it
placed my interlocutor and me around other people and amid a landscape
that itself was changing as we moved along it. There was something natural
in the pace of our thoughts and movements, and in the way our thoughts had
to respond to noises and scents, yet unnatural in that these "tours" were
planned by me,[8] and my interlocutor had come prepared to recount and remember. But the results of such planned and unplanned traversing through
the country often uncovered some of the best material for thinking about
memory work.[9]

My walk through downtown Beirut with Zuzu was a case in point. I met
him around 4 p.m. on a Tuesday by Virgin Megastore in downtown. The
Virgin building has become somewhat of a landmark, and for a long time
after the war was more famous than the absent Martyrs statue that it overlooked.[10] We walked across the street to the Martyrs Square statue. As we
approached, Zuzu began to recall for me how he was shot in the leg by a
sniper as he hoisted the Kataeb flag (a white flag with a symbol of the cedar
tree in the middle) on the statue, sometime in the early 1980s. He had made

his way, one eerily quiet morning, across the deserted space that had become the center of downtown. On both sides, ghostlike buildings, their facades peeled away by years of fighting, peered over him as he scampered across the square. Zuzu, still the preadolescent teen, climbed the statue with his small-ish hands and feet, and stuck the flag in the torch held high by one of the statue figurines. But as he was done, a bullet penetrated his leg, the only part of his body visible through the gaps in the statue from the Azarieh Building not too far away. "*Ah, inta ḥaṭeyt hal 'alam?*" ("Oh, you put that flag?") I wondered out loud.

In my own memory, I could recollect, as clear as day, a photograph, haunting me, of a destroyed and deserted Martyr Square, the statue standing alone with the Kataeb Party flag hanging from it. Zuzu did not know which picture I was talking about, and I am not certain any more if that picture even exists. I have looked for it; almost sure I had seen it in a magazine I own. Now, I do not know if the flag in the 1982 picture of downtown Beirut (Figure 19) is a Kataeb flag, an LF flag, or a Lebanese national one whitened by the perspective of the photo. I present it here (alongside an image of the same square in

Figure 19. Martyrs Square, Beirut, 1982.

Photo Credit: James Case.

2015, which is also where Zuzu and I met some years earlier—Figure 20), partly in disbelief that I know the story behind that flag, partly to visualize how we may be misled as researchers, and partly because I am not sure whether this flag on the statue is a childhood memory that comes back to me. Did I see the flag in a photograph or did I see it during one of the many times that, as a child, I crossed the Green Line between East and West Beirut with my parents to visit my grandparents? In any case, how many before and after him put up flags? Was his flag the one in the picture, or even the one in my memory, or did his flag fall a moment or two later? It certainly could not have survived till 1982, the time of this particular photograph, and I was definitely not in Lebanon that year. More important, did he really put up the flag or was he appropriating the heroics of his group to be his own? No matter, war stories get retold and passed down through filtered channels of present moods and motivations of the storyteller. Listeners must decide in the moment how critical they want to be of the validity of these stories. For me, the story becomes important because of the shivers it sent down my spine as I recalled the flag and visualized the destroyed downtown of the past with some lucidity. I then went home to frantically search for the image of this flag in magazines, both online and those physically in my possession. As Sontag reminds us, "to

Figure 20. Martyrs Square, 2015, near area where Zuzu and I took our walk.

Photo Credit: Author, 2015.

remember is, more and more, not to recall a story but to be able to call up a picture," and this seemed to hold true for me (2003: 89).

We stood in front of the statue for some time; Zuzu told me he would like to bring his children here someday just to stand in the same place and take pictures. We then began walking to Foch Street. Zuzu spent several years fighting on this front. He told me how they used to name the area, and he tried to remember different zones they called "Alpha 1," "Alpha 2," and "Alpha 3." Then he spoke of how he was trapped for some time (without specifying how long), in a building on that street. He told me about Roni, his good friend, who was shot to death as he lay injured in the middle of the street. Roni and some of Zuzu's other "comrades" had been playing a nightly game of daring each other to go into an enemy building—the buildings were a few meters across the street from one another and I could barely comprehend the meaning of such proximity in warfare when Zuzu pointed them out to me. After entering the building, they were meant to steal something symbolic as proof of accomplishment. The enemy, in this case the Al-Murabitoun (see List of Major Political Parties), finally discovered this prank and one night planted an ambush. It was during this fatal game that Roni was killed.

At one point, Zuzu said, "I told you in the past that I've been trying to forget, to not remember the past, so that I don't affect my kids with that." I cut him off and exclaimed, "But you always remember!" He could not deny this to me after all the times we had hung out together and I had seen him around family and friends. So he downplayed this issue of remembering, telling me, "Maybe when we are sitting in a social gathering, we remember. We talk about when we did this or that. 'Remember when you tied him up, do you remember when we sniped someone.' Yes, things like that we remind each other of." If these otherwise terrible events were things being remembered, then, I wondered, what exactly was he trying to forget? He vacillated between remembering and forgetting.

Moments later he would utter, "The days of the war were not good." But I called him out on this again. How many times had he said the exact opposite? He tried to recover with ambiguous statements. He told me how he had lost opportunities because of the war, whereas others did something with their lives. Then he said, "But if we did not fight then maybe the country would have been lost. Maybe if it weren't for us then all this [he points around] wouldn't be here."

Our conversation drifted and finally came to a pause. After some silence, he said, "*Shū bidnā in-khabrak?*" (What should I tell you?), followed by a pause. Then, contradicting his earlier response, he said with a sigh, "*iyem ḥilwe!*" (Those were good days!) Another pause and then in a soft voice,

> We would in the winter sit in these shops and see each other light-ing a fire and covering up in the cold. Had you seen the guys then and lived those days, you would have written the most beautiful book, *wa-ḥyēt wlādī* (I swear by my kids)! You could have found someone to bring you down here and you would have lived it and produced a great story. Because you would have been seeing, not hearing, the stories and then wondering if people are exaggerating. But I am telling you all this now, and I feel like I am there and liv-ing it, sitting on the front and as if someone is talking to me. I get sad when I remember these memories . . . I get sad about my coun-try and what happened to it. We are the victims here in Lebanon. It isn't my fault or yours, it is the big players [who are at fault].

Here is a man who by many accounts was a perpetrator, perceiving him-self as a victim as he grapples with whether to forget or remember. His sen-timents are very similar to those in cultural representations and productions of the war and to the way formerly armed people have remembered the war in the media.[11] One thing seems clear; he is not self-reflecting on what hap-pened. Instead, he chooses to accept the dominant position that the Leba-nese were all victims, to work his memory through this lens of victimization and actively forget his role as perpetrator. Collective memory is given expres-sion through such readings of the past, where even perpetrators become vic-tims, and where people like Zuzu adopt the convenient master narrative that claims "We are all victims!"

We stood for an hour on Foch Street where Zuzu spent much of his childhood as an armed militiaman, from age twelve. After that we began to head back, stopping momentarily near the statue in memory of journalist and writer Samir Kassir, assassinated in 2005; he told me that this space used to be where all the public toilets were before the war. I thought back to Freud: imagine the shock if we could actually see cities built over each other!

We walked back up to the busier Weygand Street (most people in Leba-non will know it as either the one perpendicular to Virgin or where Grand Cafe is located). From here we were able to see the Martyr statue again, and somehow this returned us back to Zuzu's opening story about getting shot as he hoisted the party flag. He wondered about the whole incident and thought again about the sniper shooting him. Then, a ten second pause, a sigh, a nostalgic release, *"ḥilwe, ḥilwe el-zikrayāt!"* (Beautiful! Memories are beautiful!)

"Oh really," I exclaimed, knowing I had hit the nerve I was trying to get at, and arrived at that ambivalent space between active forgetting (*tanāsī*) and the pleasure of remembrance.

"Yes, but then you think between yourself and you think of all the people . . ." he started to say, almost as though back tracking. I interrupted, "I'm not talking about the people that were lost, but how you remember and the 'nice' . . ."

Zuzu cut me off, "Look Sami . . . Yes, it's nice. Doesn't the saying go *tindhakar bas mā tin-ʿād*? We remember, but we don't want to repeat the story, we don't want to let war return. But they were good days (*iyēm khayr*). Sami, you would spend something like 10LL and get in return 20,000LL [an exaggeration denoting the prosperity or profit of the times]. Now you have to think twice before you spend $10 and where you are going to make your next buck."[12]

Zuzu's use of the slogan above seems like a cooptation of its original intent, and I wonder if civil society actors had in mind for people to remember the war as being "good days." Zuzu remembered the war, but not only its evil past, but its good days as well.[13] Even the evils of the past, Lebanon's war, had good elements, and to deny this would itself be to deny people of a past. Zuzu's remembering does not seem to fit in with neat ideas of memory being a panacea for Lebanon's problems. His remembrance was not a type of therapy since remembering past war in order to keep it in the past seemed to conflict with the good times he did not want to let go of. Times that he likely associated with his youth, with freedom, and getting away from the structuring limitations of both kin and state, all of which were related to a sense of power over himself.

In any case, there was, here and in many other discussions we had, a disconnect between saying one wanted to forget (*tanāsī*) and then really forgetting (*nasā*). Talk of forgetting was never far away from actually remembering, from engaging past memories and experiences, and from making those memories visible. Zuzu said he wanted to remember but not repeat the war, and he was not the first to express this to me, nor was it just people who formerly carried arms. However, few expressed an interest to confront the master narrative of equal victimization on all sides—the narrative of "No

Victor, No Vanquished"—or to deal with the moral ambiguities and ambivalence that arose from not having a clear idea of who were the victims and who the executioners. Zuzu's acceptance of the victimhood status was a symptom of this moral ambiguity. In all this, one witnesses a work of memory—as in Zuzu was remembering and engaging the parts of the past he wanted to forget—but no emphasis on truth telling and assuming responsibility for the past.

This memory is not forgotten; it can be triggered by the slightest mundane act, sight, or object. It is memory formed in the fluidity and spontaneity of everyday life. And rather than repressed memories, we may think of them in the form of archived or livable memories. For if we pay attention to the way people speak, to their behaviors, to what is written and disseminated, to art, to literature, and to the media, we start to see this archive work as a daily reminder that the past is still lived in the present and that these are livable memories people access as strategies for everyday life.

In absence of state accountability of the war, of truth-telling mechanisms, and of asserting a structure for the dissemination of history, debate has continued to focus on memory, a process so alive, spontaneous, and intense that it might be time to recognize it for what it is. One would then be able to ask if it is not necessary, instead, to accept the way society lives its memory in the present as practice, rather than as *lieux de mémoire*, and to accept the way society produces—or consumes—memory rather than force a specific notion of how to remember and forget. We would then, perhaps, be able to move away from constructing memory as a panacea, or as a process that society in Lebanon must engage with as though it were not already doing so.

Memory Versus the Master National Narrative

If, as I am saying, there has been no amnesia, and memory is being used instead as a political tool, then what are the implications for social movements working on the issue of memory?[14] To scream "the Lebanese are suffering from collective amnesia" seems to imply that if they remember, then this would solve some of their problems. But what if they remember the war as meaningless? The inability to find meaning in all the fighting of war is very powerful; it is another form of warfare.[15] So what happens when people draw from their memory that the war was useless? Should the absence or presence of collective memory be the issue, or should the question and problem be framed around finding meaning in the war and the past, and the ways in which memory can be intensified? If people remember the war, but find no meaning in it and in fifteen years of their lives and history, then would that prevent people in Lebanon from fighting again, or could it, perhaps, drive groups back to war to find their otherwise lost meaning? The activist in me wants to suggest confronting the fact that people in Lebanon do remember, and remember differently, and that it is multiple meanings of the past with which society needs to learn to coexist. Rather than confront history, by which I understand this to mean confronting memory to rewrite or rethink history, might people think of confronting the multiple misunderstandings of war experiences, and come to a shared comfort space in how these experiences shape present engagements with the world? After all, memory in Lebanon is not seized by history, so it is not a confrontation with history per se that will prevent war from returning.[16]

In the process of constituting the nation, memory appears fixed with a hegemonic narrative of what is remembered. However, in a precarious place where state and society are fighting over narratives, memory becomes a key battleground, not in its absence or denial, but rather, in its intense presence and multiplicity, and in its battle to defend itself and all its competing possibilities, refusing to compromise to the hegemonic space of a master national narrative. Memory sees the master national narrative as the death of memory.

The master narrative, that which we must agree on and subscribe to as our understanding of the past, and that becomes our memory of the past (think of appeals for a student textbook on Lebanese contemporary history), is a narrative that we hear or read about from our present position. In fact,

> The problem with the grand narratives of nationalist historiography is that they override the complex multivocality that resides within the individual and within society by giving a single authoritative expression to complex collective experiences. In so doing, they almost invariably expose nationalist history, nationalist regimes and, eventually, the nation-state itself, to popular subversion that finds an outlet in memory cultures. (Haugbolle 2010: 13)

For example, the Lebanese civil war is said to have begun on April 13, 1975, when the Lebanese Phalange Party fired at a bus carrying Palestinians,

and retaliated for an earlier attack on their leader, Pierre Gemayel. This is
how many people will narrate the beginning of the civil war, but this is not
how many, if not most, individuals who subscribe to this narrative experienced it. The master narrative substitutes for the experiential and subjective
memories of people who try to hold onto their memories and recount it for
me differently. For example, Sherif, a school bus driver in his mid-forties,
and formerly an armed member of the PSP, recounted the war as beginning
the day his father was shot, and did not remember April 13 until I reminded
him of that date.

There is a difference between a national memory and a broader collective
memory. Collective memory can be at the level of a community, but can remain fragmented at the level of the national whole (this implies there can be
multiple collective memories that construct the national memory). Similarly,
there is a difference between a master narrative and a master national narrative. The master narrative has the ability to function, as Borneman writes, "to
enable individuals to order their experiences around the repetition of specific
tropes by integrating the lifecourse into a coherent story, hence constituting a
meaningful subject. To the extent that the same master narratives are appealed
to by different subjects, they become instruments for producing social and
possibly national cohesion" (1992: 46). However, the cohesion of the master
national narrative comes at the expense of other mini-master (communal,
family or political party) narratives and at the expense of people remembering
and forgetting in different ways. Remembering is politically laden, "It is not a
simple process of evoking and recovering elements fixed in a historical moment but rather a remembering that produces narratives legitimizing, maintaining, ordering, and conditioning social life" (Íñiguez, Valencia, and Vázquez
1997: 238). This will necessarily privilege some narratives over others.

Given this, we might want to question whether a national memory is a
goal to be achieved. Should there be an agreed upon unified history taught in
schools—currently there is none—or should the goal be to provide different
possible narratives, allowing students to learn history through discussion and
debate, with the purpose of learning to confront and engage the conflict and
its disagreements? Borneman provides an alternative suggestion for reconciliation after ethnic cleansing that could apply to the argument against national memory in general. He writes that public forums

> will lead to an open acknowledgment of dissensus, of the ambiva-
> lences and complicities inherent in the exercise of power. They may

even lead to public conflict and to aggression directed toward those who have truths to tell. But because this acknowledgment affirms the power of truth-telling in creating a public sphere, it is in the interest of democratic publics. (2002: 296)

If it is democratic publics that people are asked to search for, then could the work of memory service such democratic publics, rather than being in the service of a national, highly ethnicized memory—ethnicized because the nation represents the power of certain groups to establish symbols and meanings at the expense of others (Borneman 2002)? But trying to overcome the multiple, competing processes of memory is not a simple matter, and we would have to turn on our questions with further questions to ask if a politicized—or publicized—work of memory could ever be therapeutic, and could ever produce the democratic publics a Lebanese civil society is in search of.

My point in this and the preceding chapter has been to argue that a politics of memory in Lebanon works through processes of living and spontaneous memory rather than through specific sites of memory. However, more important, is that in all these processes forgetting has had a special place, but not in order to produce loss of memory or silence, but rather, as a political act to deter an archeology of truth that the conflict's aftermath depends on, especially if such acts as forgiveness and reconciliation are to be entertained. Forgetting, in its active and agentive sense of tanāsī, has been a way to remember without carrying the weight of remembrance; it is not an act of hiding, but one of revelation where supposedly repressed memories (and emotions) can make their way out, if only for a moment, and even if not voiced.

Forgetting, and this is my primary claim, has been used by some as a rhetorical device to hide the remembering that has occurred beneath it, and where people can continue living without admitting that they remember. It is this type of forgetting that I would argue has developed into a kind of social fact in Lebanon. Through the process of tanāsī, people can rhetorically claim to forget; they can even feel like they have forgotten at certain times while going through much of their day. But through this active conscious forgetting, they can also remember the past war, and they can remember it without serious moral implications or taking responsibility, precisely because they are said to have forgotten. This active forgetting appears like a play with history, a kind of conscious performance of denial to give meaning to people's lives in the aftermath of war.

Chapter 8

Amnesty as a Politics of Protracted Conflict

There is an Arabic saying that: "A man is a man because he forgets." [In Arabic the words for "human" and "forget" are very similar.] We make a choice what to remember and what to forget but the unsaid in history must be said. The major condition for us to forgive and to forget is that we feel that truth was said. Those who committed crimes must at least admit them. This is the precondition of forgiveness.

—Elias Khoury (2015)

In 1991, with the supposed end of the war, the Lebanese government passed an amnesty law. More than fifteen years later, when I arrived for my fieldwork, and despite other wars, bombings, and continued violations of the rights of people in Lebanon, this law remained a topic of concern, both in people's recollections of how past war was concluded and when they reflected on the future political situation. Perhaps no single phrase captures the amnesty in public discourse as ʿafā Allāh ʿammā maḍā, a principle that Lebanese political society lives by. The phrase literally means "God has forgiven/pardoned what is past," but God was not the one who had pardoned, it was the state governed by many former warlords. Was this phrase suggesting, as people often do, that the state was a divine higher power? Were people resigning to a top-down decree of amnesty? Indeed, if God had pardoned, nothing could be done to reverse the decision.

ʿafā Allāh ʿammā maḍā has a history, and so does the use of amnesties in the Lebanese political sphere. In fact, rather than write a history of war, it is useful to recount the history of amnesties in the country in order to think of how each successive amnesty transformed politics. We might then begin to see how the political sectarian system has in part been produced and solidified through successive "peace agreements" and their corresponding amnesties. These amnesties have also allowed past acts of violences to be lived in the present and transitioned into the future, as people recall them and create the conditions for an intensification of memory.

Importantly, the 1991 amnesty must be analyzed alongside the idea of *lā ghāleb, lā maghlūb* (No Victor, No Vanquished), first invoked after the 1958 civil war. To recap, this policy is meant to ensure no political group or sect is eliminated from the political system, and that there is *al-'aysh al-mushtarak* (coexistence) and *al-waḥda al-waṭaniyya* (national unity). In the words of Lucia Volk, we might think of this policy as one way "culturally plural societies may work toward reconciliation after periods of violence" (2010: 23). But if this policy allowed for reconciliation at the level of the political elite, it ignored the sentiments of many victims. With no victor, all politicians were collectively to blame, as well as collectively harmed. But acts of political violence cannot be collectively shared, not to mention equally shared, and therefore this policy breeds hypocrisy for the political subjects who then use it to subvert responsibility.[1] Equally, this policy reinscribed the same politics that led to war in the first place, and, therefore, facilitated a feeling that war could return. How, I ask, does the absence of accountability that resulted from both the amnesty and its corresponding policy of "No Victor, No Vanquished," translate into people's experiences and into discourses about their political existence in the past, present, and future?

To reflect on this question, and after recounting a history of peace agreements and amnesty in Lebanon, I elaborate on the politics of *lā ghāleb, lā maghlūb*. I then look at the ways in which discourses of accountability seeped into public engagements in Beirut, and the role a policy of "No Victor, No Vanquished" played in these engagements. In the absence of any law strong enough to appear uncontested and depoliticized, it remains for the people concerned to negotiate around injustice. In this way, accountability and crime become open to contestation in public discourse, and such basic concepts become challenged and ambiguous. Who is a criminal? And what constitutes a crime? The last section in this chapter deals with these questions through an exchange with one interlocutor who asserts his ideas by laying blame on everyone, perhaps not ironically, in the tradition of a politics of "No Victor,

No Vanquished." Notions of accountability and crime get negotiated and remain ambiguous, but centrally part of the public discussion. They also seem to complicate Elias Khoury's important position in the epigraph to this chapter.

In reflecting on these issues, my point is that the amnesty law in Lebanon has produced a public discourse of justice and accountability despite being institutionally absent in writ law. This was unlike in South Africa or at the Nuremberg trials. In the former, the state laid out a clear path of accountability through a process of restorative justice (think of forgiveness and the legal structure of the Truth and Reconciliation Commission in South Africa, established to deal with the crimes of the apartheid era). In the latter, the victorious powers held criminals accountable through a process of retributive justice (handing out the death penalty in many cases). However, in Lebanon, the amnesty law was a government decree that did not require the perpetrators to come to terms with their supposed crimes, or to face victims to seek their forgiveness. In this way, accountability, and its material ramifications, were made absent in Lebanon by the law. Yet, the law, in actuality, made a discourse of accountability deeply present by opening up multiple valences of accountability in the public sphere (cafés, living rooms, lectures, media) through acts of recollection, even if this did not result in formal accountability.

A History of Amnesties

In Ussama Makdisi's seminal book, *Culture of Sectarianism* (2000), one can count three instances of amnesty in the region of Mount Lebanon predating the latest one that followed Lebanon's war.[2] The first came in 1839. The year before, fighting erupted as a result of Ibrahim Pasha's reforms in Syria to alter the power in the region from Istanbul to Cairo.[3] Ibrahim Pasha, the son of Egyptian ruler Mehmed Ali, ruled Syria and conscripted Druze to fight alongside him. Druze loyalty to Egypt and a corresponding Christian loyalty to the Ottoman Empire resulted in Christian-Druze battles in Mount Lebanon in 1838 where Ibrahim Pasha's armies were finally crushed. In 1839, the principle of "Let bygones be bygones," or *maḍā mā maḍā*, was adopted in the aftermath of these battles as a strategy to "abolish the memory of past deeds and transgressions" (Makdisi 2000: 56), and restore civil peace in the mountains.[4] It indicates the early presence of an amnesty discourse that was effectively calling for a forgetting of a recent intercommunal conflict that had sectarian underpinnings.

That year, amnesty came to restore the social order, which was based on a "discourse of loyalty" rather than sectarian allegiances. In other words, the Druze and the Christians fought not for sectarian reasons but because of competing loyalties, which were inscribed in religious affiliation. For the Ottomans, the Druze were considered heretics so long as they were loyal to Ibrahim Pasha. By extension, "the Christian identity of the Lebanese came to the fore only as a method for the authorities to separate them from the Druzes, to arm them, and to send them against the Druzes [*sic*]. Once the rebellion was over and the threat of disorder contained, the Christian-Druze dichotomy was meant to be erased; all subjects were to resume their former social standing" (Makdisi 2000: 56). The amnesty was adopted to erase the dichotomy and to return the mountain to old loyalties based on Ottoman authority. However, history could not be undone, nor could it be sent to an irretrievable oblivion, and in the 1840s we see the Maronite Church come into the political arena and try to destabilize the old social order of political families by converging religion and politics into the same institution.

The second amnesty was in 1845, when Ottoman foreign minister Sakib Efendi was asked to "pacify" Mount Lebanon after another spell of intercommunal violence. Makdisi considers that "this familiar rhetorical device discursively abolished the memory of transgression" (2000: 86), but I believe that what makes this significant for modern day discourse is precisely its attempt to abolish "the memory of transgression," but the failure to achieve that end. The process of *tanāsī* was at work, attempting to actively forget the past transgression, and instituting a mechanism such as amnesty in order to do so. The similarities between the 1839 and 1845 amnesties are striking. Both were an attempt to restore the social order that was based on popular loyalty to elites. However, in the second instance, the common people, or *ahālī*, had begun to develop new sectarian modes of allegiance. The new sectarian knowledge, based in past transgressions, could not easily be denied or forgotten. The act of giving amnesty, arguably a condition for reconciliation, here begins to appear as a metonym for the hegemony of the social order of the time and a tool for maintaining the power of the notables.

The third amnesty materialized in 1860. That year, a general rebellion led by a "commoner," Tanyus Shahin, resulted for the first time in the overthrow of a notable family: the Khazin family in Kiserwan. This was a rebellion led from outside the notable classes rather than managed, controlled, and stoked by these classes to pressure each other. In the past, it was often the case that one notable would instigate the masses to rise against the interests of another notable, but the insurrection never transgressed established loyalties, and the notables remained in control of the conflict.

Shahin's rebellion "illustrated a popular participation in politics that conflated the defense of reform with the salvation of 'the' Christian community. It shifted, in other words, the basis of loyalty away from a notable family toward an imagined political sectarian community" (Makdisi 2000: 115). Shahin had managed to convince a segment of the population that the Druze were "unbelievers," and were treating the Christians unjustly, thereby establishing a purely sectarian discourse. He maintained that the overthrow of Christian notables was a necessary step to protect the Christian community from the aligned interest of the notable classes, which was seen as being against the interest of the broader Christian community. This "Christian zeal," or al-ghīra al-masīḥiya, as Makdisi calls it, "was not simply a religious slogan . . . It marked for [the Christians] a coming of age—not a return to a primordial kinship with other Christians but a new geography that enabled them to come to the aid of 'brothers' in distress in Shiʿa and Druze regions of Mount Lebanon" (2000: 115).

That year, Shahin and his forces were defeated, ending all dreams of a unified Christian ṭāʾifa (sect). The dream, however, still continues to have appeal in the present and one can often hear in everyday discussions, and in the media, statements such as khalas baʾā, el-ṭāʾifa el-masīḥiye lā-zem tit-waḥad ("enough already, the Christian sect must unite")—to be sure, this has also seeped into the ethos of all the other sects, which have done a better job of uniting their ṭāʾifa.[5] In the Christian community, around family, or around people like Zuzu, I would often hear implicit echoes of the dream of Tanyus Shahin. This dream was one path to supposedly save Lebanon, and it was the main driver of Bashir Gemayel's program of uniting the Christian militias under his command in the late 1970s. At one point in the episode I recounted in Chapter 2, Nabil expressed the sentiment diʿān Bashīr (loosely translated to: Bashir's loss is unfortunate), and followed this by saying that Bashir was the only one who could unify the Christians and all of Lebanon. It was a sentiment I often heard.

The continual dream of a united Christian politics is also felt whenever I hear Christians talk proudly as they unite across their political parties for one reason or another. In summer 2012, one interlocutor expressed excitedly that the Christians were united against Shiʿa dayworkers striking at Electricite Du

Liban (the electricity headquarters). In this case, the major Christian factions (LF and FPM) had taken a position against these dayworkers because it gave the appearance that they were speaking out in favor of Christian economic interests, and in favor of ensuring a Christian quota.

Returning to 1860, on July 12 a peace treaty was signed in the presence of Hursid Pasha, the governor of Sayda, in which

> the purpose was to ensure "that all that has occurred from the
> beginning of the events leading up to the general war until now
> shall never become a source of litigation or allegation from either
> side, not in the present nor in the future." The peace treaty was,
> to say the least, a document of remarkable interest: in the space
> of a few sentences . . . the elites of Mount Lebanon conspired to
> write the *ahālī* out of history. As the elites pressed their seals to the
> document, some grumbling, others with relief, they vowed eternal
> peace with one another. Of course, they did not believe it. (Makdisi
> 2000: 144)

Here, again, the notables, believing in the social order, did whatever it took to write off the subaltern movement led by Shahin and establish the previously held order. These general amnesties, following the principle of *maḍā mā maḍā*, were all intended to protect the social order and restore elite political life over people who were not thought to be politically aware. When in 1958, after a brief civil war lasting a few months, the Lebanese government was to issue its first amnesty in post-independence Lebanon, it had a similar principle in mind. But in 1958 the social order was no longer simply to preserve an elite class; it came with a preservation of the 1943 National Pact (*al-mithāq al-waṭanī*), which enshrined a political sectarianism based around protecting Muslims and Christians by giving them equal share in government. Class, especially among the elite, had become an ambivalent formation. Elite classes certainly had class-consciousness and worked for similar interests, but this intersected deeply with often competing sectarian interests, making it difficult to reduce the notables to a functioning class within a national political configuration. What Hammoudi (1997) writes in the Moroccan context resonates in this case too, that the elite only work together "inasmuch as it motivates them," and they "can be found in the most diverse political parties; their political choices are guided by local factionalism and immediate interests. They act in a pragmatic rather than systematic fashion" (40).

What Makdisi does not say in his wonderful historical analysis of Lebanese state formation is that despite efforts to start anew, and despite efforts to forget and to enforce a version of history on the people—on the *ahālī*—memories of the conflicts continued to make their way into communal perceptions and to structure daily life. This was primarily because those in power never engaged in enforcing the type of forgetting Connerton identifies as "repressive erasure" (2008: 60). This erasure can be the most brutal form of forgetting employed to deny a historical rupture, and takes the form of destroying such things as images, names, and statues. We saw in Chapter 6 how the ruling elite and those with high stakes in maintaining the old social order did none of this: for example, some symbols were forbidden, but not all, communal memorials were not destroyed, and commemorations were not forbidden or suppressed, even though not always state endorsed (Volk 2010).

What seems more in line with this historical process of amnesty is Connerton's category of "prescriptive forgetting," which "is precipitated by an act of state, but it differs from erasure because it is believed to be in the interests of all parties to the previous dispute and because it can therefore be acknowledged publicly" (2008: 61). However, Connerton shows that this is not unique in any way to the Lebanese historical context, and the peace treaty signed in 1860 by the governor of Sayda has much in common with Connerton's description below:

> Whether at the resolution of civil conflict or after international
> conflict, the formulation of peace terms has frequently contained an
> explicit expression of the wish that past actions should not be just
> forgiven but forgotten. The Treaty of Westphalia, which brought
> the Thirty Years' War to an end in 1648, contained the injunction
> that both sides should forgive and forget forever all the violence,
> injuries and damage that each had inflicted upon the other. After
> Charles II ascended the English throne in 1660, he declared "An
> act of full and general pardon, indemnity and oblivion." (2008: 62)

The issue was not necessarily in the amnesty, but in what the amnesty inevitably failed to do each time: to make everyone forget. Both ordinary people and political actors, in the absence of other constructive processes for building community, "did not forget"; instead, memory intensified. After all, starting anew "contains an element of recollection," and, as Connerton writes, we cannot but "base our particular experiences on a prior context in order to ensure that they are intelligible at all" (1989: 6). Thus, what appeared to be a conflict over loyalties in 1839 spiraled into sectarian divisions and identity formation because of the perception, however minimal in 1839, that there were *political lines drawn across religious affiliations*. By 1860, the structures of a culture of sectarianism were deeply forming precisely because starting anew and forgetting were never completely detached from a process of remembrance. It was not until after the 1958 civil war that power was effectively transferred from traditional notables (Zu'ama) to political parties (this was to a large extent due to early successes of the Kataeb Party).[6] This further entrenched sectarianism as political parties became increasingly conflated with sectarian communities in people's minds and in their daily speech. With each successive consolidation of sectarianism through amnesties came a period of intensified violence or threats to violence. This consolidation, then, becomes another way in which past violences come to be lived in the present and are a part of the lived memory. In doing so, the past (amnesty and violence) continues and overlaps with the present to produce the constant anticipation and recollection of violence.

Amnesty in the Present and the Politics of "No Victor, No Vanquished"

'afā Allāh 'ammā maḍā! People in Lebanon were expected to continue to echo this in speech and sentiment when another amnesty, law 84/91, was passed on August 26, 1991.[7] The amnesty "applies to crimes committed before March 1991, including 'crimes against humanity and those which seriously infringe human dignity' (Saghieh 2002:255). Only crimes committed against religious or political leaders are exempt from the law" (Haugbolle 2010: 69). In plain terms, this meant that perpetrators of a massacre of civilians could not be prosecuted, whereas perpetrators of an assassination or attempted assassination of a political leader could be. Saghieh writes that this "direction eloquently speaks of the Lebanese people's agreement to preserve their 'leaderships' even when engaged in warfare, while they disagree on the right of the human person as a 'valued entity' to protection" (Saghieh 2006: 3). This amnesty was again meant to eliminate a history of social and political disorder and create the appearance that nobody was wrong and no one had to be held fully accountable. Saghieh is worth quoting at length to understand the logic at play in Lebanon's 1991 amnesty:

The amnesty law classified crimes against humanity under pardonable crimes on the one hand, and classified crimes committed against war leaders under unpardonable crimes. Hence, a murderer is granted amnesty in as much as his victim is innocent (a child or a group of children, for example), while his chances of indictment increase in as much as his victim played a leading role in the war. (2006: 4)

Saghieh reviews the trial of the assassination attempt against Michel el-Murr to uncover this "reversed conception of justice." In this case, the accused's defense was to try to prove Murr was an innocent, chaste victim during the war. Had the defendant tried to kill an innocent victim he would have been pardoned. On the other hand, the "prosecuting team tried to prove [Murr's] leading role in the war to justify the prosecution!" Saghieh continues:

Therefore, the cassation law—a one of a kind law, to be sure—aiming to consecrate the "leadership" as a highly valued entity for the future, no matter what its actions were, and to absent the victim and his intrinsic humanity, paved the way not only to granting amnesty, keeping the crimes under wraps—and here lies the dilemma—and to appointing the leaders to the highest positions in government, but also to glorifying them, which, often, cannot be dissociated from glorifying their crimes. In other words, while the United Nations consecrated the Universal Declaration for Human Rights as a lesson learned in the wake of the Second World War, it seemed that the lesson the Lebanese people learned at the end of their war was the necessity to protect and revere their leaders. (2006: 5)

Following from this, it is easy to see how people might struggle to define what constitutes a criminal (a point to which I will return to later in this chapter). One can also see how the political elite could reconcile with each other over mutual interests and agree that bringing political and religious leaders to justice would threaten the national peace (*al-silm al-ahli*) and set off a new war.

While, by now, critiques of reconciliation politics in South Africa are known (Wilson 2001; Meister 2012), less is known about Lebanese politics as a form of reconciliatory politics that subscribe to values of tolerating and respecting the rights of the other. This has led some scholars and civil society activists, at various times, to call for a truth and reconciliation process like the one in South Africa, without deeply considering the efficacy of such a project, especially given the ways the political leadership already subverts the reconciliation process by adapting its discourse of tolerating the other and holding up values of national unity and consensus.

In passing an amnesty law and promoting a "No Victor, No Vanquished" politics, Volk tells us that the political elite "sought to present Lebanon as a national community" that was "able to maneuver past ideological disagreements and even armed conflict" (2010: 194). This elite is invested in a politics of compromise with the other, and reconciling after war, rather than in continuing the path of annihilating the other's politics or political leadership. One can see examples in the battles of May 2008, when Hizballah stopped short of storming the palaces of Saed Hariri, leader of the Future Movement, and Walid Jumblatt, head of the PSP, or after the June 2009 parliamentary elections, when the March 14 coalition ensured that a new government would be one of national unity and consensus. The political system embeds in itself the possibility of forgiveness for past crimes (*'afā Allāh 'ammā maḍā*) and reconciliation between past foes, to the point that new alliances are made possible and emerge between them. For example, there is the case of Samir Gaegae and Walid Jumblatt, who became part of the same coalition for a period of time (Volk 2010).[8] Armed opponents are encouraged to defer their differences rather than resolve them, and this was the basis of the amnesty law passed in August 1991. The different political parties are called on to share political power and acknowledge that they are all equal; no one has lost and all have a place at the table of power.

Yet, ironically, the politics of "No Victor, No Vanquished," with its emphasis on no one losing, creates an excessive feeling of victimization. The Christian community's experience after Lebanon's war is a case in point. It was commonly acknowledged by those identifying with the Christian community that many Christians felt they were the main losers and that they were politically excluded at the end of Lebanon's war. This view held that they were the exception to the "No Victor, No Vanquished" policy, especially in that the Christian LF was banned and their leader, Samir Gaegae, jailed (though no accusation was brought against him until four years after the end of the war), and Michel Aoun was exiled for not agreeing to the emerging consensus laid out by Syria. Although this was indeed a form of political exclusion, and many Christians began to feel they were the vanquished throughout the 1990s, this feeling reinforced the status of this community's victimization and absolved them of their perpetrator status. At the same time, few outside the community saw them as the vanquished or as the primary victims of the war, and Christian parties did, in fact, remain over-represented in government in terms of their sheer demographic numbers (due to the consociational system that seeks to preserve a balance of power between the sects). Thus, instead of asking why other politicians were not jailed, and admitting to their responsibility in the war, one often heard people from various Christian sects argue that Gaegae should be released. Moreover, while these specific leaders were excluded, this was forced at the hands of Syrian rule, and when this rule ended, the politics of "No Victor, No Vanquished" kicked in more explicitly, and these leaders were freed or returned from exile with no serious apology for past transgressions.

On one hand, this type of impunity and consensus model among the political elite can preserve the security of respective communities living side by side, while denying the populace their right of redress and grievance. On the other hand, through this model, the political elite define the community based on a status quo definition of community as unchanging and homogeneous (and sectarian), thus, leaving no room for community members to seek a process of accountability outside sectarian frameworks and channels.

In this way, the post-Taif Agreement period resembled other liberal transitions in that winning was "subordinated to the maintenance of institutional arrangements aimed at compromise and reconciliation" (Meister 2012: 28). The old beneficiaries continued to benefit from the new arrangements by being promised positions in government and remaining leaders of movements. They were no longer identified as perpetrators, and, in fact, they turned into leaders of communities of victims. In this way, the old beneficiaries could join hands with victims and denounce the true common beneficiary—or enemy: the outsider (epitomized in the understanding that this was the war of others in Lebanon, ḥarb al-ākharīn fī lubnān), or even the war as a personified object. The effective beneficiaries, the warlords, some militia fighters,[9] and the political elite, were in this way also subsumed under the category of victims, allowing them to compromise among themselves and speak for all other victims without holding truth commissions or public spaces for apology.

To be sure, the distinction I draw between political elites and non-elites, such as ex-militia fighters, is blurrier than it might at first seem. The category of elites and non-elites should be understood relationally, where elites cannot exist without non-elites reproducing them, affiliating with them, and helping reinscribe their power. As such, the issues and questions raised by amnesties are not so much about responsibility, for analytically speaking all are responsible and implicated in reproducing the system of elite status and power. Rather, the concern is with accountability and who is to be held accountable, a question fundamentally interested in power, where it lies, and how it operates.

Discourses of (Un)accountability: Confronting Perpetrators

While formal, institutional accountability of war crimes along with punitive measures was absent, discourses of accountability and its lack materialized in various kinds of public and private engagements, both before and during my fieldwork. These included public lectures, conferences, film screenings, and even political party gatherings and private encounters among friends and family. Engaging in and producing discourses of (un)accountability were a way for people to make sense of, find meaning in, account for, and attempt closure of the political violence of the past, in a context where no actual accountability was possible.

During my fieldwork, I attended dozens of lectures and events organized in Beirut that brought together former combatants and noncombatants from Lebanon's war. Some of these were organized by UMAM,[10] but other civil society groups organized similar events as well—these included film screenings followed by discussions with combatants, or panel discussions in commemoration of the war or previewing a new project about memory. In these events, time and again, I observed ex-fighters being confronted by the question: "*hal intū nadmānīn*? Do you regret what you did?" Overwhelmingly, the response would come back negative; rarely (maybe never) did the fighters admit to regretting their armed participation in the war. Even when they apologized, they still maintained they would do it all over again. As if the apology was meant not to break the past from the present, but rather to conjoin the two temporal moments so the past would continue to threaten the present.[11]

Later on, in separate conversations with male and female ex-fighters, I would bear witness to their frustration and anger at audience questions continually asking them if they regretted. "Why should we regret? Why? We fought for them! I sacrificed my life for them." Who was "them," I wondered? Was there really a singular sacrificial community as they imagined it? Nevertheless, this is what I heard them say. To make matters worse, these were ex-fighters who were coming out to speak in public. At some level, their acceptance to face public scrutiny was a source of their let-down as they expected a more understanding and forgiving audience. Was the public not ready for this? It seemed like the question whether or not fighters regret should have been directed to ex-fighters who did not care about the public's gaze. I felt, in those settings, that the exchange was a substitute for the desire to confront the absent ex-fighter, the one who was not willing to face the public, and the one the public was itself not willing to face. Instead, the public directed the tribunal at the ex-combatants willing to stand in front of them to answer their questions.

While the government did not facilitate any mechanism for holding people accountable, through civil society organizations, people were forming their own spaces for processes of accountability, even if these had no formal legitimacy, punitive power, or consensus, and remained in a discursive realm. "I always feel like I am under attack by them [the audience]. Like I am the guilty one," one female ex-fighter, Mme Rita, who fought with the Kataeb Party, told me in distress and amazement at what she saw as a naïve public.[12] Her sense that this public was also guilty suggests that, for the ex-fighters, there is a thin line between complicity and participation in violence. This "public" as a unified mass was itself an imagined community given form by Mme Rita in ways that could make it easier for her to justify her actions and motivations.

In several public forums, the "public" revealed itself to be ambiguous with regard to its participation in the wars. In a few instances where I was present, someone in the "public" would stand and identify himself as someone who carried arms (ḥiml slāḥ) and then proceed in a number of ways, such as justifying his own actions, a form of on-the-spot public confession, or attacking the speakers on stage for their positions. People in the public would often turn this into the tribunal they never got—and the response of ex-fighters was one that could never satisfy the social, and perhaps collective guilt of war. I felt, in the public settings, whether at a post-film screening at UMAM, at a talk during the April 13 war remembrance day, or among students of church groups, that there was a type of confrontation, both physically and psychologically felt, between those perceived to be former fighters and the public that was not armed, too young, or not alive during the war. Each was, in these instances, trying to rise above the other and take the moral high ground. Each was trying to establish a sense of power and dignity in the new space of "not-war," a space from which there was a keen sense that war was just around the corner. The anticipation of war meant that while the decision to take up arms was technically in the past, it was salient in the present and had potential to emerge as a question once again.

Surely, there were generational differences in how these acts manifested themselves. Thus, for example, I witnessed some of those who were alive and old enough during the war responding to the combatants with anger. Whereas younger generations born toward the end of the war or in the space of "not-war," in some cases, confronted the situation with a feeling that their own generation was smarter, more aware, and would never engage in war. In other cases, I saw them view the combatants as role models defending the nation.

These public settings present all sides with moments of confusion as to where power is located and with whom. The noncombatants during Lebanon's war seemed to project their guilt onto the armed men and women, but the ex-fighters refused to play the part and refused to carry any collective guilt, which seemed, in Freudian terms, to trigger a "return of the repressed" emotions that so-called noncombatants thought they could transfer without incidence. For Freud (1989), primitive impulses, especially sexuality, threatened to destabilize the smooth functioning of civilization, and people otherwise repressed these impulses, which always threatened to return, hence, "the return of the repressed." In the case of Lebanon, people have repressed such things as their complicity, guilt, regret, horror, anger, and disgust in order to move on. These encounters with combatants threatened to bring back these repressed emotions and disrupted their ability to smoothly and actively forget (tanāsī) the war.

In the absence of former fighters, people could generally take solace in notions that fighters are guilty, are monstrous, and do not really retain power in the "dead certain" way they did during wartime.[13] In public settings, when confronted with former fighters who refused to follow the accepted script proposed by those who considered themselves noncombatants and nonparticipants in the war, the location of power became ambiguous. In this way, a lack of official mechanisms of accountability gave way to people trying to produce their own forms of accountability, but largely left with ambiguous practices and discourses, and often burdened with frustrations, anxieties, and the feeling that war was not in the past but visibly seeping into the present.

Ambiguities of the War Criminal

The amnesty law has been written about as if it "encouraged the Lebanese to forget their crimes" (Young 2000:45). The perpetrators of supposed crimes, however, did not face trial, were not found guilty, and did not have to admit or confess to their crimes, so what were people being called on to forget? By pardoning violations against innocent civilians and leaving the possibility open to prosecute violations against the political leadership, the amnesty law effectively deemed the latter form of transgression (against leaders) a crime, while the former transgression, through an act of pardon, was silenced and its status as crime left ambiguous and open to interpretation. Thus, rather than forgetting and leaving wartime acts in the past, we might want to think of former fighters as engaged in processes of reinterpretation very much in the present, whereby their past acts are repackaged and intertwined with self and group interests in mind. In some cases, acts one can determine as being criminal were actually being reinterpreted as a social good.

A revealing moment takes place with Basil, who is probably an extreme case, but nevertheless a case that can lead us to understand the complexities of remembering and forgetting crime in the absence of accountability and agreed upon frameworks. I first met Basil one evening in April 2008, when Zuzu invited me to a restaurant-pub owned by his relative. The two of us got along right away and he felt like a person I could get close to. We went out quite often over the course of my fieldwork and I got to meet his children and wife, paying them visits a few times at home. Once, in June 2008, Basil and I went to the shooting gallery, an event I had naïvely hoped would help me better understand those who fought during the war—suffice it to say that this was a futile effort. After an hour at the shooting range, we went to a restaurant in the northern Beirut suburb neighborhood of Dora.[14] Over cordon bleu and green salad, he with a glass of Black Label whisky and I sipping on a vodka tonic, I began to talk to Basil about my research in more detail to get his perspective on things. I asked his opinion about the May 7 battles that broke out the month before and referred to it as a war. "War! You call what happened a month ago a war?" he clamored. And then, "All these kids who are screaming about war, none of them know what war is. . . . War isn't a word; it isn't easy; war isn't a word; it is so much more than that. It is killing and torture and watching your friends die and get handicapped, and homes be destroyed. That is war. The young these days don't know war."

I had heard this a few weeks earlier after the fighting in May from both Basil and relatives. In addition to being employed as a "currency of memory" based on what they knew of war in their past (Connerton 1989), it was said with a sense that if it were a "true war," then they would not anticipate things to be so safe. This notion of the "true war" or "real war," articulated as *haydā mish harb* (this is not a war) or rhetorically as *bit-sammū haydā harb?* (You call this a war?), was echoed by my relatives who expressed the same sentiment as Basil, claiming that a war is when you fear people will come into your house and pillage it and harm you. War could be many things, but I was increasingly getting the sense that for the people around me, it was in the way people died, the intensity of the destruction, and the fear it cultivated in people. But most of all, its meaning was contested, ambiguous, and not fixed.

So, when a month later Basil mentioned the idea that the May battles were not a war, I did not argue with him. In fact, it was in instances like this that I most clearly saw the hegemonic work of memory implicated in power relations, as if remembering the past in a certain way was used to assert one's power over another (Basil's power over me in this case). Choosing how to remember and what to forget could be seen as giving the agent legitimacy or credibility in a certain setting; it could be used to focus attention on the person remembering and silence a political debate if, for example, a memory was too cruel to be argued with rationally. In such an instance as the one above with Basil, it was clearest how people were using Lebanon's war as a "currency of memory"—a tool to assert power.

After *harb tammūz*, I thought the experience of living through a full-blown war would be a way to identify with the generation that lived Lebanon's wars in the 1970s and 1980s—namely, older members of my family—after all I had war memories of my own now. This claim to a personal experience with violence changed things to a degree. I could now share jokes about the war and instead of hearing a war memory told to me in the following way, "We would spend the night playing cards during the bombing raids," I would get the added, "You remember? Similar to how it was during the July war."

But still, my claim to experiencing war would often get brushed away (probably for good reason) as nothing compared to Lebanon's war. "That [the July 2006 war] was nothing compared to what we went through in the 70s; you watched it from afar," I would be told, and this may or may not be followed with memories of past wars for comparison's sake. In May 2008, when I experienced fighting in the streets of Hamra, the old war memories were used again to compare and to dismiss the present battle as child's play.

Haydā mā kān ḥarb; haydā mashī (This was not a war, this was nothing), some would say. The memories would return to be used as currency: to discipline (children), to privilege (the experienced), and to inform (the present). This currency meant that living violence could become a form of or barrier to identification.

It was in this sense of "currency" that Basil was using his memories of the war, and from which he drew a type of agency where I had to defer to him. However, there was something else taking place in these memories, for people were also accounting for their past, and if this included participation in political violence, then the question of justice and accountability for these actions inevitably became a part of the conversation, either explicitly through a series of questions, or implicitly through what was left unsaid. My discussion with Basil was moving along quickly, from topic to topic, and at one point I asked him directly, "Are you a criminal?"

"*akīd!* Of course, I'm a criminal. 80% of *sha'b el-libnānī* (the Lebanese people) are criminals," he responded cynically and without a pause. If everyone was a criminal, however, then he could hide behind them and take solace in the idea that 80 percent of the population cannot possibly be tried.[15] He would go on to tell me, "There was never a cause. Sure people thought they were fighting for a cause at the time, but then it was proved that there was never a cause. Even in the days of the most heated battles, Bashir Gemayel was meeting with Arafat. What cause?" he asked. Basil was too young at the time of Bashir Gemayel's rule of the LF and did not participate in all the battles of the war. He was only involved in the late 1980s, primarily in the Aoun-Gaegae War of Elimination. He had taken up arms as "the thing to do" at the time, when the war system was just another hegemonic social structure. "We fought because it was a hobby. We enjoyed it. We talked about our kills between each other. The guys would say I killed 10, or 1 or none today." But this begs the question why, if killing was a hobby, did he not kill whoever he wanted, or whenever he wanted, or continue to kill after the war? I grew to take Basil's bravado with a grain of salt, and while one has to be skeptical of his seemingly decisive demeanor, it is telling of how the lack of official accountability or punitive actions for acts of war manifests in an ease to speak, maybe even to exaggerate, about these acts in private spaces (but also, as we saw earlier, in public spaces). Not having to fear the law, he can talk as he pleases so long as he does not admit to harming any important political leader.

A year later, in the summer of 2009, I would again hear Basil refer to criminality as a form of social good. This time we were at his house. His children were watching TV in the room, his wife was busy in the house, and with us was his childhood friend who had fought alongside Basil with the LF and was now a soldier in the army. Basil told me, again over whisky—he and his friend would finish a little over a bottle by the end of our three-hour conversation—that the Christians were criminals (*mujremīn*). He said with pride, that contrary to what people think, Christians are not calm people. I challenged him by telling him that if they were to be considered criminals, this would reflect badly on the Christians. His response was that in a region like ours, it is necessary to be criminal, and if the Christians were not seen as criminals, then their opponents would not take them into consideration before making their strategic moves. It was important that their opponents know they are criminal so that they don't belittle them.[16]

Basil seemed to be confusing criminality with being fierce. What I thought he should have said was that the Christian is fierce (*shiris*), rather than criminal (*mujrem*). But the confusion is meaningful because it was not a mistake. He insisted that the Christians committed criminal acts and these are things to be proud of because in this way Christians were able to defend their existence. It was as if he was turning the legal category of the criminal on its head and contextualizing the morality of this criminality—Robin Hood might offer us the historico-mythical comparison. To be sure, this is not unique in any way to Basil, only that his language was blunter. Conventional warfare has long used terror to inflict harm on populations, and this ability to unleash obscene violence is perceived as a sign of strength and power.

Crime, as defined by the *Oxford English Dictionary*, is "an act punishable by law, as being forbidden by statute or injurious to the public welfare." The problem with this definition of crime is that killing in wartime may not always be a criminal act because a person often does not commit "an act punishable by law." In fact, Martti Koskenniemi writes that "not every killing of the innocent is a crime" and international law has a difficult time trying to determine "whether the death of innocent civilians in some situation is an atrocious crime or an inevitable by-product of action that was necessary to protect some more fundamental interest" (2002: 32). This ambiguity of what constitutes a crime in international law is even more complicated at the local level because individual warring groups may have their own understanding of what determines a criminal act much in line with their political and military objectives, and it is this framework the fighter will acknowledge over any international one—this legal relativity is important and not to be dismissed. More important, as an act for the greater good or for a cause, the killing is not even "injurious to the public welfare" (public here to be read as communal not national) and can be perceived as a public good.

Given that what constitutes a crime is not a natural designation, and producing this category is fraught with difficulty at both international and local levels, it remains ambiguous for people in Lebanon as to who committed crimes of war and what constitutes such crimes, and especially that people are free to produce these designations communally rather than nationally, and may not defer to international norms. The amnesty law in Lebanon is perhaps the most authoritative and designates what a crime is in a general sense. But it did not say that in Lebanon such things as it designates as crimes to be forgiven were actually committed. Thus, perpetrators were not tried and found to have committed crimes—based on predetermined norms and legal foundations—after which they were given amnesty; had this been the case, it might have been a reconciliatory act. Had some tribunal in the postwar era deemed the acts of some politicians or armed militia people as crimes after an investigation, this would have created a new way for the said criminals, and their victims, to interpret their past.[17]

However, the amnesty law did not allow people to interpret their past in this way and to come to grips with their crimes and with justice. Basil was not asked to account for, or admit, his "crimes," and was free to interpret being criminal as a necessity, and criminals, as he told me, as "heroes." Since there was no trial, people were left to judge in their own ways, and I would often hear friends tell me that armed people were criminals needing to be tried, only to turn around and defend their own warriors. In the absence of legal accountability, the amnesty did not produce anything such as forgiveness. What it did was allow the political elite to reconcile with each other and to forgive each other not for killing other political leaders—which was not pardoned—but for perpetrating crimes against civilians under their opponent's jurisdiction. Since there was no trial, and no guilty verdict, it holds that there was nothing to be forgiven.

Final Remark

Memory is not fixed in the past; the way we remember the past is constantly on the move, changing, and subject to different perspectives—for example, the amnesty law calls on us to remember the past from the perspective of our wartime communities and beliefs rather than from the perspective of a state-sponsored tribunal. This form of amnesty encourages the least interpretive effort or grounds for self-reflection. Therefore, the way an act is perceived, whether as a crime or as heroism, is not simply a fixed process of either remembering or forgetting; it is first and foremost an interpretation based on a certain narrative and recognized value-judgments of past events.

What was taking place in the two decades after the war was not about one side trying to forget crimes and another—civil society—trying to raise the debate about the past war.[18] What seems to have been taking place, and what collective amnesia and issues around memory concealed, was a power struggle between different players in society over how to interpret the war and who had the rights to a process of history making. It is no secret that the political leadership won out in preserving the regime. They absented the innocent victims by writing the crimes against them out of history, and, thus, the crimes simply did not exist in order to be forgotten. And this is exactly the point: civil society was forced to try to redeem these violent acts as crimes, and as the only and final space for possible closure, and, just maybe, for the hope of some accountability. In doing so, civil society ensured the continual recollection of Lebanon's war into the present, but, unable to deal with the war's causes, facilitated war's anticipation into the future.

Continuations.
The Anticipation of War in 2009–2014

It feels like only yesterday I was conducting interviews around the country that more or less ended in 2009. Every year since, however, I have returned for several months in summer and again in winter. Invariably, with every return there have been conversations about the coming war and, by extension, memories of past political violence. In July and August 2010, I found myself surrounded again by the anticipation of war. On the street, in Hamra, I bumped into an acquaintance who was not very familiar with my work. After greeting each other quickly, and as we were about to depart on our separate ways, she asked, "Do you think there is going to be a war?" Later, a shopkeeper down my street told me he could almost guarantee that a war would break out in September. The investigation into Hariri's assassination was said to release a formal accusation to accuse Hizballah (it finally did), and people were predicting such an outcome might result in all-out war. At the end of August 2010, an altercation in the neighborhood of Burj Abi Haidar, in Beirut, exploded into armed fighting for several hours, with the use of semi-heavy weapons such as RPGs. These are just brief examples from that summer.

In December 2010, a protest broke out in Tunisia that in a few weeks, would culminate in a kind of world historical event people would later call the Arab Revolutions, Arab Spring, or still later, the Arab winter of counter-revolutions. Initially, there was a protest movement that developed in Lebanon that was short lived (Hermez 2011). Soon after, with the transformation of the revolution in Syria into a full-fledged war, life in Lebanon began to witness huge changes. Most critical has been the influx of about one million Syrian refugees (as of April 2014).[1]

When I returned in the summer of 2011, after the start of the Syrian uprising, people were already beginning to worry that the instability there would lead to war in Lebanon. Some speculated that Syrian leader Bashar al-Assad would try to divert world attention to Syria by creating a conflict in Lebanon. Others anticipated that Israel would do this since it had an interest in seeing the Syrian regime stay intact (the regime was seen as keeping the Syrian-Israeli border stable). Unarmed civil society protests on the Lebanese-Israeli front, which resulted in the Israeli army opening fire on and killing protestors, flamed some of the rumors of possible war. In my notes that summer, I noted that in response to the ongoing revolutions, people continued to feel "that war is inevitable and there is nothing to be done since all roads will lead to war."

One day in August 2011, I was walking down Makhoul Street, in the Hamra neighborhood of Beirut, when I bumped into a man in his mid-seventies, Ghassan, whom I had seen many times before in the neighborhood. Ghassan, an old-time resident of the area, had told me he worked on the staff at AUB for around forty-four years. I had seen his living conditions before and wondered how miserably the university pays its employees.

I passed Ghassan and we made eye contact. I said hello, *Kīfak ʿam? Kīf el-ʾumūr? Kīf el-ḥayāt?* (How are you uncle? How are things? How is life?). These are the usual formalities one might give another when they meet in the street before walking on. In this case, however, I stopped. After both of us responded with the usual good tidings, he began to talk about how the situation is terrible or spoiled (*kherbēne*). *Kil khamstaʿshar sine fī ḥarb, wal-ḥarb jāye. Mish ʾanā ʿam bʾūl bas ʿam bismaʿ wa-ʿam shūf el-akhbār* (Every fifteen years there is a war, and the war is coming. It's not me who is saying but I am hearing and I am watching the news).

Ghassan began to talk about how the situation in Lebanon is a disaster and is always like this. He spoke to me about Syria and how the Americans want to destroy it. I listened to him for a few minutes, but then tried to change the topic as I didn't want to argue. There was a beautiful Mediterranean breeze cooling us on this otherwise hot summer day. The remaining trees that lined the street were composing a remarkable symphony as their leaves rustled calmly. I took this as a moment to subtly steer the conversation to the weather. Ghassan approved of my observation: the breeze was indeed beautiful, but there was humidity. He followed this perceptively with *ʿafek, ʿam bit-ghayyer el-ḥadīs lal-ṭaʾs!* (Good job, you are changing the conversation to the weather). I laughed, and told him that the politics aren't going to change; all we could hope for was the best. But he saw no hope there, and he used this moment to return us to the political situation, as if talking might be the only hope of expressing certainty of the uncertain future.

Summer 2012 brought more of the same. However, with violent escalation of the conflict in Syria, some people were beginning to argue with me that the feeling of a possible war was more intense. On the news, one could observe patterns similar to the discussion in Chapter 5. On June 11, 2012, I noted that one talk show host, George Saliba, asks his guest, Samir Gaegae, whether we are *'alā 'abwāb el-ḥarb* (at the gates of war), referring to a newspaper article suggesting this possibility. Fighting in Tripoli, as well as in the Tareeq el-jdeedeh and Caracas areas of Beirut, had intensified in May that year, and Rasheed mentioned he was not optimistic about the future. Other interlocutors talked about how the city streets were emptied after these May events. I got the sense that the way they talked about it this time was different, that this time people didn't have a stomach for war, and were slowly being broken. Yet in this book one should notice that this has been a continual process at least since the period of my observations after 2005 (but I would argue that this was so even throughout the 1990s with varying degrees of intensity). People seem to have a need constantly to refresh the expectation of violence and consciously forget (*tanāsī*) their anticipations in times past. Perhaps it allows them to be nostalgic for a time when they were more resilient in facing the violence, or to deny that they have always been affected and depressed by their presents.

In August, there were a series of kidnappings by the "Moqdad clan"[2] in retaliation for one of their own being kidnapped in Syria days earlier. Over two days, the clan took it upon itself to kidnap approximately forty people, mostly Syrians. Initially, they had said this was their first step, and that the country hadn't seen even 1 percent of their mobilization. However, two days later they declared an end to their military activity. In the meantime, the situation got very tense. At one point, the airport road was shut down and a plane from Paris was apparently diverted to Amman, Jordan. There were reports that a Turk and two Saudis were kidnapped, and the news was reporting—primarily through the voice of protesters—that people from the Arabian Gulf were at risk.[3] The media, arguably using unethical, irresponsible, and amateur tactics to draw out a story, were giving random protesters, sometimes in their very early teens, the chance to voice their grievances and speak. One announced that they would go to Tripoli and that "the people in Tripoli will see what will happen." Another threatened that no Gulf Arabs could leave through the airport and must leave as they did on May 7.[4] When asked what would happen to these people, the threats came back in the form of "they know what will happen."[5] One could only speculate, at the time, whether these were empty threats.

One interlocutor told me that Hizballah certainly knew what was going on, and there was no way the party, which knew their own streets so well, would have relations with this clan operating with arms in its area. One could argue (or speculate) that in order to put pressure on the Free Syrian Army (FSA) without starting an all-out war,[6] Hizballah opted for using clan relations to turn this into a feud rather than a war. In this way, pressure could be used without escalation of talk of war.[7] Resorting to clan politics could also allow a show of strength within the Shi'a community, while at the same time Hizballah could distance itself from such acts, reclaim the situation, and show itself as a mediator rather than a war-maker. On the whole, the outcome of such incidents was to hear people predict that things were going to get worse, and that the FSA was mobilizing to confront Hizballah in Lebanon. The violence did indeed escalate over the next years, though two years later, by 2014, the war was still said "to be coming," and as this book goes to press, people continue to wait.

On October 19, 2012, Wissam Hassan (head of the intelligence branch of the Lebanese Internal Security Forces) was assassinated. Days after the assassination, a relative posted on Facebook that "even though we were expecting something to happen, this tragic terrorist attack is still a shock to all of us." It was a sentiment shared by many, and it speaks to the attempt, and subsequent failure, of the anticipation of war to find complete certainty—or security—in uncertainty. An electronics store owner in my neighborhood expressed similar shock and aggravation months earlier, during the Moqdad kidnappings, when he shared his anger about the breakdown of the Lebanese state as if it were a new discovery. The assassination and kidnappings made explicit and undeniable what people already knew about the inability of the state to control the implements and outcomes of political violence. People's anticipation of these forms of violence could build certainty of the uncertain future. The anticipation could even soften the shock once the events did happen by normalizing them in the smooth functioning of social life in Lebanon; however, it could eliminate the effects of uncertainty altogether.

In the summer and winter of 2013, the situation took a turn for the worse as Hizballah declared open armed involvement in the conflict in Syria, during the battle of Qusayr, and groups fighting in Syria promised to retaliate in Lebanon. Besides the ongoing battles in Tripoli, the southern city of Sidon witnessed armed conflict in June between the Lebanese army and militants tied to Sheikh Ahmed Al-Assir. The army was able to root out Al-Assir in a matter of days, and his group went into hiding; Assir was caught trying to leave through the Beirut airport in 2015. At the end of the summer, and especially in the winter, there was an increase in bombings and assassinations, mostly in areas where majority inhabitants were Sunni and Shi'a. By one count, there were sixteen bombings between the assassination of Hassan on October 19, 2012, and February 19, 2014.[8]

The assassination of Mohammed Chatah, foreign policy advisor to Saed Hariri, on December 27, 2013, is an example of these bombings that brings home my own personal witness and positioning to the political violence. It was shortly after 9:30 a.m. when I walked out of my building. The area around my house was not yet infested with the midday traffic and bustle that is Beirut. I had taken only a few steps away from my building when I heard a loud explosion and felt the tremors that accompanied it. I looked around. It felt like people in the streets had mixed looks. I couldn't determine if they were afraid, shocked, or just slightly confused. I overheard someone wonder if it was a supersonic boom of a plane. Someone else said that it was definitely a bomb.[9] Then I saw in the distance smoke billowing over the city. It was a dense white smoke. I pointed up in the air, slightly panicked. People followed my hand and looked up, but in those early moments everyone seemed to be moving on with their lives. I sensed confusion. They were moving on but hesitant to do so. These were perhaps the first moments of shock.

In those early moments in the street, I felt my nerves tighten and weaken. I could sense my panic. Ambulances zoomed by me to the site of the explosion. I overheard people speculate about the bomb's exact location, intensity, and target. I stopped people to ask for more information, but no one was really sure. Those of us in the streets had no way of knowing any details, and in that unknowing, at least for myself, there was a sense of uncertainty and nervousness. Where exactly was the bomb, who could have been passing by, did I know anyone in that location, how big was it? I counted seven or eight ambulances passing me from the bombsite to the AUB Hospital. At home, things were more certain because I could turn on the news and learn the exact location and magnitude of the bomb. On the streets, people were left with their own speculation and those of the people around them; one hoped these people would have more news, but they were often equally speculating.

As anthropologists, we have the privilege to share our stories with the world, to frame events and think through their meaning. But everyone has a personal story about these explosions, everyone knows someone who knows someone who was there, or who experienced it like me, or who was supposed to be in the vicinity that morning, but, as fate would have it, changed his or her mind.[10] People try to place themselves within the event, to share what they were doing "in the meanwhile," and to place their ordinary day within such extraordinary moments, perhaps to share in what is a collective pain, or to make out of a public event a personal and private meaning. Almost everyone I encountered that day made explicit a narrative that placed him or her a stone's throw from the event.

Some days after the assassination of Mohammed Chatah, a friend commented, "Sami, you need to publish your book soon. The war is coming. You need to get this published before it begins." Indeed, "the war is coming," as one can sense from this final summary; it is always coming if it isn't, in some manner, always already upon us.

The Intensification of Political Violence

People often think of events in terms of periodizations. The latest period is commonly seen to have begun in 2012, with the assassination of Wissam Hassan and the escalation of war in Syria that has brought a gradual armed involvement of Lebanese political groups, especially Hizballah. Yet this periodization is problematic because it leads to easily forgetting the ways the past continues into the present as we analyze current events. One example is to conclude that the war in Syria is spilling over into Lebanon, or that armed conflict in Tripoli is a result of the Syrian war.[11] If, however, one considers the political violence of the present period an intensification, then one can have a more holistic analysis that allows for thinking about the continuity of political violence. In such an analysis, the conflict in Tripoli, for example, can be remembered as ongoing, almost consistently, since the summer of 2008, and its preparation dating to as far back as the end of Lebanon's war.

One of the arguments in this book has been to think about political violence as a question of scaling and intensity. Rather than the absence or presence of violence, I have argued that political violence is always present, but it moves between the realm of invisible and visible, and that we should think about it as intensifying and deintensifying. Intensity implies that political violence is unfolding; it does not simply emerge from nowhere but rather has a prior presence. The intensity increases gradually, even if oftentimes the intensification appears so quick as to make people feel it is instantaneous. As intensity, political violence, then, continues even after the event fades away (Badiou 2012), and, in fact, has a social life prior to it (Hoffman 2005).

The intensification of political violence, as I have written about it, does not appear out of thin air; it does not just rear its ugly head through some sort of supernatural power. Violence might appear ambiguous in its functions, structures, practices, and effects, but our inability to see clearly does not mean it does not have its source(s), rationale, and agents. The intensification is people-driven, and it comes about through a confluence of practices, objects, and subjects acting together and against each other. The intensification is also a result of a dialectic of power and relations of domination. In the case of Lebanon, I have stressed the large role a continual politics of "No Victor, No Vanquished" plays in facilitating both the intensification and deintensification of political violence. I have also argued that intensity works through subjective forms of energy, such as emotions, desires, and memories, which give sense and meaning to particular actions and allow action and reaction to build into an event. But, importantly, this subjective energy operates in and through people, their memories, practices, and the objects they encounter (which also act upon them).

By thinking of the intensity of political violence, we can understand the two parts of this book, anticipation and recollection, the future and the past, and the way these meld into each other to produce strategies for everyday life. People are left feeling different intensities of political violence, and with these intensities they recollect past war to inform them of present and future political violence, or they expect future war and thereby remember the past to make sense of what is yet to come.

The political violence people experience, the latest of which I outlined in this chapter, is very real in a material sense; people can hear it and see it, and they can physically feel it on their bodies. Yet, this physicality and materiality does not tell the whole story. To grasp the full value and meaning of this political violence, we must also consider the circulation of affects, discourses, and practices that ensue from it. The way people anticipate future war, how they live "in the meanwhile," and the way they remember past wars, all play a role in the ways aerial bombings, car bombings, assassinations, armed street battles, and other forms of political violence gain meaning in society, and come to be embodied.

Broader Implications

While this book has focused on the case of Lebanon, it has implications for a broader understanding of violence and of life in precarious states with protracted conflict. That my argument is insistent on the importance of a local context, and that my claim is based on anticipation being politically informed and varying in time and space, means that one could use these arguments as a lens by which to look at other conflict states. One could see, for example, how memory as an everyday lived experience might apply to such places as Colombia, Sudan, Sri Lanka, Afghanistan, Palestine, Iraq, and any number of other Arab states experiencing post-2011 revolutionary and counterrevolutionary action.

In Colombia, the persisting conflict has created a sense of normalcy where the anticipation of violence becomes subconsciously factored into everyday life. As in Lebanon, people generally do not "speak of violence, but of war. Of narco-war, dirty war, guerrilla war, the president's war, the bandas' war" (Sanchéz 2000: 19). My work in this regard would add a new dimension to an already existing literature that is concerned with the normalcy of an extended war in everyday Columbian life (Taussig 2003). I ask that we inquire into the kind of interactions and experiences that are exposed through people's anticipation of war.

My main lines of argumentation offer an alternative means of understanding zones of conflict, where I find that emphasis on remembrance as a panacea for breaking cycles of violence is often well intended but not enough. One must, in these zones, find ways to confront politics, and recognize the susceptibility of one's self and one's own community to engage in horrifying acts of political violence. Instead of focusing on tolerance and dialogue with the other, my interpretations call on us to engage in a more challenging, but I believe more fruitful project of finding ways to confront hegemonic political systems and powers. How, for one, can we confront the politics of compromise embedded in the policy of "No Victor, No Vanquished"? And how, as I wondered in the opening chapter of this book, can we build a new politics (in Lebanon or elsewhere) to reflect the moral imperatives of protecting minorities with the practical implications of building a state for *all its residents*? My hope is that this book pushes people to think in these terms and provides a modest step for finding some answers.

How people anticipate war should not only be confined to states witnessing protracted internal conflict. One could also examine how warzones affect people around the world and how people might anticipate war from anywhere. For example, people in America also anticipate global wars in which their troops go off to battle, or in which their cities are put on high alert. How, one might ask, does this anticipation affect their daily lives? Surely there would be some contrast to the ways of anticipating violence in Lebanon. Wars in one country affect the lives of people not only in neighboring countries, but across the globe. Lebanon's war, for example, resulted in mass migration, including militia fighters who settled in urban and suburban centers in countries in Europe or the United States. In Berlin, a Palestinian refugee from Lebanon once told me how he was beaten half to death at age twelve by Amal fighters (during Lebanon's war), and how he watched his male friend get raped. This is just one example of how a war in Lebanon can come to affect the lives of people this man encounters in Berlin. This is not to mention that nations might have to send troops to keep the peace, and that such missions might create counter-reactions in the form of terrorism.

The global war on terror, declared in 2001, ensures that people around the world feel a sense of fear that they might be attacked at any time. This kind of war turns anticipation into a tool for preparing, fighting, and feeling the war—one need simply to think of the color-coded threat levels of the U.S. Department of Homeland Security (now done away with) to show how the anticipation of war is controlled and utilized as a tool of power. The very war on terror plays on our levels of anticipation and on our fear of the violence our future might bring. Anticipating terrorism is just another form of a constant feeling of anticipation of political violence, one that can be observed in communities around the world. In light of the war on terror and, perhaps more specifically, in view of a war against transnational non-state actors, I expect that the themes of this book can be applied beyond Lebanon and beyond communities at the frontlines of war.

Continuations

One could keep writing. The violence is continual after all, and the stories keep coming. As this book is about to go to press, it is now exactly ten years since my first encounters with Dima. The two of us are sitting once again at a café, not too far from where this fieldwork all began. "You should look at videos of the war. I see them and can't believe how beautiful our city was," she tells me. "I watch the videos and feel like, today, we are living the effects of *their* war as the city is being destroyed all around us." Dima echoes what I've heard before. Beirut's heritage is being erased as we live in these times of a never-ending postwar. Dima shows me the videos on her smartphone, and where there is a burning building, she notices beautiful artisanal windows; where there is a sandbag barricade (*mitrās*), she sees stunning architecture giving character to the city. She'd take those times over ours any day. It is nostalgia to cope with the present, I'm sure. But, she tells me, she'd rather live the past war than its not-so-subtle effects that destroy our city a hundred times over today. There is at one and the same moment a past that is dead and another that continues so destructively into our future; a past that kills, if not our bodies, then our homes, our cities, our villages, and our futures. It is between this past and these futures, a space where we live "in the meanwhile," that this book has tried to excavate.

Appendix 1. The Cairo Agreement

3 November 1969

Resolution No. 2550/D 52, on 13 September 1969 Strictly Confidential

On Monday, 3 November 1969, the Lebanese delegation headed by Army Commander General Emile al-Bustani, and the Palestine Liberation Organization delegation, headed by Mr. Yasir 'Arafat, chairman of the organization, met in Cairo in the presence of the United Arab Republic Minister of Foreign Affairs, Mahmud Riyad, and the War Minister, General Muhammad Fawzi.

In consonance with the bonds of brotherhood and common destiny, relations between Lebanon and the Palestinian revolution must always be conducted on the bases of confidence, frankness, and positive cooperation for the benefit of Lebanon and the Palestinian revolution and within the framework of Lebanon's sovereignty and security. The two delegations agreed on the following principles and measures:

The Palestinian Presence

It was agreed to reorganize the Palestinian presence in Lebanon on the following bases:

1. The right to work, residence, and movement for Palestinians currently residing in Lebanon;
2. The formation of local committees composed of Palestinians in the camps to care for the interests of Palestinians residing in these camps in cooperation with the local Lebanese authorities within the framework of Lebanese sovereignty;
3. The establishment of posts of the Palestinian Armed Struggle

[PASC] inside the camps for the purpose of cooperation with the local committees to ensure good relations with the Lebanese authorities. These posts shall undertake the task of regulating and determining the presence of arms in the camps within the framework of Lebanese security and the interests of the Palestinian revolution;

4. Palestinians resident in Lebanon are to be permitted to participate in the Palestinian revolution through the Armed Struggle and in accordance with the principles of the sovereignty and security of Lebanon.

Commando Activity

It was agreed to facilitate commando activity by means of:

1. Facilitating the passage of commandos and specifying points of passage and reconnaissance in the border areas;
2. Safeguarding the road to the 'Arqub region;
3. The Armed Struggle shall undertake to control the conduct of all the members of its organizations and [to ensure] their non-interference in Lebanese affairs;
4. Establishing a joint command control of the Armed Struggle and the Lebanese Army;
5. Ending the propaganda campaigns by both sides;
6. Conducting a census of Armed Struggle personnel in Lebanon by their command.
7. Appointing Armed Struggle representatives at Lebanese Army headquarters to participate in the resolution of all emergency matters;
8. Studying the distribution of all suitable points of concentration in border areas which will be agreed with the Lebanese Army command;
9. Regulating the entry, exit, and circulation of Armed Struggle personnel;
10. Removal of the Jiyrun base;
11. The Lebanese Army shall facilitate the operation of medical, evacuation, and supply centers for commando activity;

12. Releasing detained personnel and confiscated arms;
13. It is understood that the Lebanese authorities, both civil and military, shall continue to exercise all their prerogatives and responsibilities in all areas of Lebanon in all circumstances;
14. The two delegations affirm that the Palestinian armed struggle is in the interest of Lebanon as well as in that of the Palestinian revolution and all Arabs;
15. This agreement shall remain Top Secret and for the eyes of the commands only.

Head of Lebanese delegation Emile Bustani
Head of Palestinian delegation Yasir Arafat

The agreement was revoked in 1987 by a resolution of the Lebanese Chamber of Deputies: Resolution adopted by the Lebanese Chamber of Deputies, 21 May 1987:

1. Abrogation of the law issued by the Chamber of Deputies on 14 June 1983, authorizing the Government to ratify the agreement signed by the Government of the Lebanese Republic and the Government of the State of Israel on 17 May 1983.
2. The agreement signed on 3 November 1969 between the head of the Lebanese delegation General Emile Bustani and the Chairman of the PLO and which is known as the "Cairo Agreement" is hereby null and void as if it had never existed. Further, all annexes and measures related to the Cairo Agreement are hereby null and void as if they had never existed.
3. This law will become effective upon its publication in the Official Gazette.

Source: http://www.marsad.eg/wp-content/uploads/publications-pdf/Lebanese _ Reconciliation_ EN.pdf.

Appendix 2. Doha Agreement on the Outcome of the Meeting of the Lebanese National Dialogue

Under the generous sponsorship of His Highness Sheikh Hamad bin Khalifa Al-Thani, Emir of the State of Qatar;

In continuation of the efforts of the Arab Ministerial Committee on the Lebanese crisis under the leadership of His Excellency Shaikh Hamad bin Jassim bin Jabr Al-Thani, Prime Minister and Minister for Foreign Affairs of the State of Qatar and of Mr. Amre Moussa, Secretary-General of the League of Arab States, and Their Excellencies the Ministers for Foreign Affairs of the Hashemite Kingdom of Jordan, the United Arab Emirates, the Kingdom of Bahrain, the People's Democratic Republic of Algeria, the Republic of Djibouti, the Sultanate of Oman, the Kingdom of Morocco and the Republic of Yemen;

On the basis of the Arab Initiative on containing the Lebanese crisis;

And in implementation of the agreement concluded in Beirut among the Lebanese parties under the aegis of the Arab Ministerial Committee on 15 May 2008 (annexed), which is an integral part of the present declaration;

A meeting of the Lebanese National Dialogue was held in Doha from 16 to 21 May 2008, with the participation of the Lebanese political leaders who are members of the Lebanese National Dialogue, who affirmed their desire to rescue Lebanon from the current political crisis with its dire implications for communal existence and civil peace among Lebanese, and their commitment to the principles of the Lebanese Constitution and the Taif Accords. As a result of the proceedings of the meeting and of bilateral and group consultations conducted with the participants by the Chairman and members of the Arab Ministerial Committee,

Agreement was reached on the following:

I. The parties agreed that the Speaker of Parliament will call on the Lebanese Parliament to convene in accordance with established rules within 24 hours to elect the consensus candidate General Michel Sleiman as President of the Republic, this being the best way from a constitutional point of view to elect the President under these extraordinary circumstances.

II. A Government of national unity will be formed with 30 ministers to be allocated as follows: 16 to the majority, 11 to the opposition, and three to the President. All parties pledge by virtue of this Agreement not to resign or obstruct the work of the Government.

III. In accordance with the electoral law of 1960, the district (qada') will be adopted as the electoral constituency in Lebanon, and the two districts of Marj 'Uyun-Hasbayya will remain a single electoral constituency, as will Baalbek- Hirmil and Western Bekaa-Rashayya.

Beirut will be divided as follows:

First Constituency: al-Ashrafiyya—al-Rumayl—al-Sayfi;

Second Constituency: al-Bashurah—al-Mudawwar—al-Marfa';

Third Constituency: Mina' al-Hus—'Ayn al-Muraysah—al-Mazra'ah—al-Musaytibah—Ra's Beiru—Zuqaq al-Balat.

It was agreed to refer the reform clauses contained in the draft law submitted to Parliament, drafted by the National Electoral Law Drafting Commission under the chairmanship of Minister Fuad Butros, for debate and consideration in accordance with established procedures.

IV. The above-referenced agreement concluded in Beirut will be implemented, and in particular paragraphs 4 and 5 thereof, which state that:

4. The parties pledge to refrain from a return to the use of weapons or violence for the purpose of achieving political gain.

5. Dialogue will be launched to strengthen the authority of the Lebanese State over all its territory, and its relations with the various organizations in the Lebanese arena to ensure the security of the State and its citizens . . ."

Accordingly, dialogue was launched in Doha on strengthening the authority of the State in accordance with paragraph 5 of the Beirut agreement, and agreement was reached on the following:

• Resort to the use of weapons or violence to resolve differences of any kind under any circumstances is prohibited, in order to ensure that there is no violation of the national contract of partnership based on the determination of the Lebanese to coexist within a democratic system. Security and military authority over Lebanese nationals and residents is reserved to the State, to guarantee continued communal existence and civil peace for all Lebanese. The parties pledge to this.

- The law is to be applied and the sovereignty of the State honoured in all Lebanese regions. There will be no regions in which fugitives from justice may take refuge, out of respect for the rule of law, and anyone who commits crimes or violations will be brought before the Lebanese justice system.

This dialogue will be resumed under the leadership of the President of the Republic immediately upon his election and a national unity Government will be formed, with the participation of the League of Arab States, with a view to strengthening confidence among Lebanese.

I. The Lebanese political leaders reaffirm their commitment to stop using the language of treason and political and sectarian incitement immediately.

The Arab Ministerial Committee undertakes to deposit this Agreement with the Secretariat of the League of Arab States upon its signature.

This Agreement was signed in the city of Doha on 21 May 2008 by the Lebanese political leaders who took part in the meeting.

(Signed) His Excellency Speaker Nabih Berri
His Excellency Prime Minister Fouad Siniora
Shaykh Amin Gemayel
General Michel Aoun
Member of Parliament Michel Murr
Shaykh Saad Hariri
Mr. Walid Jumblat
Member of Parliament Boutros Harb
Member of Parliament Ilyas Sakkaf
Member of Parliament Ghassan Tueni
Member of Parliament Muhammad al-Safadi
Member of Parliament Muhammad Raad
Member of Parliament Agop Baghradounian
Member of Parliament Samir Ja'ja'
Witnessed by:
His Excellency Shaikh Hamad bin Jassim bin Jabr Al-Thani Prime Minister

and Minister for Foreign Affairs of the State of Qatar Chairman of the Arab
Ministerial Committee
Amre Moussa Secretary-General of the League of Arab States

Source: UN Security Council S/2008/392, http://www.securitycouncilreport
.org/atf/cf/%7B65BFCF9B-6D27-4E9C-8CD3-CF6E4FF96FF9%7D/Leb-
anon%20S2008392.pdf.

Notes

1. For more on Hizballah see Saad-Ghorayeb (2002), Norton (2007), and Hamzeh (2004). To begin to think of Hizballah beyond its armed resistance and within its social surroundings, see Deeb (2006), Harb and Leenders (2005), and Harb (2007). Harb and Leenders (2005) argue against referring to Hizballah as either a terrorist or "lebanonized" organization, and to think of it instead as an integrated network of services and values.

2. This research is influenced by broader theorizations on war and violence. On the notion of "new war," in which nonstate actors play an increasing role and where the lines between peace and war are distorted, see Kaldor (1999), Kalyvas (2001), and Duyvesteyn and Angstrom (2005). For a focus on the blurred lines between political and personal causes for violence in civil war, see Kalyvas (2003, 2006). See Richards (2004) and Lubkemann (2008) on the notion that war is socially organized rather than something that breaks out due to ripe conditions; on objective forms of violence as that which allow for the smooth functioning of everyday life, see Zizek (2009); on the idea of violence and terror as culturally informed, see Sluka (1999), Zulaika and Douglass (1996), Nordstrom (1997), and Warren (1993). To explore the structures and politics behind violence see Tsing (1993), Appadurai (1998), and Scheper-Hughes (1993). See Daniel (1996) on the embodiment of violence in social life and its effect on identity.

3. As this book goes to press, Aleppo, Syria, faces another round of massive destruction as part of the revolution turned war that began in March 2011. On May 3, 2016, as Aleppo is under heavy government forces bombardment, I hear an interview on the Al-Jazeera English news broadcast by a doctor in Aleppo who reminds me of this everyday life and death "in the meanwhile" of war that I write about. The doctor tells his audience that everyone focuses on the inability of hospitals to treat trauma, but forget that people still need to deal with everyday health. People need to see doctors for the flu and other illnesses like diabetes, children need their checkups, and women need to visit the gynecologist. The doctor's comments jolt me into remembering existing daily life in war that we unjustly erase.

4. I write this paragraph in memory of Ambassador Adib Alamuddin, the father of a dear friend, Rayane Alamuddin, and my mother's maternal uncle-in-law, Theodore (Doro) Hembekides, both succumbing to cancer during war.

5. Gilles Deleuze quoted in Veena Das (2007: 135).

6. For an account of my time in military prison, see http://electronicintifada.net/content/prisoner-my-own-land/6281 (accessed July 29, 2012).

7. See Strathern, Stewart, and Whitehead (2006) for a discussion of terror and the imagination, and the connections between the anticipation of violence and memory.

8. A large number of short films and documentaries about the various wars further attested to the way war preoccupied people's lives and tried to bridge the past with phenomenological experiences of the present (El Chamaa 2009; Abi Samra 2010). A variety of books about wartime events (Saade 2005; N. Sayigh 2008; R. Hage 2006) and fictional films, among them *Under the Bombs* (Aractingi 2007) and *The Mountain* (Salhab 2010), also ensured that experiences of the wars were constantly remembered. This is in addition to the war torn landscape of the country that presented a daily reminder of the war years.

9. I have used the construction "people in Lebanon" in this book, rather than the more obvious "Lebanese" because I find the latter to exclude residents and other communities like the Palestinian community. "People in Lebanon" is a non-nationalist construction that assumes non-Lebanese nationals may also be affected by the processes in question.

10. Lubkemann writes that the "totalizing and sensationalizing effects [of violence] influence how the analysis of war and war-time behavior is framed. . . . Our understandings of what war involves as an experience for subjects and societies thus tends to be organized almost exclusively around our understanding of what coping with violence involves" (2008: 10). I write with this in mind.

11. Although in the chapters that follow I look specifically at the case of Lebanon, my approach to political violence, thinking in terms of its anticipation and recollection, can be observed in other field sites. A prime example from the region is the political instability facing several countries in the Arab world in the aftermath of the 2011 Arab revolutions. With varying degrees, Tunisians, Egyptians, Libyans, Yemenis, Bahrainis, and Syrians fear the uncertainty the future holds. In other places in the world, like Colombia, Uganda, or Afghanistan, people also experience the uncertainty that comes with possibilities of future political violence. In all these cases, political violence of the past and its expectation in the future serve as signposts for thinking about and living in the present.

12. The phrase "No Victor, No Vanquished" can be represented in Arabic as either *lā ghāleb wa lā maghlūb* or, dropping the article *wa* (and), as *lā ghāleb, lā maghlūb*. I use the latter version throughout.

13. In 1958, a short-lived conflict erupted, sometimes known as the 1958 civil war. The conflict began when president Camille Chamoun stood against Egypt's Gamal Abdel Nasser, and refused to join Egypt and Syria's United Arab Republic. Chamoun invoked the Eisenhower Doctrine calling for American intervention in the face of communist threats. This forced a split within Lebanon between Arab nationalist supporters of Nasser, and those, primarily Maronite Christian, who were against this unity and aligned instead with the Baghdad Pact, a group of countries allied with the British and the United States (see Traboulsi 2007).

14. Meister (2012) makes a similar claim about global politics more generally, where he says this politics is governed by fear, whereby political decision-making and alliances are based on a fear of the always possible genocide rather than on what is good. Fear of genocide in a war context might demand intervention or compromise to end the war at the expense of continuing the struggle for justice, which in itself is said to possibly lead to genocide.

15. Little anthropological work has been done so far on political violence and everyday life in Lebanon. Gilsenan (1996) tackles this, but he mostly deals with the violence and anticipation of the feud rather than war. War can be more destructive because it occurs at a larger scale, and on a national stage rather than confined to a village or town. Much of the wartime violence has been dealt with in novels (Khoury 1981, 2002; Barakat 1995; R. Hage 2006; Samman 2010) or biographies and autobiographies (Sneifer 2008; 'Aleq 2008; Saadeh 2005; Bechara 2003; Bazzi 2005), but otherwise one finds far more by way of political analysis and historical and sociological accounts (Hanf 1993; Picard 1996; Fisk 2002; El-Khazen 2000; Khalaf 2004; Traboulsi 2007).

16. For more on the za'im (pl. zu'amā'), see Khalaf (1968), El-Khazen (2000), Hamzeh (2001), and Clark and Salloukh (2013). Henceforth, I will drop the diacritics and use Za'im and Zu'ama.

17. The state in Lebanon resembles a fantasy (Navaro-Yashin 2002), and is certainly imagined (Anderson 1991), elusive (Mitchell 1991), porous (Greenhouse, Mertz, and Warren 2002), and an illusion masking other relations (Abrams 1988). All this does not mean it is fictional, however. It is most definitely a very real category for the people who benefit from it, are oppressed by it, and demand services from it.

18. For more on the way the state operates in Lebanon see Obeid (2010), Hamzeh (2001), Clark and Salloukh (2013), Fawaz (2008), Hermez (2015). See also Joseph (1997) for an analysis of the state building enterprise, especially as a function of patriarchal kinship processes.

19. Zizek (2009) creates a binary between what he calls subjective and objective violence. Subjective violence is what one feels and experiences in a physical sense, and it is usually measured against a backdrop of a normal state of zero violence or nonviolence. What we normally refer to and understand as violence is what Zizek would call subjective violence, opposed to ordinary or normal life where there is nonviolence. Objective violence, on the other hand, is inscribed into the smooth functioning of our entire system, whether economic, political, or social. This type of violence is invisible, and Zizek argues that it is the type of violence that sustains the normal zero-level standard. The invisibility of this form of violence is from where we then perceive and measure subjective violence. Objective violence is structural and symbolic. It can be ascribed to language through what is silenced and unsaid (Scheper-Hughes 1993), or through the words we choose that may anesthetize subjective violence (Cohn 1987). For more on structural violence, see Bourdieu and Wacquant (1992), Scheper-Hughes (1993, 1997), and Bourgois (2003).

20. I understand politics in a materialist Weberian sense as a struggle over distribution of power and resources (Weber 1946: 78). However, I am also influenced by Schmitt's

definition of the political as a relation between friend and foe, even though we might argue that these categories may not present themselves in everyday life as absolute subject positions. Still, I take seriously Schmitt's point, based on these relations, that war, "as an ever present possibility" is "the leading presupposition" that "determines political behavior" (2007: 34), and the possibility that if war were eliminated, then so might politics. This leads me to Foucault's "permanent war," not to say that Schmitt and Foucault understand the political in the same way, but that they are not mutually exclusive. For Foucault (1997), the political is a set of conditions, practices, and power relations that include Schmitt's dichotomy. When I call for a need to address the political at various points in this book, I am specifically advocating, in Foucauldian terms, a need for tackling these conditions, practices, and power relations, in light of friend-foe divisions and conflicts over resources.

21. On the notions of rupture and interruption of conflict see Taussig (1992), Das (2007), Jeganathan (1997, 1998), Daniel (1996), Hoffman (2005), and Lubkemann (2008).

22. The Sabra and Chatilla massacre occurred on September 16–18, 1982. During this time, the Christian Phalange Party massacred several thousand unarmed Palestinian refugees in the Sabra and Chatilla camps.

23. On December 6, 1975, Christian Phalange Party members went on a killing spree and massacred 200–600 Muslims near the Beirut port. See Saadeh (2005).

24. On January 20, 1976, factions in the Palestine Liberation Organization (PLO) alongside the Lebanese National Movement (LNM), a coalition of Lebanese leftwing parties, attacked the coastal town of Damour, massacring around 500 Christian residents and forcing the rest to flee.

25. In saying that incidents meld and are not instantly felt as events, or that they continue rather than succeed other events, I am giving a nod to the notion of Bergsonian duration that does not necessarily see time as space or as a homogeneous category that can be separated into segments (Caton 2014).

26. Similarly, Monroe (2016: 70) finds that mobility for the younger generation is often marked by consumer and cultural sensibilities rather than violence. So it is people's socioeconomic interests, not just their political interests or how they identify, that determine how they will think, act and feel with regard to the violence.

27. In moving beyond the dichotomy of absent/present, I am indebted here to feminist thought, and in particular to the work of Anne Orford (2007, 2011).

28. For the study of emotion and affect see Diphoorn (2013), Beatty (2010), Hume (2007), G. Hage (2009), and Davies and Spencer (2010).

29. I take everyday practices, following Michel de Certeau, not as "merely obscure background social activity" but a place of possible articulation through a "body of theoretical questions, methods, categories, and perspectives" (1984: xi). Like de Certeau, my project concerns modes of operation or schemata of action, not directly the subjects (or persons) who are their authors or vehicles (xi).

30. In 1989, Michel Aoun, leader of the FPM, was general of the Lebanese military and had waged a war against the LF and its leader, Samir Gaegae, in what was called ḥarb al-ilghāʾ. Ever since, a large section of the Christian community has been divided between

the LF and supporters of Aoun, who later established the FPM. In the 1990s, the LF and FPM both operated underground since their leaders were jailed (Gaegae) and exiled (Aoun), and had common interest in fighting the Syrian military presence. Soon after the assassination of former prime minister Hariri in 2005 and the exit of the Syrians, Gaegae was released from prison and Aoun returned from exile, and they returned to (politically) battling each other for control of the Christian community.

31. Zuzu used the word *'ird* to express the man's shame. *'ird* is associated with woman's honor; the idea is that attacking a woman's honor brings shame to a man. Honor, however, is not a simple reified notion. In this case, it is entangled with respect for person, kin, and political party, and with pride, safety, and responsibility. While there are rhetorical employments of the language of honor, through the notion of *'ird*, it would be simplistic to reduce their actions and make them overdetermined by honor. Overall, I don't want to reduce such violence, or other political violence, to a question of honor. In this sense, I take issue with Michael Johnson (2002) who draws connections between Lebanon's war and the honor of communal leaders.

32. For a discussion of how families regulate violence, and how the regulation of violence can shape people's views of the future, see Farha Ghannam (2013).

33. I am reminded of Campbell's (1964) Greek mountain people who had similar experiences of knowing the limits of a quarrel.

34. On April 13, 1975, Phalange Party militiamen opened fire on a bus carrying Palestinians in the Ain el-Ramaneh neighborhood. This is generally seen as the catalyst for the war.

35. See Meister for a similar logic regarding evil (2012: 40).

36. The Tripartite agreement was reached between Elie Hobeika as a leader of the Lebanese Forces, Nabih Berri's Amal Movement, and Walid Jumblatt's Progressive Socialist Party. It was signed in Damascus and reached agreement on political reforms and special relations with Syria.

37. This is in reference to lawyers who chase ambulances to find clients to file personal injury claims.

38. It's not that I did not recognize the religious identities of my interlocutors, but I took it upon myself not to record this identity, and not to ask people (though most times I would know from names, residence, or political affiliation without needing to ask them).

39. I have ultimately decided to leave out Dima's original sect, as I imagine she might be offended if she were to be reified in this text by her sect background.

40. For an analysis that transcends, but does not ignore, sectarian identity, see Naber and Zaatari (2014). They provide an intersectional analysis of Lebanon that considers gender, class, sex, religion, family, and other identities. See also Joseph (1983) for a study of how certain political leaders fought heterogeneous working-class networks as this heterogeneity in socioeconomic relations threatened sectarian power.

41. I spent long periods of fieldwork in the South and North of the country with diverse groups of people (in terms of class and sect), but most of the episodes in this book come from Beirut and its surroundings.

42. There is also the fact that I fall victim to the male gaze and to the presumptions, both in society and the literature, that violence is in the realm of men. This also contributes to glossing over the specific problematic of how women and men's experiences with violence can be differently gendered.

43. The HTS program was launched in February 2007, and "embeds anthropologists and other social scientists in military teams in Iraq and Afghanistan." See American Anthropological Association, http://www.aaanet.org/issues/AAA-Opposes-Human-Terrain-System-Project.cfm, accessed October 2009.

44. "Spies as Scholars: Anthropologists in the Field of War," *Al-Akhbar*, April 20 and May 1, 2008.

45. By Human Rights Discourse (capitalized), I borrow from Meister and refer to a specific discourse that "became globally predominant after the fall of Communism in 1989, a moment of apparent closure to the discourse of global revolution and counterrevolution that followed from the 1789 Declaration of the Rights of Man" (Meister 2012: 2). Such a discourse is meant to set a new global power apart from "the cruelties perpetrated by both revolutionaries and counterrevolutionaries during the previous two centuries," and to suggest that today's global powers supersedes such cruelties (3). It promotes humanitarian forms of intervention and is less concerned with victims of cruelty than with the beneficiaries who no longer identify with perpetrators. This specificity is important, as it would be presumptuous for my comments to be an indictment of all human rights discourse (lowercase).

CHAPTER 2.

WAR, POLITICS, AND LUNCH: CONVERSATIONS OF EVERYDAY LIFE

1. I use the word "discern" to suggest that the retelling of history undergoes a process of filtering whereby subjects choose what they will from a larger oeuvre they cannot possibly recount. I borrow the word from Bergson by way of Caton (2014: 240).

2. See Caton (2014) for a discussion of Bergson's duration and how time endures.

3. The events in this chapter were unfortunately not recorded, as I was not prepared for the sequence of events as they unfolded at the time. I attempted to reconstruct as much of the day as I could immediately upon my return home. In writing this chapter, some of the dialogue is reconstructed based on general descriptions in my notes. I have tried to remain as accurate as possible to the characters, representing them from what I know after years of contact with them, but the dialogue must be understood as a product of my own framing afterward. In order to be as representative as possible of their words, I returned to record my relatives as they discussed some of the historical accounts below. Although it was not necessary to take this path of historical reconstruction beyond rewriting the notes I had taken the day of my encounter, I chose to do so with the belief that this would give the reader an added sense of being there, and more depth and thickness to that encounter.

4. In this particular family, the women's space for political expression is often implicitly restricted through the assertiveness of male perspectives. Women are not relegated to an apolitical space, and certainly take part in heated political debate. Still, often it is the male voices and opinions that dominate and I notice that women must fight for legitimacy and space.

5. I had decided not to vote in this election, not even to put a blank "protest" ballot. My reasoning was twofold. First, I believed that engaging these elections was a cynical way to give the regime legitimacy. Even a blank ballot would be a form of participation that assumed the very act of voting had significance, and I was set against this. Second, based on the above, I felt it more important to conduct research on this day and spend it with former militia fighters. To vote would have meant leaving the city to my voting district in the mountains (Lebanese vote where they are historically registered, not where they currently reside). This would have prevented me from conducting ethnographic fieldwork. My feeling was that in a place where citizenship is a tool to maintain a status quo I rejected, I preferred to exercise my role as researcher rather than citizen.

6. See the International Foundation for Electoral Systems (IFES) for a list of voting districts in the 2009 elections at www.ifes.org/publication/.../IFES_Lebanon_ESB_Paper030209.pdf (accessed June 23, 2012). "Beirut 1" is one such district.

7. The seats went to the pro-March 14 pro-Kataeb list: Nayla Tueni, Jean Augusabian, Michel Faroun, Nadim Gemayel, and Serge Torsarkasian.

8. Cammett and Issar explain the voting system as follows: "Lebanon has a majoritarian party block system to elect representatives to its 128-member parliament, in which seats are evenly divided between Christians and Muslims (who are further subdivided into four Muslim sects and seven Christian sects). In each multimember district a pre-established quota of seats is reserved for candidates from different sects, so that the main axes of competition occur within rather than across sects. All voters regardless of sect vote for candidates from all sects and vote for as many candidates as there are seats available; the seats from a given sect go to the candidates from the corresponding sect who win the most votes. For example, the Baabda district of Mount Lebanon reserves three seats for Maronite Christians, one for a Shia, and one for a Druze. All voters can cast ballots for six candidates as long as they vote for no more than three Maronites, one Shia, and one Druze. They cannot vote for a candidate from a sect that is not represented in the district" (2010: 386). For the election law and entire results of the 2009 election see http://www.elections.gov.lb/Parliamentary/default.aspx?lang=en-us, accessed July 22, 2015.

9. I personally saw people throw rocks at Syrian workers in one such opposition protest during those weeks, and in other instances scores of Syrian workers were killed and injured with no repercussions against the perpetrators.

10. Some of the larger parties included in the March 14 coalition are the LF, Kataeb Party, Future Movement, and PSP (see list of party descriptions). The Free Patriotic Movement had originally been part of this coalition. However, as a result of being pushed out by other parties in the March 14 coalition, and entering into a pact with Hizballah, it later joined the March 8 coalition.

11. Some major parties of the March 8 coalition are Hizballah, Free Patriotic Movement, Amal Movement, Marada, and SSNP.

12. It is important to note that the Progressive Socialist Party (PSP) has shifted its position between these coalitions, effectively making it the party all sides want to seduce, as it carries the parliamentary swing votes. Originally a fundamental component of March 14, Walid Jumblatt, leader of the PSP, switched sides in January 2011, giving the March 8 coalition his support.

13. See, for example, WikiLeaks id 06BEIRUT2443 7/23/2006 or id 06BEIRUT2540 8/6/2006, and others published in *Al-Akhbar*, http://alakhbar.spiru.la/taxonomy/term/136?page=8.

14. El-Solh was the first prime minister of Lebanon and some credit him for uniting the sects, while Chehab was a military man who was able to bring the nation together in 1958 when it had descended briefly into its first civil war (Salibi 1966).

15. The one-third-plus-one, or blocking third, is the idea that the minority in the government has enough voting representation to block any unpopular decisions proposed by the majority. Since all cabinet-level resolutions need two-thirds of the votes to pass, having one-third-plus-one voting power would ensure the minority voting block had the power to block any resolutions it did not agree with. This principle forces the government to always work toward consensus.

16. The Islamic militant group Fateh al-Islam had found a base in the Nahr al-Bared camp and had armed itself over several years. Many Lebanese felt that the Palestinian camp residents were responsible for the rise of Fateh al-Islam and justified the army's indiscriminate shelling of the camp in response to militants killing a number of Lebanese soldiers. My interlocutors and I, who were active with relief work, thought otherwise, and believed there was no justification for such bombing that amounted to collective punishment. These politics should be kept in mind when reading about my encounters during this conflict in subsequent chapters.

17. Tying the fate of the country to one event is a recurring theme, as we see the same tactic used during the 2006–2007 March 8 demonstrations, which also promised to save the country. People saw this tactic again in the May 2008 battles that promised to overhaul the political system.

18. For a recipe of this dish, see Tony Tahhan, blog, April 27, 2010, http://www.antoniotahhan.com/2010/04/27/middle-eastern-dumplings/, accessed July 31, 2012.

19. See Gilsenan (1996), Johnson (1986), and Hamzeh (2001) for discussions of structures of clientelism.

20. Nabil voted for Frangieh, but he did not confirm whether he voted only for Frangieh or for his entire list.

21. Winners in this district were: Michel Al-Murr, Ibrahim Kanaan, Sami Gemayel, Ghassan Mukhaiber, Nabil Nicola, Edgar Maalouf, Agop Pakradounian, and Salim Salhab.

22. The common abbreviation to refer to members of the SSNP is 'awmiye, which translates to "Nationalists," and it is pronounced this way in the Lebanese dialect rather

than as *qawmiya*. The singular form, referring to one member, is *'awmi*, or in Modern Standard Arabic, *qawmi*.

23. Hanssen and Genberg (2001) suggest the official end to the war could be seen as being on October 1989, with the signing of the Taif Agreement, on October 13, 1990, following the ousting of General Aoun, on August 26, 1991, with the issuance of the Amnesty Law, or even in December 1991, with the release of the last foreign hostages (235). Regardless, this speaks to the ambiguity of the ending of war. The perception of an end often depends on the will and force of hegemonic powers.

24. See Traboulsi (2007) for a detailed history of the roots of the war.

25. Opponents of the Christian factions often call them "isolationists" in reference to the type of political agenda the Christian factions sought.

26. The famous Christian narrative goes that Arafat wanted to create a Palestinian state in Lebanon in lieu of the one lost to the Israelis. Proof for this is in a statement Arafat gave in 1976 that the road to Jerusalem runs through Jounieh.

27. One could claim that December 7, 1975, was a watershed in solidifying the sectarian nature of the war. On that day, the Kataeb Party carried out reprisal attacks on Muslims in the city, killing over 350, as a response for the kidnap and killing of four Christians a day earlier (see Tabbara 1983: 54).

28. Cobban (1985) and Salibi (1988) are proponents of the primordialist view. Others, like El-Khazen (2000), promote the theory that this was primarily a conflict about and against the Palestinians. Trabousli (2007) locates the war in politico-economic factors and does not reduce the conflict to one of sectarian identity, while for Hudson (1988) it is the political system itself that is unable to prevent conflict. In this last view, the Lebanese consociational system of power sharing was the root problem and is doomed to reproduce violence.

29. Tel el-Zaatar is an area in Beirut that hosted a Palestinian refugee camp. During the Tel el-Zaatar battle in July 1976, the Kataeb massacred 1,500–3,000 Palestinians and annihilated the camp. One interlocutor who left the Kataeb Party in the 1970s speculated that William Hawi was killed not by the Palestinians but by the Kataeb, to make room for Bashir Gemayel. Even if this claim is untrue, it shows how rumor and speculation can have dire and drastic impact for people on the ground during an armed conflict. It can shift allegiances and consolidate power bases.

30. For an interview with Habib al-Shartouni see "Habib al-Shartouni: Striking the Head of Collaboration," *Al-Akhbar English*, July 23, 2012

31. One interlocutor I spoke with, a former fighter with the Phalange Party, took this war as proof that no one wanted it to conclude and that there were greater regional interests at work. She wondered out loud with me why the Syrians did not just come in to East Beirut and wipe out the fighters. The Christians would not have been able to hold onto their positions, and it would have been the end of the Lebanese Christian resistance.

32. In fact, at one point toward the end, someone mentioned that it has been like this at least since 1860, if not for a thousand years, in reference to sectarian conflict that broke out between Druze and Christians in Mount Lebanon that year. This is seen as the

beginning of sectarianism in the country by some, and proof of the predisposed nature of Lebanese to sectarianism by others.

CHAPTER 3. "AT THE GATES OF WAR":
TIME, SPACE, AND THE ANTICIPATION OF POLITICAL VIOLENCE

1. Lebanon has experienced high rates of emigration over the last 150 years. Between 1975 and 1990, around 40 percent of the population emigrated due to political instability. One survey suggests that around 67 percent of Lebanese expressed an intention to emigrate in 2008 (Tabar 2009).

2. For different ways of thinking about anticipation see Strathern (1988, 1992), who considers social relations being formed as a function of the anticipation of the gift; Bourdieu (1977), who conceives of habitus as being those "strategy-generating principle[s] enabling agents to cope with unforeseen and ever-changing situations" (72); and Taussig (1992), who thinks of the anticipation of violence as "terror as usual."

3. Tobias Kelly argues that the ordinary can be constituted within violence, and that violence and what we think of as the ordinary are not mutually exclusive or opposite (2008: 353). For Kelly, during the second Intifada in Palestine there were many ordinary moments, such as watching TV or preparing food, within supposedly violent times. This chapter builds on Kelly, and further suggests that such ordinary moments as he describes can also be inflected with a form of violence.

4. For similar definitions of war, see Richards (2004) and Lubkemann (2008). Lubkemann also blurs the distinction between war and "normal everyday life" (158).

5. This understanding of the divisions between war and peace, what I refer to as "not-war," follows Richards (2004), who calls on us to think of these periods as a continuum and writes of war as being "long periods of (uneasy) peace interrupted by occasional eruptions of violence." He then quotes Begoña Aretxaga: "Peace and war are not so much two opposed states of being as they are multi-faceted, ambiguous, mutually imbricated areas of struggle" (Richards 2004: 5).

6. One can notice that Rola's very subjectivity seems to be influenced by living in duration and negotiating recollection and anticipation. Das confirms this when she writes that, "duration . . . is the very condition of subjectivity" (Caton 2014: 239).

7. A housing contract, for example, exists because we do not know the future and attempt to seal an agreement in writing.

8. Let this point, however, not be confused as being unique to Lebanon lest I contribute to a widespread discourse that imagines the country and its people as violent. One can look to other places like the United States, for example, where military traditions are handed down within generations of families, or more collectively, in the way American society imagines its relation to the wars it fights. Violence, in one form or another, is part of every society's social traditions. The way violence is implemented, its practices, the how, when, and why of violence, are what determine the social traditions of societies differently.

9. According to Slavoj Žižek, Lacanian anxiety occurs when we are in danger of getting too close to the object-cause of desire and thus lose the lack (Žižek 1992: 8). In other words, our anxiety comes about when we sense we are realizing our desires and are therefore losing the state from which we desire. Vocalizing the anticipation of violence leads to anxiety in this sense. The anxiety of future violence is brought about in the realization that we are dangerously close to sacrificing others or ourselves. In such instances, we realize that we are perilously close to having to make life and death decisions and to a place of decisive action, where we lose "the lack," or the position from which to dream of the "what ifs."

10. Most refugees fled to the Baddawi refugee camp because it was closest to the Nahr al-Bared camp of the twelve remaining Palestinian refugee camps in Lebanon.

11. The process by which the ordinary comes to be ordinary is often itself a violent one. See Foucault (1994, 1979), Mitchell (1988), Žižek (2009), and Hall (1986) on Gramsci. All discuss the structural roots of order and the way order and the ordinary can come to fruition.

12. Das (2007) tackles similar issues by exploring the way violence continues to reappear in the present through language and what is heard and unheard, said and unsaid.

CHAPTER 4. "THIS IS OUR LIFE":
EXPERIENCING THE INTENSIFICATION OF POLITICAL VIOLENCE

1. Navaro-Yashin (2002) writes of this voyeurism as being one aspect of public life, where she understands public life as a site that generates the political. It is not to be taken lightly. The gaze of the voyeur, she says, is one location of the state. Indeed, during the war, the state itself was an onlooker, giving way to another powerful insight by Navaro-Yashin that we should look at sameness within and between the domains of power and resistance.

2. Sontag (2003) explains this by drawing on the example of passersby in a traffic accident. People stop to watch, not just out of curiosity, but also for a desire to see something gruesome. She has several other examples of how people revel in the pain of others (2003: 96).

3. The phenomenon of people going out to beaches, restaurants, bars, and clubs crosscut class backgrounds (between middle and upper at least) and was relatively widespread, but one should also be careful not to over-exaggerate the numbers of people who were clubbing, especially in Faraya or Brummana. Kegels (2007) says that most upper-class people she spoke with after the 2006 war had only gone out once or twice, not every day as some perceive.

4. Fawaz, Harb, and Gharbieh (2012) reach similar conclusions about how people experience Beirut's security zones, with some of this being influenced by a person's political position.

5. The meaning of the state itself, and the way it is sensed and confronted, is

contested. Generally, I found that people were looking for its "ideal face" (Obeid 2010). There is a more thorough discussion of the state in Chapter 1. See also Hermez (2015).

6. It should also be noted that whereas my primary argument is that politics affects what type of violence we anticipate and how we behave in light of this anticipation, it is important that one not overdetermine the relation of the political to people's thoughts and behaviors. Isolating the political motivations embedded in what and how people anticipate provides another way to think about the seeming contradictions present in social life, without necessarily resolving them.

7. See Yassin (2012) for some observations on the perceptions and practices of youth in Beirut vis-à-vis different sectarian communities.

8. Kegels (2007) finds a similar discourse of resilience and resistance, and argues that this shapes Lebanese identity.

9. Journalist and writer Bilal Khbeiz (2009) captures this same sentiment when he writes of the difference between witnessing war in Lebanon in July 2006 and following it from New York or London. He writes that "Witnessing the full impact of the 2006 July War in Beirut, or the 2008–2009 Israeli invasion in Gaza, is a very different sensory experience to that of following it from afar in New York or London. The edited scenes broadcast in New York or London are replays of the protracted events to which war subjected Beirut and Gaza. The reverberation of shelling is evidence in itself of death and destruction, yet the lengthy process of establishing the extent of the damage and the identities of the victims delays the broadcast of that event by several hours. Because of this interval, the residents of Beirut-Gaza experience the attacks as two distinct events, one vague and obscure and the other clear and documented. Of the two, the obscure event is undoubtedly the one experienced more sorrowfully." To this I add that the anticipation after the moment of physical destruction is experienced vastly differently in New York or London than in Beirut or Gaza.

10. When the war was all said and done there were around 1,109 dead, 4,399 injured, and approximately one million displaced on the Lebanese side. See "Why They Died: Civilian Casualties in Lebanon During the 2006 War." Human Rights Watch, September 2007, https://www.hrw.org/report/2007/09/05/why-they-died/civilian-casualties-lebanon-during-2006-war, accessed May 2016.

11. See Mermier (2013) for reflections on Beirut during and after the May 2008 battles, and for thoughts on how frontiers were drawn.

12. Generally, this armed escalation was defined as an "event" and called "the events of May 7" or *aḥdāth sabʿa ʾayyār*, though depending on political affiliation some would venture to call it an "invasion of Beirut." This suggests there was no consensus about the scale and type of battle this was.

13. Marwan is an Arab foreign national living in Lebanon. He went to university in the United States and is a web designer in his early thirties. Anna worked as a clinical psychologist. She grew up in the Arabian Gulf and moved to Lebanon at age ten, where she continued her schooling in a village in the North. She is Greek Orthodox with family roots in the SSNP but herself not politically aligned. She did not live through the war of

1975–1990, and was in her late twenties at the start of my research. For descriptions of Rasheed and Dima, see the List of Characters.

14. Sontag tells of how Hollywood has informed the way we experience reality, since, she writes, "a catastrophe that is experienced will often seem eerily like its representation" (2003: 21).

15. Cosmopolitan is here defined as it was used by people in the field around me: to refer to a place where there were people from all walks of life and where there was a perceived atmosphere of tolerance and acceptance, even if this was not always true.

16. I am skeptical of the amount of planning by the Future Movement, for a former militia fighter and current member of the Future Movement had granted me an interview only a few days before in the Caracas area. I imagine that if they were expecting a battle on the scale they saw, my interview would have been postponed. But this is purely speculation on my part, especially that one could also see more Future Movement affiliated youth lingering in and patrolling the streets in the weeks leading up to May.

17. In retrospect, the clashes that week in Hamra were no more intense than some of the battles that took place in the 1970s or 1980s, and certainly small in comparison to the Israeli siege of Beirut in 1982. For an account of some Hamra clashes, see Yousef Bazzi (2005).

18. Deeb and Harb (2013) speak of how safety is sometimes directly connected with sectarian politics and determines how people maneuver within the city. For example, one informant tells them, "the security situation affected our outings a good deal" (184).

19. Every time one points to a kind of oasis of partying amid the armed conflict, or to spaces of luxury and enjoyment (a beach party, or the plethora of pubs and restaurants), they are implicitly subscribing to the idea that certainty and uncertainty cannot exist, and that when they do exist together, they open a space of contradiction or, at least, exception.

20. It would be useful to keep in mind the types of people that are continually painted as public enemies due to the structure of these speculations. For example, fearing the possibility of the Palestinian camps being used as a counteraction to the May battles was a way to reinforce the demonization of Palestinians and maintain a fear of them.

21. I find this to be a vastly different experience from the one Carolyn Nordstrom observes in Mozambique. In that context, she writes that people in Mozambique felt that "to go 'home' is to court danger, to have no home is to be safe. But to have no home is not to be human" (Nordstrom 1997: 166).

22. There is by now significant literature on the politics of mourning and grieving (Butler 2004; Sontag 2003), but also on how this relates to a politics of recognition (Povinelli 2002).

23. I am quite confident, from my discussions with Zuzu in the years after this encounter, that he was trying to convince me of something he was not entirely convinced of himself. I believe his role in a future battle remains ambiguous to him and would be decided from within the conditions of that future.

24. Aida is Syrian and only moved to Lebanon after marrying Zuzu in the 1990s. She

is a housewife and never came out with us when I went with Zuzu to social events. When I met her, she was vocal in her opinions and assertive.

25. I am keenly aware that Basil was sometimes a *fannās* (Gilsenan 1976: 198). Gilsenan describes this word as a technique of showing off and of survival, where it is used in times of crises when "the self will be challenged and defined" (198). Still, others corroborated many of his stories.

26. The camps are more akin to neighborhoods, in most cases economically and socially connected to the surrounding community of which they are a part. For an explanation of the camps and the context of the Nahr al-Bared war and its aftermath, see Newman (2007) and Makarem (2012)

27. To understand the crisis of Palestinian refugees in Lebanon see R. Sayigh (1995). For a period of relative autonomy and social and cultural development in the Palestinian camps in Lebanon see Khalidi (1984).

28. In hindsight, the better word would have been "Messiah," since this sentiment crossed all religious lines.

29. It is worthwhile to note that my own internal conflict and the reason nighttime outings got embroiled with ethics in times of conflict is partly because spaces such as nightclubs are impregnated with symbolic value so that they are seen as spaces of pleasure that are hedonistic and guilt-free. These spaces are then seen as somehow immoral spaces to visit during a war, whereas sitting in a café, walking in the street, or being at school don't carry the same symbolic value. Hence, in these latter spaces people are less often caught in ethical debates.

30. One can see this over and over again on social media (such as Facebook and Twitter). Members of a political group are quick to comment on bombings that target their group but have fewer words when a bomb targets civilians in areas affiliated to another political group.

31. See Hermez (2015) as well as Žižek (1989), Sloterdijk (1988), Navaro-Yashin (2002), Shea (2006), Allen (2013), and Wedeen (1999) for conversations on cynicism as I use it here.

CHAPTER 5. ENFRAMING THE ANTICIPATION OF WAR

1. I borrow here from Sarah Ahmed (2004) who, from a Marxist analysis, thinks of emotions as gaining value through their circulation.

2. See Mitchell (1988) for a similar discussion of enframing as a process of ordering and containment (44). See also Heidegger (2010).

3. See Picard (2000) for a discussion of economies of war in Lebanon.

4. There are numerous other examples one could point to, and a quick online search for the keyword "no war" in the *An-Nahar* and *Al-Akhbar* websites turns up dozens of results of politicians saying there will be no war.

5. See Riskedahl (2007) for other examples.

6. Local political actors are not alone in trying to exploit people's feelings of uncertainty. The U.S. government is one example of a foreign actor that sends warning letters and messages to its citizens in Lebanon (http://lebanon.usembassy.gov/sm_010514.html). These warnings travel as U.S. citizens share them with others in Lebanon. The messages will often map general and broad locations of insecurity that appear meaningless to those who are informed about the country. Still, however, they play a part in increasing levels of the anticipation of war, as people trust that the Americans have inside information.

7. I focus on television, but it was certainly not the only medium, and the printed press was replete with articles about the potential for war. Take, as one example, the front-page headline in *Al-Akhbar* dated September 17, 2007, which read: "The Shadow of War Engulfs the Region." Of course, all this is by no means unique to Lebanon and may be indicative of media on a global scale. For example, U.S. media is replete with images and accounts of war, and played a key role in the lead-up to the Iraq war in 2003 to muster American public support for that war.

8. "Comedic television programs have long been a platform for caustic political satire" in the Arab world (Kraidy 2006).

9. Schulthies (2013) discusses a similar scenario with viewers in Morocco who react to news about armed conflict.

10. In thinking about the news and media programming, I remained attentive to some of the reactions the shows engendered and the way they fit into a larger repertoire of practices of speculation and representation of the future. Like Abu-Lughod, I recognize that these shows, and representations more broadly, are received and experienced in a variety of ways. I maintain, however, that one of the byproducts of this programming is to capitalize on a predominant social feeling of a coming war, as even when the coverage is of present political violence, it is overwhelmed by forms of analysis and speculation of what this means for the future.

11. Future TV is a channel founded by assassinated prime minister Rafiq Hariri and run by the Future Movement.

12. Khatib (2007) rightfully claims that the opposite was also true, and the public influenced media coverage in the days and months after the Hariri assassination. However, this is not the case most of the time, especially when it comes to non-news programming such as *Star Academy* and others previously mentioned. In such cases, the audience is "least powerful," to quote Gurevitch and Blumler in Khatib (2007: 34), and the media "have the power to be selective" and present their own frames (34). The rare call from the audience (when not monopolized by calls from famous political personalities) and text messages, or interviews on the streets, can hardly be considered public influence on the media.

13. Fortunetellers are generally more accepted than say, miracle makers like Dr. Dahesh. He was a personality in the 1960s and 1970s who saw many elites flock to him, including the sister-in-law of a former president. He was eventually persecuted and his followers believe the civil war was a karmic reaction to this treatment (Leah Caldwell, "The Lingering Legacy of Doctor Dahesh," *Al Akhbar English*, March 12, 2012, https:// english.al-akhbar.com/content/lingering-legacy-doctor-dahesh, accessed July 25, 2015).

14. For the full list of Michel Hayek's 2007 predictions, see the "Streets of Beirut" blog at http://streetsofbeirut.wordpress.com/2007/01/08/michel-hayek-predictions-finally -translated/, accessed March 30, 2014.

15. More recently, in 2013, Volvo had an advertisement on the occasion of Lebanon's Independence Day based on the Jean-Claude Van Damme video in which he does a split on top of two Volvo trucks. In the Lebanese print version, we see him standing atop the same trucks but not doing a split. The caption reads: "This nation does not need an epic split— United We Stand." Volvo is here playing on ideas of ethnic splits, and on the Sunni-Shi'a sectarian conflict to appeal to people's desires. See http://ginosblog.org/2013/11/20/win-volvo-lebanon-customizes-jean-claude-van-dammes-epic-split/, accessed July 5, 2015.

16. Their July 12, 2007, press release claimed: "Our products reflect our values, mission and concerns. We had previously confirmed our concern for the country on several occasions . . . Today we are confirming it more and more by launching this credit card as we believe that a country cannot be without its army and the security forces that protect it." See http://www.zawya.com/story/ZAWYA20071101104448/, accessed June 24, 2014.

17. Another name for the Zira'a neighborhood is Menshiya neighborhood.

18. Deeb and Harb write of how martyr images in Dahiyeh, similarly, identify and "visually materialize" that area as the Resistance community (2013: 177).

19. To a large degree, I would argue that political parties understand some of the consequences in producing and allowing for the public display of these objects of representations (banners, posters, etc.). I would not hesitate to refer to these as strategies for mobilizing constituents. My argument is based on a decision political leaders took after the May 2008 battles to take down all images of political leaders and not display political slogans. They abided by this for quite some time. It is a decision that speaks to the fact that they understood the implications and repercussions of these objects. For an in-depth look at political posters from Lebanon's war, especially martyr posters, see Maasri (2009). For a discussion of martyr images in Dahiyeh, see Deeb (2006).

20. In Arabic, the term for checkpoint is either *nuqtat taftīsh* (checkpoint) or *ḥājez* (obstacle, barrier). In Lebanon, the latter is more common, and it is always used when referring to the name of a checkpoint. So, for example, there are checkpoint names like *ḥājez el-bashūra* or *ḥājez el-barbāra*. People will also often say *fī taftīsh* (there is checking) or *'am bi-fatshū* (they are checking) to refer to the presence of checkpoints. Someone might say this as a caution before a person they know leaves the house, or they might call to warn a driver that there is a checkpoint ahead. The term, *ḥājez*, captures a certain harshness of the checkpoint, in which it was an obstacle in people's lives, and in the continuation of their lives, rather than simply a place where people were checked before they could continue on with their movements.

21. There are other types of barricades and blockades, including mobile security, whereby "caravans of security personnel" accompany political figures (Monroe 2011: 94). While all these also play a role in framing the anticipation of political violence, I deal specifically with the military checkpoint in this section. See Monroe (2011, 2016) for a discussion of these security installations and their impact on mobility in the city.

22. During Lebanon's war, checkpoints produced their own economies, especially around the Green Line. See Tawil-Souri (2009) for an analysis of how economies emerge around a checkpoint in the Palestinian context. During my fieldwork, this kind of economy was no longer prevalent, and, in fact, in some cases the checkpoints destroyed the already existing economy in the area (especially around security zones of political leaders). Tawil-Souri also elaborates on how checkpoints in the occupied West Bank are built, the materials used, and the requirements for passing. See also Hammami (2004) for the role of checkpoints as well as the economy of checkpoints in the Palestinian context.

23. See Kapuściński (2001) for a similar but thicker description of checkpoints in the Angolan context.

24. People and politicians in Lebanon will refer to Israel as the enemy (al-'aduw) and local opposition political parties as opponents or adversaries (khasm). Hage writes that "The key difference between enemies and adversaries is that the latter, no matter how antagonistic to each other they may be—and no matter how much their interests diverge—remain committed to the reproduction of the social or at least the spatial-environmental common grounds where such divergence and antagonism are played out" (G. Hage 2015:22).

25. In this section, I use the term "civil society" simply to designate a loose collection of people and groups that are independent of political parties and the state. I do not mean to create a clear division between civil and political society; and certainly individuals in civil society may also be employed in the state. My usage is not meant to be critical of the term; I employ it simply to separate from the other actors I have been discussing.

26. This particular picture was taken in 2011, at a time when people were afraid that events in Syria would have violent implications in Lebanon.

27. Graffiti has long been used as a form of political expression in the country, but most of this is generally connected to party politics, such as party symbols, slogans, and other expressions of support. Often, it also takes the form of quick scribbles without much time, effort, or creativity, and political party art has not been of superb quality. Murals would appear from time to time, especially when connected to a political party message, but it has definitely been more visible in the last years by independent graffiti artists. In fact, according to one artist, Ali Rafei, good quality graffiti spray was not readily available before 2010, and this is one reason I didn't see much during my fieldwork (personal communication, February 24, 2014). Political posters, flags, and banners (such as in Figures 9, 10, and 13) were traditionally far more prevalent as a form of street expression.

28. Lara Deeb (2008: 370) reminds us "that representations of the past are frequently about the present and hold implications for the future."

29. There are so many excellent examples, too many to recount here, of these impromptu social representations that play on the feelings of anticipation of war. One recent example in the performance art genre saw a woman dress up as a suicide bomber and walk along the seafront in Ras Beirut. See https://www.youtube.com/watch?v=WwHo7Ux-oK7M, accessed February 23, 2014. I notice another on my Facebook page when a relative writes that, walking in the city one day in February 2014, he sees a taxi with a sign that

reads, "For your safety, please open your jacket before entering the taxi." The sign can be read as dark humor, but certainly reminds people of the present danger of suicide bombers.

30. For detailed accounts of the massacre and death tolls see al-Hout (2004) and Fisk (2002).

31. See Chapter 2 for more details of this episode.

CHAPTER 6. ACTIVE FORGETTING AND THE MEMORY OF
WAR IN EVERYDAY LIFE

1. Amnesia, as I understand it, is a loss of memory, and as Boon writes of loss, "Figuratively, loss pertains to what can neither be repaired nor redeemed by receiving-from-elsewhere" (1999: 156), implying that amnesia is a memory that cannot be redeemed.

2. I am particularly influenced by Hanssen and Genberg's notion of hypermnesia, as an antonym to amnesia, and as "a situation where memory is constantly present, multiple and celebrated" (Hanssen and Genberg 2001: 233).

3. Similarly, Meister (2012) says of Human Rights Discourse that it calls on us to consider that we are in a time after evil by remembering that evil is in the past; to forget this is thus necessarily to invite evil, or war, back into our lives.

4. This discussion of lived memory, especially as it relates to sites of memory, moves beyond Nora's (1989) dichotomization of memory as being between *lieux de mémoire* and his "true memory."

5. While I focus on individual accounts in this chapter, it would be a methodological error to think that individual memories are automatically collective memories (Kansteiner 2002). Thus, I show how these accounts reflect wider practices and also supplement them with references to cultural productions and public displays of memory work.

6. Riskedahl's informants expressed similar sentiments about the war years (2007: 308).

7. Halbwachs, generally seen as the father of collective memory, was an advocate of the idea that people did not remember coherently outside the group, making memory work heavily structural and lacking in agency (Kansteiner 2002). Yet, and important for our purposes here, he also locates a space for the individual's agency by believing that we come to learn about the individual's memory through the individual's public expressions, which he recognizes as occurring within society. In other words, he should not be dismissed as he is able to attribute agency to the individual by claiming that an interpretation of collective memory can only occur through the individual's open and public expressions of that memory (Halbwachs 1992).

8. Although the term has communist connotations, it is a word used among militia members from across the spectrum of left to right.

9. Saadi Nikro makes a similar point about how "dismemory" was not successful, and argues that there are multiple processes of memory work taking place in the country (2012: 1)

10. See Battaglia (1993) for a discussion on the intentionality and agency embedded in forgetting, and how social forgetting can produce forms of sociality rather than oblivion in Papua New Guinea.

11. Some might argue that the forms of remembrance I observed were a memory cycle marked by Syria's military withdrawal in 2005 and the period of Syrian hegemony pre-2005. However, this was likely not the case, given that forms of cultural production and debates around memory of the war date back to the 1990s and did not begin post-2005 (Haugbolle 2010). Though unlikely, the idea of a memory cycle is appealing and would be partly due to: (1) a "psychological distance" from the war years that remembering might require (Igartua and Paez 1997); (2) a sudden political change that caused many in the country to feel—or perceive—a sense of greater freedom and more control of the country's direction; and (3) a return of political instability and uncertainty that resembled the days of Lebanon's war and thus served as a trigger for those memories to surface.

12. I visited the *An-Nahar* newspaper archives for several months during my fieldwork. I collected articles from a number of sources that included *Ad-Diyar, Al-Mustaqbal, As-Safir, An-Nahar, Sharq El-Awsat, Al-Hayat,* and the weekly magazine *Al-Afkar. An-Nahar* and *As-Safir* alone have a distribution of about 45,000 copies daily. Overall, I collected more than fifty articles published between 1991 and 2002 (the years most relevant to the emerging discourse on amnesia), which were specifically written around April 13, the anniversary of the war. These articles comprised investigative pieces and long interviews with both politicians and regular citizens. The articles included everything from confessions (*As-Safir*, April 14, 2002), to studies about how the war began (*Al-Mustaqbal*, April 13, 2000), to how it was lived and how it affected people (*Ad-Diyar*, October 22, 1999). On April 13, 2000, an article in *As-Safir* published results from a poll showing that only 38 percent of people believed the war to be over, and 70 percent of these believed it could start again. These articles are besides the hundreds of others I came across that referenced the past war as part of other stories. Together, these articles reveal the inconsistencies and complexities of post-conflict memory work in Lebanon. The sample speaks to an overall mood and discourse within civil society that was advocating for remembering the war, and shows that the state could not control the effort to remember and speak about war, nor could it control the way it seeped into everyday spaces in society. In one example, *An-Nahar* (April 14, 1992) republished an interview conducted by the London-based Monte Carlo radio station that interviewed former president Suleiman Frangieh, exiled former president Amin Gemayel, former speaker of Parliament Kamal al-Asaad, former prime minister Saeb Salam, former military commander Reymond Edde, and leader of the LF Samir Gaegae, who all recounted their memories of the war. This interview in a London-based station also indicates that local processes of national forgetting are nearly impossible given global interconnections and processes of remembering in the Lebanese diaspora and the global community. Through the circulation of these articles, which referenced past war as they spoke of impending war, memory took the form of everyday practices located in people's political conversations, in their encounters with each other, and in their interactions with their surroundings.

13. As Hanssen and Genberg (2001) write, the effacement of the city "ironically produced a public sphere pregnant with divergent versions and visions for past and future of city and country" (234).

14. For one relation between memory and power, consider also Derrida's "archive fever." Derrida writes, "There is no political power without control over the archives, without control over memory" (quoted in Hanssen and Genberg 2001).

15. I borrow this thought from Adrienne Rich's poem, *Cartographies of Silence* (1978: 17), as in the epigraph to this chapter.

16. For readings on forgetting, see Augé (2004), who writes, "Oblivion is a necessity both to society and to the individual. One must know how to forget in order to taste the full flavor of the present, of the moment, and of expectation . . . memory itself needs forgetfulness" (3). See also Borges's famous essay "Funes the Memorious" (1962), where he echoes a similar sentiment, and Slyomovics (1998), who discusses different significations of forgetting in Palestinian and Jewish contexts.

17. See Osman's (2001) architectural master's thesis on Beirut's postwar development that suggests an interesting role for forgetting. Osman developed a conceptual model whereby a poem can be read by operating a dial that is simultaneously connected to a paper shredder. He explains it as such: "the only way that the reader can come to know the poem is by destroying it; the poem can only be presenced through its own annihilation. The roll of paper, however, contains multiple copies of the poem; thus the work operates on a repetitive cycle of reading/destroying." This leads Osman to title his project after Pablo Neruda's poem, "There's No Forgetting." For Osman, the move toward oblivion requires agency, and presence is in need of self-consciously annihilating, or forgetting, the poem.

18. For a similar view on memory struggling to forget in order to live, see Mueggler (2001).

19. See Freud (1989) on archiving memory versus forgetting, and the difference between heritage and memory of the mind. For Freud, what differentiates memory of the city (heritage) from the mind is that while the mind's memory can be effaced like the city (think of the various cities underneath the current Beirut), it is generally "the rule rather than the exception for the past to be preserved in mental life" (20). Any effacement, for Freud, is a repression that is bound to return distorted. According to Freud, it is forgetting that takes work through "repression and substitution of 'screen' memories that block access to more disturbing ones" (Olick and Robbins 1998: 109).

20. In articulating his idea of sites of memory (*lieux de mémoire*), Nora says that these sites came about, "at a particular historical moment" in France (1989: 7), when there was a clear scientific process and an objectification of the past, and methods to categorize, record, and archive it. Nora traces this through the period of industrialization and modernization in France. The *lieux de mémoire* is in the archives as well as commemorations, anniversaries, museums, dictionaries and libraries. They emerge from memory seized by history, where memory is "no longer a retrospective continuity but the illumination of discontinuity" (16). Nora claims, "If we were able to live within memory, we would not have needed to consecrate *lieux de mémoire* in its name. Each gesture, down to the most

every day, would be experienced as the ritual repetition of a timeless practice in a primordial identification of act and meaning" (8).

21. UMAM Documentation and Research is a center that strives to document the violence of Lebanon's past. It was one of the more popular centers that were active in the field of memory work during this research.

22. The idea of "confronting history" is best represented in a quote by one of UMAM's founders, Monica Borgmann. Borgmann is a German who grew up in post-Nazi Germany, bringing with her much of the valuable experiences and lessons of memory work from that context. In a speech delivered at a conference in Istanbul in 2007, she said: "Lebanon shows quite well that 'forgetting' is not the way to ensure civil calm and also, that confronting history could be the less perilous path" (Barclay 2007: 47).

23. I don't deal here in any length with cultural production as discussed in depth in Haugbolle (2010) and Westmoreland (2008). Suffice it to say that works about the war were not absent from cultural space. There are documentary films like *Massaker* (2004) and several by Mai Masri and Jean Chamoun, and feature films such as *West Beirut* (1998). There were also novels by Jean Said Makdisi (1990), Hanan el-Sheikh (1995), and Hoda Barakat (1995), among many others.

24. There were other dates that had significance for various communities and, like sites of memory, were manifested in documents, such as the 1969 agreement between the PLO and the army, or the May 17, 1983, defunct peace agreement with Israel. These would often be referenced in conversations and take on varying meanings from community to community—often defined along sectarian lines.

25. I borrow from de Certeau, who develops a critique of consumption and argues that consumption is really another form of production—the production of "ways of using" something (de Certeau 1984: xiii). The idea is that a product is never really completely produced until consumption further produces the way it will be used.

26. Since they are trying to challenge or align their interests with power, it is not unusual to see representatives of civil society groups speaking out on the importance of war memory to engage politicians and seek their approval, like Amal Makarem, founder of the organization Memory for the Future, or to be involved and start their own political organizations, like UMAM founder Lokman Slim.

27. This was not my last visit to Lebanon, but I had planned this particular departure to coincide with the end of fieldwork for this project.

CHAPTER 7. AMBIGUITIES OF WAR'S REMEMBRANCE: TWO EPISODES

1. Many of these buildings, built in the late 1990s and beyond, are one story over their legal height, a floor known as *ṭābe' el-mur* (the Murr floor) after member of Parliament Michel el-Murr, who is said to have authorized this as part of his clientalist services in the Metn district where he commands much political power.

2. See Chapter 2 for details of this group.

3. Numur el-Ahrar is the Arabic name for the militia wing of the Ahrar, also known as "The Tigers."

4. In everyday language, often there is a term added after *tin-dhakar* so the sentence would read *tin-dhakar ta-mā tin-ʿād*, *tin-dhakar wa-mā tin-ʿād* or *tin-dhakar bas mā tin-ʿād*. This latter version slightly changes the meaning to become "Remember but do not repeat." I have used these phrases interchangeably.

5. *Tanāsū* is the plural form of *tanāsī*.

6. See Larkin (2012) for accounts of how memory is transmitted down to youth between the ages of fifteen and twenty-two who do not have personal memories of the war.

7. Transmitted memory between generations in Lebanon is very present. One should not claim, as one newspaper article did, that the younger generation searches for a memory of this war but does not find it (Rola Mikael, *An-Nahar*, April 14, 2002). I observed, during fieldwork, political party members discuss wartime experiences, and often brag about them, in front of people in their early to mid-twenties.

8. I took several walks with formerly armed people during my research; for example, to Khiam prison, and through the streets of Ashrafieh, to name a couple. These walks informed much of my understanding of my informants' relationship to place, to the city, and to their social surroundings.

9. Movement in anthropological literature is explored in a variety of ways. Claude Lévi Strauss speaks of the journey in *Triste Tropique* (1992). Erik Mueggler (2001) talks of how we forget ourselves on walks, and looks at walking through its embeddedness in exorcism rituals as healing and as therapy. He writes that, "Walking creates a delicate interplay of perception and reflection. Surprises emerge from the landscape and are left behind; new thoughts come into being; old ones gradually loosen their hold. 'A kind of fluid oscillation between external objects and inward ideas and images may ensue, one whose very rapidity blurs the borderline between physical and mental experience'" (Mueggler 2001: 248). I see my movements through the city with people as "experiences" in the way Hammoudi defines them as an "ethnographic encounter in which the anthropologist meets people as they engage in their own activities" (2009: 48). However, I recognize that in some cases there is some cueing by the anthropologist, which complicates, but I believe does not detract from Hammoudi's sense of experience—these interlocutors were, after all, engaged in daily practices.

10. The statue was removed in 1996 for safekeeping during the reconstruction of downtown, and to be refurbished. It was returned in 2004, with its wartime scars still visible and an arm still missing after being blown apart during the years of fighting.

11. See Haugbolle (2010: 151–56) for examples of these representations.

12. Both U.S. dollars and the Lebanese lira are used as currency in Lebanon. The lira is pegged to the dollar, and 1 dollar equaled roughly 1,500 LL during the time of my fieldwork. Lebanese generally take into account the devaluation of the Lebanese pound when they speak of the war and postwar days, as Zuzu does in this case.

13. Recall from Chapter 1 that Human Rights Discourse calls on us to remember evil

to be in the past (Meister 2012). Zuzu turned this on its head by remembering the war as good days.

14. During my research, I spent hundreds of hours working with different social movements and civil society groups and attending closed meetings, public meetings, lectures, and workshops.

15. Traboulsi writes, in a very different context, and referring to a photograph of an Algerian woman in agony over violence in her country: "We know from our Lebanese wounds that meaninglessness is the deepest wound, and that meaninglessness is the harshest ['aqṣa] slaughter" (2002: 341; my translation from Arabic). Traboulsi is, here, suggesting that a lack of meaning is like another form of war.

16. In this thesis on memory I am not alone. I am building partially here from Hourani (2008) when he says that "the generation of narrative memories is more than a process of working through or providing closure to a difficult and traumatic past," that it is also the "narrative constitution of the nation." The nation, Hourani says, "is the unstable product of multiple and sometimes contradictory narratives that cohere through a process of 'making-other'—defining which groups, behaviors, and beliefs belong to the nation and which are excluded, marginalized, or to be guarded against" (Hourani 2008: 288).

CHAPTER 8. AMNESTY AS A POLITICS OF PROTRACTED CONFLICT

1. For the relation between collective blame and hypocrisy, see Trouillot (2000).

2. I am assuming here that the policies of Mount Lebanon had a large role to play in the structure of modern-day Lebanon, and only consider major communal amnesties, although there were many more individual pardons before this date.

3. Official Lebanese history tends to begin in 1860 or 1840 at the earliest. My intent in this brief historical narrative is not to locate a beginning, but to show that current practices have their roots in past accounts that have built up over time. Makdisi's argument is that sectarianism arises through multiple factors involving Ottoman reforms known as the tanzimat, Western colonial encroachment, and the local population's negotiations between these forces and their own affiliations. Makdisi considers Egyptian power plays and military advancements to be part of the local element in his analysis. He writes that, "sectarianism occurred not in the distant past but in an era of the in-between, when old-regime society had collapsed but an independent nationalist society had not yet formed—a period of indigenous, European, and Ottoman interaction and collaboration that spawned the contested culture of sectarianism" (2000: 166). And later, "The beginning of sectarianism did not imply a reversion. It marked a rupture, a birth of a new culture that singled out religious affiliation as the defining public and political characteristic of a modern subject and citizen. To overcome it . . . requires *another* vision of modernity" (174).

4. *maḍā mā maḍā* is a variant of *'afā Allāh 'ammā maḍā*, except that God is not present in the former construction. This distinction may be important as it might imply

people thinking of this as an agreement between communities, rather than a top-down amnesty relying on law or the state (both having godlike qualities).

5. The Druze are led by Walid Jumblatt, the Shiʻa by Hizballah and their allies in the Amal Movement, the Sunni by Saed Hariri (at least up till 2009, since by 2014 this leadership began to experience cracks), whereas the Christians are divided among several political parties that are in conflict.

6. Entelis writes that "The [Kataeb's] successful performance in the [1958] civil war and its crucial role in the resulting political compromise was indication of a major power realignment; the defense of Lebanon's national integrity (in ideological rather than strictly military terms) and the guarantee of its future viability in its current multi-confessional form now passed from the hands of traditional Zuʻama to a modern political organization" (1973: 333).

7. There were other general amnesties such as in 1969 but they are relatively minor to this discussion.

8. Samir Gaegae, leader of the Christian LF, and Walid Jumblatt, leader of the Druze PSP, had been archenemies ever since Gaegae led the LF in the War of the Mountain that began in 1982, where the Druze and Maronite fought for control of the Chouf region. In 2005, the two leaders entered into a coalition involving other political parties. A few years later, it was not uncommon to hear coalition members turn a blind eye to the past crimes of these leaders against their community. In an interview, one Druze fighter claimed it was time to forgive Gaegae, who had served his time for his crimes and should be forgiven. For more on the War of the Mountain, see Traboulsi (2007).

9. I say only some, since many indeed did not benefit and remain disenfranchised today, being taxi drivers, security guards, or jobless.

10. See Chapter 6 for a description of this organization.

11. See Trouillot (2000) for an understanding of individual and collective apologies and the way apologies are meant to register a new era.

12. Mme Rita is a woman in her early fifties with a short boyish-cut hairdo that is slowly graying. She lives with her sister in an old Ashrafieh apartment. Her father, who passed away a few years before we met, had received an injury to his head from a rocket explosion near the house toward the waning years of the war. Her mother passed away around the time we met. She was never married and spends a lot of her free time with her nieces and nephews, the children of her two brothers. She is Maronite, from Saida, but she moved to Beirut during the war after Saida was made unsafe for her family. Her father was a supporter of the Phalange Party and she and her brothers took up arms for the party. She left them in 1985 to join other Phalange women in a woman's peace organization that later became involved in family planning issues.

13. On "dead certainty" see Appadurai (1998).

14. Suburb is a misnomer if one thinks of it in the American suburban sense, since Beirut's urban sprawl means that Dora feels almost like a central part of the city.

15. This echoes Eichmann's defense, in which the argument was that the entire German population was guilty and Eichmann was just doing his job as a member of society. Arendt (and the prosecution) argues that Eichmann cannot hide behind the German

population, and that if we cannot prosecute everyone, this does not mean we cannot prosecute anyone. There are people who are guiltier and more responsible than others, and therefore should be held to account (Arendt 1994).

16. Basil may be seen as coming from a place where *haybi* (reverence) is an important value. Crucially, in this context, *haybi* projects fear, not just awe and respect. Zecher (1967) explains the role of *haybi* in being able to command influence. She writes that if a person "cannot or does not threaten to harm an opponent, he will lose his *haybi*" (1967: 130). In devising strategies in wartime, *haybi* is taken into account at some level. Just as Zecher's man of influence, who, when threatened, failed "to make people afraid," and ended by losing his respect and position as influential (130), so the community is seen to lose its respect and position in Lebanese society if it fails to instill fear in its opponents. Some men then believe they must take it upon themselves to enforce the community's *haybi*—one can see this for example in needing to enforce the Christian community's position (*yifrud haybet el-mujtamaʿ el-masīḥi*). Zecher also adds that "excessive cruelty," at least according to the formal structures of *haybi* that Zecher outlines, can lead to a loss of respect and resentment (131). For the relation between violence and respect in another context, see Bourgois (2003).

17. See Wilson (2001) for a critique of Truth and Reconciliation Commissions.

18. Barak (2007) sets up the state's action of forgetting in opposition to civil society's (supposedly more positive) act of remembering.

CONCLUSION. THE ANTICIPATION OF WAR IN 2009–2014

1. See UN High Commissioner for Refugees (UNHCR) data on Syria, https://data .unhcr.org/syrianrefugees/country.php?id=122, accessed April 4, 2014.

2. The Moqdad family are from the Beqaa Valley, and it is said they are part of the hashish cartel. The militarization is linked to this cartel, which has effectively kept state security out of the Beqaa Valley in any meaningful way.

3. These nationals (especially Turkish and Saudi Arabian) were targets because of their country's involvement in the Syrian uprising on the part of the Free Syrian Army and opposition to the regime.

4. Presumably he meant they would have to leave through Syria, or even by boat, as some nationals did in the July 2006 war.

5. While varying levels of fear did occupy people's feelings, there were also many jokes that developed. People started to call them "Moq-daddy," and there was even a Twitter account by this name. Others would joke about the idea that a family had a military wing, and questioned how one could get one for their own family.

6. The FSA is in some respects a misnomer because it is not one army with a central command, but rather a loose collection of armed groups opposed to the Syrian regime under Bashar al-Assad. The name speaks to a concerted effort to bring opposition groups under one banner to unite against the Syrian regime army.

7. Such an argument is based on an understanding of feudal politics. See Gilsenan (1996), Bourdieu (1966), and Jamous (1992).

8. See Alex Rowell, "Vehicle Explosions in Lebanon Since 2011," NOW Lebanon, February 17, 2014, https://now.mmedia.me/lb/en/reportsfeatures/535852-vehicle-explosions -in-lebanon-since-2011, accessed April 6, 2014.

9. Interestingly, after I wrote some of these thoughts in my notes later that day, I came across a video on Future TV showing a live broadcast where the presenter and her guest express similar confusion. The studio is much closer to the site of the bombing, so it is clear they are more frightened, but they go through a similar guessing process, and the host asks her producer off-camera if the sound they heard is a supersonic boom or a bomb. https://www.youtube.com/watch?v=Nh23onaDgxY, accessed April 6, 2014.

10. See, e.g., Tania el-Khoury, *Sabāḥ al-infijār* (The morning of the bombing), Jadaliyya, http://tinyurl.com/nkpabq9, accessed April 6, 2014.

11. The predominantly Sunni Bab al-Tabbaneh neighborhood in Tripoli, now against Syria's Bashar al-Assad, and the predominantly pro-Syrian regime Alawite neighborhood of Jabal Muhsin, have been engaged in low-intensity armed conflict for years.

Bibliography

'Aleq, Rami. 2008. *Tarīq al-naḥel* (The Path of the Bee). 2nd ed. Beirut: Tareeq el-Nahel Press.

Abrams, Philip. 1988. Notes on the Difficulty of Studying the State. *Journal of Historical Sociology* 1, 1: 58–90.

Aguilar, Paloma. 2002. *Memory and Amnesia: The Role of the Spanish Civil War in the Transition to Democracy.* Trans. M. G. Oakley. New York: Berghahn.

Ahmed, Sarah. 2004. *The Cultural Politics of Emotion.* London: Routledge.

Al-Hout, Bayan N. 2004. *Sabra and Shatila: September 1982.* London: Pluto.

Allen, Lori. 2013. *The Rise and Fall of Human Rights: Cynicism and Politics in Occupied Palestine.* Stanford, Calif.: Stanford University Press.

Anderson, Benedict R. 1991. *Imagined Communities: Reflections on the Origin and Spread of Nationalism.* 2nd ed. New York: Verso.

Appadurai, Arjun. 1998. Dead Certainty: Ethnic Violence in the Era of Globalization. *Development and Change* 29, 4: 905–25.

Arendt, Hannah. 1994. *Eichmann in Jerusalem: A Report on the Banality of Evil.* New York: Penguin.

Augé, Marc. 2004. *Oblivion.* Trans. Marjolijn de Jager. Minneapolis: University of Minnesota Press.

Badiou, Alain. 2012. *The Rebirth of History: Times of Riots and Uprisings.* London: Verso.

Barak, Oren. 2007. Don't Mention the War? The Politics of Remembrance and Forgetfulness in Postwar Lebanon. *Middle East Journal* 61, 1: 49–70.

Barakat, Hoda. 1995. *The Stone of Laughter.* Trans. Sophie Bennett. Brooklyn, N.Y.: Interlink Books.

Barclay, Susan. 2007. Performing Memory, Violence, Identity, and the Politics of the Present with UMAM. M.A. thesis, American University of Beirut.

Battaglia, Debbora. 1993. A Play in the Fields (and Borders) of the Imaginary: Melanesian Transformations of Forgetting. *Cultural Anthropology* 8, 4: 430–442.

Bazzi, Yousef. 2005. *naẓara illeyī Yasser Arafat wa-ibtasam: yawmiyāt muqātel* (Yasser Arafat Looked at Me and Smiled). Trans. Rasha Salti. Beirut: Dar al-Kotob.

Beatty, Andrew. 2010. How Did It Feel for You? Emotion, Narrative, and the Limits of Ethnography. *American Anthropologist* 112, 3: 430–43.

Bechara, Soha. 2003. *Resistance: My Life for Lebanon.* New York: Soft Skull.

Bergson, Henri. 1946. *The Creative Mind*. Trans. Mabelle L. Andison. New York: Philosophical Library.

———. 1960. *Creative Evolution*. New York: Macmillan.

Boon, James. 1999. *Verging on Extra-Vagance: Anthropology, History, Religion, Literature, Arts . . . Showbiz*. Princeton, N.J.: Princeton University Press.

Borges, Jorge Luis. 1962. Funes the Memorious. In *Ficciones*, ed. Anthony Kerrigan, 107–16. New York: Grove Press.

Borneman, John. 1992. *Belonging in the Two Berlins: Kin, State, Nation*. Cambridge: Cambridge University Press.

———. 2002. Reconciliation After Ethnic Cleansing: Listening, Retribution, Affiliation. *Public Culture* 14, 2: 281–304.

Bourdieu, Pierre. 1966. The Sentiment of Honour in Kabyle Society. In *Honour and Shame: The Values of Mediterranean Society*, ed. J. G. Peristiany, trans. Philip Sherrard, 191–41. Chicago: University of Chicago Press.

———. 1977. *Outline of a Theory of Practice*. Trans. Richard Nice. Berkeley: University of California Press.

Bourdieu, Pierre and Loïc Wacquant. 1992. *An Invitation to Reflective Sociology*. Chicago: University of Chicago Press.

Bourgois, Philippe. 2003. *In Search of Respect: Selling Crack in El Barrio*. Cambridge: Cambridge University Press.

Butler, Judith. 2004. *Precarious Life: The Powers of Mourning and Violence*. London: Verso.

Cammett, Melanie and Sukriti Issar. 2010. Bricks and Mortar Clientelism: Sectarianism and the Logics of Welfare Allocation in Lebanon. *World Politics* 62: 381–421.

Campbell, John. 1964. *Honour, Family and Patronage: A Study of Institutions and Moral Values in a Greek Mountain Community*. Oxford: Clarendon.

Caton, Steve. 2006. *Yemen Chronicle: An Anthropology of War and Mediation*. New York: Hill and Wang.

———. 2014. Henri Bergson in Highland Yemen. In *The Ground Between: Anthropologists Engage Philosophy*, ed. Veena Das et al. Durham, N.C.: Duke University Press.

Clark, Janine A. and Bassel F. Salloukh. 2013. Elite Strategies, Civil Society, and Sectarian Identities in Postwar Lebanon. *International Journal of Middle East Studies* 45: 731–49.

Cobban, Helena. 1985. *The Making of Modern Lebanon*. Boulder, Colo.: Westview.

Cohn, Carol. 1987. Sex and Death in the Rational World of Defense Intellectuals. *Signs* 12, 4: 687–718.

Connerton, Paul. 1989. *How Societies Remember*. Cambridge: Cambridge University Press.

———. 2008. Seven Types of Forgetting. *Memory Studies* 1, 1: 59–71.

Corvisier, André and John Childs, eds. 1994. *A Dictionary of Military History and the Art of War*. Trans. Chris Turner. Oxford: Wiley-Blackwell.

Daniel, Valentine. 1996. *Charred Lullabies: Chapters in an Anthropology of Violence*. Princeton, N.J.: Princeton University Press.

Das, Veena. 2007. *Life and Words: Violence and the Descent into the Ordinary*. Berkeley: University of California Press.

Davies, James and Dimitrina Spencer, eds. 2010. *Emotions in the Field: The Psychology and Anthropology of Fieldwork Experience*. Stanford, Calif.: Stanford University Press.

de Certeau, Michel. 1984. *The Practice of Everyday Life*. Berkeley: University of California Press.

———. 1986. *Heterologies: Discourse on the Other*. Minneapolis: University of Minnesota Press.

Deeb, Lara. 2006. *An Enchanted Modern: Gender and Public Piety in Shi'i Lebanon*. Princeton, N.J.: Princeton University Press.

———. 2008. Exhibiting the "Just-Lived Past": Hizbullah's Nationalist Narratives in Transnational Political Context. *Comparative Studies in Society and History* 50, 2: 369–99.

Deeb, Lara and Mona Harb, eds. 2013. *Leisurely Islam: Negotiating Geography and Morality in Shi'ite South Beirut*. Princeton, N.J.: Princeton University Press.

Diphoorn, Tessa. 2013. The Emotionality of Participation: Various Modes of Participation in Ethnographic Fieldwork on Private Policing in Durban, South Africa. *Journal of Contemporary Ethnography* 42, 2: 201–25.

Dunmire, Patricia. 2013. "New World Coming": Narratives of the Future in US Post-Cold War National Security Discourse. In *Discourses of War and Peace*, ed. Adam Hodges, 23–46. Oxford: Oxford University Press.

Duyvesteyn, Isabelle and Jan Angstrom, eds. 2005. *Rethinking the Nature of War*. London: Frank Cass.

El-Khazen, Farid. 2000. *The Breakdown of the State in Lebanon, 1967–1976*. London: Tauris.

El-Sheikh, Hanan. 1995. *Beirut Blues*. New York: Doubleday.

Entelis, John P. 1973. Party Transformation in Lebanon: Al-Kata'ib as a Case Study. *Middle Eastern Studies* 9, 3: 325–40.

Fawaz, Mona. 2008. An Unusual Clique of City-Makers: Social Networks in the Production of a Neighborhood in Beirut (1950–75). *International Journal of Urban and Regional Research* 32, 3: 565–85.

Fawaz, Mona, Mona Harb, and Ahmad Gharbieh. 2012. Living Beirut's Security Zones: An Investigation of the Modalities and Practice of Urban Security. *City & Society* 24, 2: 173–95.

Feldman, Allen. 1991. *Formations of Violence: The Narrative of the Body and Political Terror in Northern Ireland*. Chicago: University of Chicago Press.

Fisk, Robert. 2002. *Pity the Nation: The Abduction of Lebanon*. 4th ed. New York: Nation.

Foucault, Michel. 1979. *Discipline and Punish: The Birth of the Prison*. Trans. Alan Sheridan. New York: Vintage.

———. 1994. *The Order of Things: An Archeology of the Human Sciences*. New York: Vintage.

————. 1997 [2003]. *"Society Must Be Defended": Lectures at the Collège de France, 1975–1976*. Trans. David Macey. New York: Picador.

Freud, Sigmund. 1989. *Civilization and Its Discontents*. New York: Norton.

Ghannam, Farha. 2013. *Live and Die like a Man: Gender Dynamics in Urban Egypt*. Stanford, Calif.: Stanford University Press.

Gilsenan, Michael. 1996. *Lords of the Lebanese Marches: Violence and Narrative in an Arab Society*. London: Tauris.

————. 1992. *Nizam ma fi*: Discourses of Order, Disorder and History in a Lebanese Context. In *Problems of the Modern Middle East in Historical Perspective: Essays in Honour of Albert Hourani*, ed. J. Spagnolo, 79–104. Reading: Ithaca Press.

Goldie, Janis L. 2013. Culture Clash: Framing Peacekeeping and Its Role in a Canadian Context. In *Discourses of War and Peace*, ed. Adam Hodges, 119–44. Oxford: Oxford University Press.

Greenhouse, Carol J., Elizabeth Mertz, and Kay B. B. Warren, eds. 2002. *Ethnography in Unstable Places: Everyday Lives in Contexts of Dramatic Political Change*. Durham, N.C.: Duke University Press.

Hage, Ghassan. 1996. Nationalist Anxiety or the Fear of Losing Your Other. *Australian Journal of Anthropology* 7, 2: 121–40.

————. 2009. Hating Israel in the Field: On Ethnography and Political Emotions. *Anthropological Theory* 9, 1: 59–79.

————. 2015. *Alter-Politics: Critical Anthropology and the Radical Imagination*. Melbourne: Melbourne University Press.

Hage, Rawi. 2006. *De Niro's Game*. Toronto: House of Anansi Press.

Halbwachs, Maurice. 1992. *On Collective Memory*. Trans. and ed. Lewis Coser. Chicago: University of Chicago Press.

Hall, Stuart. 1986. Gramsci's Relevance for the Study of Race and Ethnicity. *Journal of Communication Inquiry* 10: 5–27.

Hammami, Rema. 2004. On the Importance of Thugs: The Moral Economy of a Checkpoint. *Middle East Report* 231: 26–34

Hammoudi, Abdellah. 1993. *The Victim and Its Masks: An Essay on Sacrifice and Masquerade in the Maghreb*. Chicago: University of Chicago Press.

————. 1997. *Master and Disciple: The Cultural Foundations of Moroccan Authoritarianism*. Chicago: University of Chicago Press.

————. 2009. Phenomenology and Ethnography: On Kabyle *Habitus* in the Work of Pierre Bourdieu. In *Bourdieu in Algeria: Colonial Politics, Ethnographic Practices, Theoretical Developments*, ed. Jane E. Goodman and Paul A. Silverstein, trans. Patricia Fogarty, 199–254. Lincoln: University of Nebraska Press.

Hamzeh, Ahmed. 2001. Clientalism, Lebanon: Roots and Trends. *Middle Eastern Studies* 37, 3: 167–78.

————. 2004. *In the Path of Hizbullah*. Syracuse, N.Y.: Syracuse University Press.

Hanf, Theodor. 1993. *Coexistence in Wartime Lebanon: Decline of a State and Rise of a Nation*. London: Centre for Lebanese Studies in association with I.B. Tauris.

Hanssen, Jens-Peter and Daniel Genberg. 2001. Beirut in Memorium: A Kaleidoscope Space Out of Focus. In *Crisis and Memory in Islamic Societies: Proceedings of the Third Summer Academy of the Working Group Modernity and Islam held at the Orient Institute of the German Oriental Society in Beirut,* ed. Angelika Neuwirth and Andreas Pflitsch, 231–42. Würzburg: Ergon Verlag in Kommission.

Harb, Mona. 2007. Deconstructing Hizballah and Its Suburbs. *Middle East Research and Information Project* 242: 37.

Harb, Mona and Reinoud Leenders. 2005. Know the Enemy: Hizbullah, "Terrorism" and the Politics of Perception. *Third World Quarterly* 26, 1: 173–97.

Haugbolle, Sune. 2010. *War and Memory in Lebanon.* Cambridge: University of Cambridge Press.

Hedges, Chris. 2009. Celebrating Slaughter: War and Collective Amnesia. *Truthdig* 5 (October).

Heidegger, Martin. 2010. The Question Concerning Technology. In *Technology and Values: Essential Readings,* ed. Craig Hanks, 99–113. Oxford: Blackwell.

Hermez, Sami. 2011. On Dignity and Clientelism: Lebanon in the Context of the 2011 Arab Revolutions. *Studies in Ethnicity and Nationalism* 11: 527–37.

———. 2015. When the State Is (N)ever Present: On Cynicism and Political Mobilization in Lebanon. *Journal of the Royal Anthropological Institute* 21: 507–23.

Hoffman, Danny. 2005. Violent Events as Narrative Blocs: The Disarmament at Bo, Sierra Leone. *Anthropological Quarterly* 78, 2: 328–53.

Hourani, Najib. 2008. The Militiaman Icon: Cinema, Memory, and the Lebanese Civil Wars. *CR: The New Centennial Review* 8, 2: 287–307.

Hudson, Michael C. 1988. The Problem of Authoritative Power in Lebanese Politics: Why Consociationalism Failed. In *Lebanon: A History of Conflict and Consensus,* ed. Nadim Shehadi and Dana Haffar Mills, 224–39. London: Centre for Lebanese Studies in association with I.B. Tauris.

Hume, Mo. 2007. Unpicking the Threads: Emotion as Central to the Theory and Practice of Researching Violence. *Women's Studies International Forum* 30, 2: 147–57.

Huyssen, Andreas. 2003. *Present Pasts: Urban Palimpsests and the Politics of Memory.* Stanford, Calif.: Stanford University Press.

Igartua, Juanjo and Dario Paez. 1997. Art and Remembering Traumatic Collective Events: The Case of the Spanish Civil War. *In Collective Memory of Political Events: Social Psychological Perspectives,* ed. James W. Pennebaker, Dario Paez, and Bernard Rim, 79–102. Mahwah, N.J.: Lawrence Erlbaum.

Information International. 2007. *Al-'aḥzāb al-lubnāniyya: "'aj'at" ta'sīs fī al-'ām 2006 (Lebanese Political Parties: The Year 2006 Sees "Traffic" in New Parties),* 42.

Îñiguez, Lupicinio, Jose Valencia, and Félix Vázquez. 1997. The Construction of Remembering and Forgetfulness: Memories and Histories of the Spanish Civil War. In *Collective Memory of Political Events: Social Psychological Perspectives,* ed. James W. Pennebaker, Dario Paez, and Bernard Rim, 237–52. Mahwah, N.J.: Lawrence Erlbaum.

Jamous, Raymond. 1992. From the Death of Men to the Peace of God: Violence and

Peace-Making in the Rif. In *Honor and Grace in Anthropology*, ed. J. G. Peristiany and Julian Pitt-Rivers, 167–92. Cambridge: Cambridge University Press.

Jeganathan, Pradeep. 1997. After a Riot: Anthropological Locations of Violence in an Urban Sri Lankan Community. Ph.D. dissertation, University of Chicago.

——. 1998. In the Shadow of Violence: "Tamilness" and the Anthropology of Identity in Southern Sri Lanka. In *Buddhist Fundamentalism and Minority Identity in Sri Lanka*, ed. Tessa J. Bartholomeusz and C. R. de Silva, 89–109. New York: State University of New York Press.

——. 2004. Checkpoint: Anthropology, Identity, and the State. In *Anthropology in the Margins of the State*, ed. Veena Das and Deborah Poole, 67–80. Santa Fe, N.M.: SAR Press.

Johnson, Michael. 1986. *Class and Client in Beirut: The Sunni Muslim Community and the Lebanese State 1840–1985*. London: Ithaca Press.

——. 2002. *All Honourable Men: The Social Origins of War in Lebanon*. London: Tauris.

Joseph, Suad. 1983. Working-Class Women's Networks in a Sectarian State: A Political Paradox. *American Ethnologist* 10, 1: 1–22.

——. 1997. The Public/Private: The Imagined Boundary in the Imagined Nation/State/Community: The Lebanese Case. *Feminist Review* 57 (Autumn): 73–92.

Kaldor, Mary. 1999. *New and Old Wars: Organized Violence in a Global Era*. Stanford, Calif.: Stanford University Press.

Kalyvas, Stathis N. 2001. "New" and "Old" Civil Wars: A Valid Distinction? *World Politics* 54, 1: 99–118.

——. 2003. The Ontology of "Political Violence": Action and Identity in Civil Wars. *Perspectives on Politics* 1, 3: 475–94.

——. 2006. *The Logic of Violence in Civil War*. New York: Cambridge University Press.

Kansteiner, Wolf. 2002. Finding Meaning in Memory: A Methodological Critique of Collective Memory Studies. *History and Theory* 41, 2: 179–97.

Kapuściński, Ryszard. 2001. *Another Day of Life*. Trans. William Brand. New York: Vintage.

Kegels, Nicolien. 2007. Nothing Shines as Bright as a Beirut Night. *Etnofoor* 20, 2: 87–101.

Kelly, Tobias. 2008. The Attractions of Accountancy: Living an Ordinary Life During the Second Palestinian Intifada. *Ethnography* 9, 3: 351–76.

Khalaf, Samir. 1968. Primordial Ties and Politics in Lebanon. *Middle Eastern Studies* 4, 3: 243–69.

——. 2004. *Civil and Uncivil Violence in Lebanon: A History of the Internationalization of Communal Conflict*. New York: Columbia University Press.

Khalidi, Rashid. 1984. The Palestinians in Lebanon: Social Repercussions of Israel's Invasion. *Middle East Journal* 38, 2: 255–66.

Khalili, Laleh. 2007. *Heroes and Martyrs of Palestine: The Politics of National Commemoration*. Cambridge: Cambridge University Press.

——. 2012. *Time in the Shadows: Confinement in Counterinsurgencies*. Stanford, Calif.: Stanford University Press

Khatib, Lina. 2007. Television and Public Action in the Beirut Spring. In *Arab Media and Political Renewal: Community, Legitimacy and Public Life*, ed. Naomi Sakr, 28–43. London: Tauris.

Khbeiz, Bilal. 2009. Gaza-Beirut-Tel Aviv: In Praise of Selfishness and Opportunism. *E-flux* 3 (February).

Khoury, Elias. 1981. *abwāb al-madīna (City Gates)*. Beirut: Ibn Rushd.

———. 2002. *Yalo*. Beirut: Dar-al-Adab.

———. 2015. Interview by Samir Rahim. *Prospect Magazine* website.

Kochan, Jeff. 2010. Latour's Heideggar. *Social Studies of Science* 40, 4: 579–98.

Koskenniemi, Martti. 2002. Between Impunity and Show Trials. *Max Planck Yearbook of United Nations Law* 6, 1:1–35.

Kraidy, Marwan. 2006. Reality Television and Politics in the Arab World: Preliminary Observations. *Transnational Broadcasting Studies* 15, 1 January.

———. 2010. *Reality Television and Arab Politics: Contention in Public Life*. New York: Cambridge University Press.

Kusno, Abidin. 2003. Remembering/Forgetting the May Riots: Architecture, Violence, and the Making of "Chinese Cultures" in Post-1998 Jakarta. *Public Culture* 15, 1: 149–77.

Larkin, Craig. 2012. *Memory and Conflict in Lebanon: Remembering and Forgetting the Past*. New York: Routledge.

Leenders, Reinoud. 2012. *Spoils of Truce: Corruption and State-Building in Postwar Lebanon*. Ithaca, N.Y.: Cornell University Press.

Lepore, Jill. 1998. *The Name of War: King Philip's War and the Origins of American Identity*. New York: Vintage.

Lubkemann, Stephen. 2008. *Culture in Chaos: An Anthropology of the Social Condition in War*. Chicago: University of Chicago Press.

Maasri, Zeina. 2009. *Off the Wall: Political Posters of the Lebanese Civil War*. London: Tauris.

Maček, Ivana. 2009. *Sarajevo Under Siege: Anthropology in Wartime*. Philadelphia: University of Pennsylvania Press.

Makarem, Ghassan. 2012. Interview by Ziad Abu Rish, *Jadaliyya* website.

Makdisi, Jean Said. 1990. *Beirut Fragments: A War Memoir*. New York: Persea.

Makdisi, Saree. 2006. Beirut, a City Without History? In *Memory and Violence in the Middle East and North Africa*, ed. Ussama Makdisi and Paul Silverstein, 201–14. Bloomington: Indiana University Press.

Makdisi, Ussama. 2000. *The Culture of Sectarianism: Community, History, and Violence in Nineteenth-Century Ottoman Lebanon*. Berkeley: University of California Press.

Massumi, Brian. 2002. *Parables for the Virtual: Movement, Affect, Sensation*. Durham, N.C.: Duke University Press.

Mauss, Marcel. 2006. *Techniques, Technology, and Civilization*, ed. Nathan Schlanger. London: Berghahn.

Meister, Robert. 2012. *After Evil: A Politics of Human Rights*. New York: Columbia University Press.

Mermier, Franck. 2013. The Frontiers of Beirut: Some Anthropological Observations. *Mediterranean Politics* 18, 3: 376–93.

Mitchell, Timothy. 1988. *Colonizing Egypt.* Cambridge: Cambridge University Press.

———. 1991. The Limits of the State. *American Political Science Review* 85, 1: 77–96.

Monroe, Kristin. 2011. Being Mobile in Beirut. *City and Society* 23, 1: 91–111.

———. 2016. *The Insecure City: Space, Power, and Mobility in Beirut.* New Brunswick, N.J.: Rutgers University Press

Mueggler, Erik. 2001. *The Age of Wild Ghosts: Memory, Violence, and Place in Southwest China.* Berkeley: University of California Press.

Naber, Nadine and Zeina Zaatari. 2014. Reframing the War on Terror: Feminist and Lesbian, Gay, Bisexual, Transgender, and Queer (LGBTQ) Activism in the Context of the 2006 Israeli Invasion of Lebanon. *Cultural Dynamics* 26, 1: 91–111.

Nagel, C. 2002. Reconstructing Space, Re-Creating Memory: Sectarian Politics and Urban Development in Post-War Beirut. *Political Geography* 21, 5: 717–25.

Narayan, Kirin. 1993. How Native Is a "Native" Anthropologist? *American Anthropologist* 95, 3: 671–86.

Navaro-Yashin, Yael. 2002. *Faces of the State: Secularism and Public Life in Turkey.* Princeton, N.J.: Princeton University Press.

Newman, Marcy. 2007. Dreaming of Nahr al-Bared. Electronic Intifada. https://electronic intifada.net.

Nietzsche, Friedrich. 1989. *On the Genealogy of Morals.* Trans. Walter Kaufmann and R. J. Hollingdale. New York: Vintage.

Nikro, Saadi. 1999. Madness Cannot Be Thought. http://www.111101.net/Writings/Author /Saadi_Nikro/, accessed September 1, 2010.

———. 2012. *The Fragmenting Force of Memory: Self, Literary Style, and Civil War in Lebanon.* Newcastle: Cambridge Scholars Publishing.

Nora, Pierre. 1989. Between Memory and History: Les Lieux de Mémoire. *Representations* 26 (Spring): 7–24.

Nordstrom, Carolyn. 1997. *A Different Kind of War Story.* Philadelphia: University of Pennsylvania Press.

Norton, Augustus Richard. 2007. *Hezbollah: A Short History.* Princeton, N.J.: Princeton University Press.

Obeid, Michelle. 2010. Searching for the "Ideal Face of the State" in a Lebanese Border Town. *Journal of the Royal Anthropological Institute* 16, 2: 330–46.

Olick, Jeffrey K. and Joyce Robbins. 1998. Social Memory Studies: From "Collective Memory" to the Historical Sociology of Mnemonic Practices. *Annual Review of Sociology* 24, 1: 105–40.

Orford, Anne. 2007. *Reading Humanitarian Interventions: Human Rights and the Use of Force in International Law.* Cambridge: Cambridge University Press.

———. 2011. *International Authority and the Responsibility to Protect.* Cambridge: Cambridge University Press.

Osman, Ashraf. 2001. "Memory for Forgetfulness": Registering/Effacing the Memory of the Lebanese War. M.A. thesis, School of Architecture, Syracuse University.

Panourgiá, Neni. 1995. *Fragments of Death, Fables of Identity: An Athenian Anthropography*. Madison: University of Wisconsin Press.

Picard, Elizabeth. 1996. *A Shattered Country: Myths and Realities of the War in Lebanon*. Trans. Franklin Philip. New York: Holmes and Meier.

———. 2000. The Political Economy of Civil War in Lebanon. In *War, Institutions, and Social Change in the Middle East*, ed. Steven Heydemann, 292–322. Berkeley: University of California Press.

Pietruska, Jamie. 1995. Propheteering: A Cultural History of Prediction in the Gilded Age. Ph.D. dissertation, Brown University.

Povinelli, Elizabeth. 2002. *The Cunning of Recognition: Indigenous Alterities and the Making of Australian Multiculturalism*. Durham, N.C.: Duke University Press.

Rich, Adrienne. 1978. *The Dream of a Common Language*. New York: Norton.

Richards, Paul. 2004. *No Peace No War: Anthropology of Contemporary Armed Conflicts*. Athens: Ohio University Press.

Ricoeur, Paul. 2004. *Memory, History, Forgetting*. Chicago: University of Chicago Press.

Riskedahl, Diane. 2007. A Sign of War: The Strategic Use of Violent Imagery in Contemporary Lebanese Political Rhetoric. *Language & Communication* 27: 307–319.

Saad-Ghorayeb, Amal. 2002. *Hizbu'llah: Politics and Religion*. Critical Studies on Islam Series. London: Pluto.

Saadeh, Joseph. 2005. *'anā al-ḍaḥiya wa-al-jallādu 'anā (Victime et Bourreau)*. Trans. Pascale Tabet and Said Al-Jin. Paris: Calmann-Levy.

Saghieh, Nizar. 2006. Crimes Against Humanity in a Charismatic State. Speech given at the Srebrenica: Crime and Punishment forum, organized by UMAM Documentation and Research together with Heinrich Boll Foundation Middle East Office in Lebanon. Original in Arabic.

Salibi, Kamal. 1966. Lebanon Under Fuad Chehab 1958–1964. *Middle Eastern Studies* 2, 3: 211–26.

———. 1988. *A House of Many Mansions: The History of Lebanon Reconsidered*. London: Tauris.

Samman, Ghada. 2010. *Beirut Nightmares*. London: Quartet Books.

Sanchéz, Gonzalo. 2000. War and Politics in Columbian Society. *International Journal of Politics, Culture, and Society* 14, 1: 19–49.

Sawalha, Aseel. 2010. *Reconstructing Beirut: Memory and Space in a Postwar Arab City*. Austin: University of Texas Press.

Sayigh, Nasri. 2008. *Al-qatel in ḥaka: sirat al-ightiyālāt al-jāmiʿiya* (Thus Spoken a Killer: A Story of Mass Assassinations). Beirut: Riad El-Rayyes.

Sayigh, Rosemary. 1995. Palestinians in Lebanon: Harsh Present, Uncertain Future. *Journal of Palestine Studies* 25, 1: 37–53.

Scheper-Hughes, Nancy. 1993. *Death Without Weeping: The Violence of Everyday Life in Brazil.* Berkeley: University of California Press.

———. 1997. Specificities: Peace-Time Crimes. *Social Identities: Journal for the Study of Race, Nation and Culture* 3, 3: 471–98.

Schmitt, Carl. 2007. *The Concept of the Political: Expanded Edition.* Trans. George Schwab. Chicago: University of Chicago Press.

Schulthies, Becky. 2013. Reasonable Affects: Moroccan Families Respond to Mediated Violence. In *Discourses of War and Peace,* ed. Adam Hodges, 193–224. Oxford: Oxford University Press.

Shadid, Anthony. 2007. "In Beirut, Crisis Settles into Routine." Washington Post Foreign Service, April 9.

Shea, Louisa. 2006. Sade and the Cynic Tradition. *Modern Language Quarterly* 67, 3: 313–31.

Sloterdijk, Peter. 1988. *Critique of Cynical Reason.* Minneapolis: University of Minnesota Press.

Sluka, Jeffrey. 1999. *Death Squad: The Anthropology of State Terror.* Philadelphia: University of Pennsylvania Press.

Slyomovics, Susan. 1998. *The Object of Memory: Arab and Jew Narrate the Palestinian Village.* Philadelphia: University of Pennsylvania Press.

Sneifer, Regina. 2008. *alqeytu al-silaḥ: ʾimraʾa fī khiḍami al-ḥarb al-lubnāniya (J'ai déposé les armes: Une femme dans la guerre du Liban).* Trans. Roula Thubian. Beirut: Dar al-Farabi.

Sontag, Susan. 2003. *Regarding the Pain of Others.* New York: Picador.

Sorabji, Cornelia. 2006. Managing Memories in Post-War Sarajevo: Individuals, Bad Memories, and New Wars. *Journal of the Royal Anthropological Institute* 12: 1–18.

Staudigl, Michael. 2013. Towards a Relational Phenomenology of Violence. *Human Studies* 36, 1: 43–66.

Strathern, Marilyn. 1988. *The Gender of the Gift: Problems with Women and Problems with Society in Melanesia.* Berkeley: University of California Press.

———. 1992. *Reproducing the Future: Essays on Anthropology, Kinship and the New Reproductive Technologies.* New York: Routledge.

Strathern, Andrew, Pamela J. Stewart, and Neil L. Whitehead, eds. 2006. *Terror and Violence: Imagination and the Unimaginable.* London: Pluto.

Strauss, Levi. 1992. *Tristes Tropiques.* Trans. John Weightman and Doreen Weightman. New York: Penguin.

Tabar, Paul. 2009. Immigration and Human Development: Evidence from Lebanon. Human Development Research Paper 2009/35, United Nations Development Programme.

Tabbara, Lina Mikdadi. 1983. *Surviving the Siege of Beirut: A Personal Account.* London: Onyx.

Taussig, Michael. 1992. *The Nervous System.* New York: Routledge.

———. 2003. *Law in a Lawless Land.* New York: New Press.

Tawil-Souri, Helga. 2009. New Palestinian Centers: An Ethnography of the "Checkpoint Economy." *International Journal of Cultural Studies* 12, 3: 217–35.

Torgler, Benno. 2007. Determinants of superstition. *Journal of Socio-Economics* 36: 713–33.

Traboulsi, Fawwaz. 2002. *'aks al-ser: kitābāt mukhtalifa* (Against the Mainstream: Writings of a Different Kind). Beirut: Riad El-Rayyes Books S.A.R.L.

———. 2007. *A History of Modern Lebanon*. Ann Arbor, Mich.: Pluto Press.

———. 2011. Does Guilt Matter? *Jadaliyya* website.

Trouillot, Michel-Rolph. 2000. Abortive Rituals: Historical Apologies in the Global Era. *Interventions: International Journal of Postcolonial Studies* 2, 2: 171–86.

Tsing, Anna Lowenhaupt. 1993. *In the Realm of the Diamond Queen: Marginality in an Out-of-the-Way Place*. Princeton, N.J.: Princeton University Press.

Tueni, Ghassan. 1985. *Une guerre pour les outres*. Paris: Lattes.

Valsiner, Jaan. 1993. Making of the Future: Temporality and the Constructive Nature of Human Development. In *Developmental Time and Timing*, ed. Gerald Turkewitz and Darlynne Devenny, 13–40. Hillsdale, N.J.: Erlbaum.

Volk, Lucia. 2010. *Memorials and Martyrs in Modern Lebanon*. Bloomington: Indiana University Press.

Warren, Kay B., ed. 1993. *The Violence Within: Cultural and Political Opposition in Divided Nations*. Boulder, Colo.: Westview.

Weber, Max. 1946. *From Max Weber: Essays in Sociology*. Trans. and ed. H. H. Gerth and C. Wright Mills. New York: Oxford University Press.

Wedeen, Lisa. 1999. *Ambiguities of Domination*. Chicago: University of Chicago Press.

Westmoreland, Mark Ryan. 2008. Crisis of Representation: Experimental Documentary in Postwar Lebanon. Ph.D. dissertation, University of Texas, Austin.

Wilson, Richard A. 2001. *The Politics of Truth and Reconciliation in South Africa: Legitimizing the Post-Apartheid State*. Cambridge: Cambridge University Press.

Yassin, Nizar. 2012. Sects and the City: Socio-Spatial Perceptions and Practices of Youth in Beirut. In *Lebanon: After the Cedar Revolution*, ed. Are Knudson and Michael Kerr, 203–18. London: Hurst.

Young, Michael. 2000. The Sneer of Memory: Lebanon's Disappeared and Postwar Culture. *Middle East Report* 217 (Winter): 42–45.

Zecher, Linda. 1967. The Men of Influence and the Exercise of Influence in Nabatieh, Lebanon. M.A. thesis, American University of Beirut.

Zizek, Slavoj. 1989. *The Sublime Object of Ideology*. New York: Verso.

———. 1992. *Looking Awry: An Introduction to Jacques Lacan Through Popular Culture*. Cambridge, Mass.: MIT Press.

———. 2009. *Violence: Six Sideways Reflections*. London: Picador.

Zulaika, Joseba and William A. Douglass. 1996. *Terror and Taboo: The Follies, Fables and Faces of Terrorism*. New York: Routledge.

FILMS

Abi Samra, Maher, dir. 2010. *shiyūʿiyīn kinā* [We Were Communists]. 85 min. Orjouane Productions, Lebanon.

Al-Issawi, Omar, dir. 2001. *ḥarb lubnān* [Lebanon's War]. 15 hours. Al-Jazeera Satellite Channel, Qatar.

Aractingi, Phillipe, dir. 2007. *taḥt al-qasf* [Under the Bombs]. 98 min. Capa Cinema, France.

Borgmann, Monika, Lokman Slim, and Hermann Theissen, dirs. 2004. *Massaker.* 99 min. Lichtblick Film and UMAM Production, Germany-Lebanon.

Doueiri, Ziad, dir. 1998. *West Beirut.* 105 min. Beirut.

El Chamaa, Sabine, dir. 2009. *Promenade.* 11 min. Neosfilm, Germany-Lebanon.

Salhab, Ghassan, dir. 2010. *al-jabal* [The Mountain]. 80 min. Abbout Productions, Lebanon.

Note: Figures and tables are denoted by "f" and "t," respectively, following page numbers.

Acknowledgments

From the very beginning, loss has followed this project like an unwanted traveling companion: the loss of over a thousand lives in Lebanon the year I began research, the loss of Syria as my book went out for review, the loss of my paternal grandmother the year I sent my final draft for copyediting, the loss of my mother's sister, Miralda, as this book went to production, and losses in between. As I think of my own losses, I remain in respect of how magnificently others have endured the tragedies in their lives. In the face of this loss, I must, above all, acknowledge the deceased, all those victims of war, and all those victims of time who suffered the in-betweens and aftermaths of war, even if ultimately succumbing to illnesses and natural causes. They give this project its spirit.

I have been blessed with so many caring people who continue to be in my life and who had a part in this book. First, and perhaps most important, I could not have gained the deep insights into Lebanon's social life without the help of interlocutors whose own ideas and analysis are everywhere visible in this book. Unfortunately, many of them will have to remain anonymous, but they should know that my gratitude to them is endless.

The seeds of this book came about during my time at New York University. For this I thank Anthony Alessandrini, Charles Anderson, Amahl Bishara, Sherene Seikaly, Anjali Kamat, and Naomi Schiller for teaching me about solidarity and how to challenge power; Rabab Abdulhadi, for pushing me to pursue my career path in anthropology; and John Gershman and Paul Smoke for their encouragement.

Later, at Princeton University, I came to hone my critical outlook of the world. Abdellah Hammoudi and John Borneman challenged me in this regard, pushing me to think theoretically in ways I had never imagined. Their influence should be recognizable in this book. I am eternally grateful to Carol Greenhouse for inspiring and humbling me during our numerous email correspondences and conversations, and for pushing me to pursue Penn Press. I would also like to thank Lawrence Rosen, James Boon, João Biehl, Isabelle Clark-Decès, and Rena Lederman for teaching me to read and observe the world, and for their insights that helped form this project. And in the Political Science Department, Amaney Jamal for her support and intellectual guidance. Thanks also go to Carol Zanca, Mo Lin Yee, and Gabriela Drinovan at the Department of Anthropology, without whom I could not have navigated Princeton. I am grateful to Charis Boutieri, Christopher Garces, Su'ad Abdul-Khabeer, and Erica Weiss, who were there for me throughout my time at Princeton, and offered me support on many levels. I also wish to thank Leo Coleman, Talia Dan-Cohen, Erin Fitz-Henry, Megan Foreman, Will Garriott, Anton Khabbaz, Peter Locke, Ricky Martin, Ali Nouri, and Jamie Sherman for contributing to budding ideas through our many conversations.

At Northwestern University in Qatar, I am grateful for the time and space I was given to complete this book. My colleagues have been welcoming and supportive, and I would especially like to thank Sandra Richards for her mentorship, and Zachary Wright, Joe Khalil, and Andrew Mills for helping me to navigate a new space, and for their conversations, advice, and friendship.

This book would not have been completed without the generous support of the Centre for Lebanese Studies at Oxford University, Zentrum Moderner Orient (ZMO), Humboldt University, the Graduate School at Princeton University, the Princeton Near East Studies Department, and Princeton Institute for International and Regional Studies (PIIRS). I would also like to thank Bill Benter and the Benter Foundation for generously supporting my time as visiting professor at the University of Pittsburgh. In Beirut, I would like to acknowledge UMAM Documentation and Research and its director, Monica Bergman, for the wealth of information and access that they provided me.

My thanks to Tobias Kelly, editor of the Ethnography of Political Violence series, and Peter Agree, my editor at Penn Press, for believing in this project and having the patience to see it through. I am also grateful to Amanda Ruffner, Alison Anderson, and the rest of the staff at Penn Press for making this manuscript a reality.

I have benefited from discussing this project with many amazing people, including Fawwaz Traboulsi, Samir Khalaf, Sari Hanafi, Rami Khouri, Kari Karame, George and Alexandra Asseily, Youssef Khlat, Carole McGranahan, Eugene Rogan, Morgan Clarke, Sharad Chari, Henrike Donner, Martha Mundy, Robert Hayden, Yasmine Ipek, Joshua Roth, Nancy Condee, Andrew Strathern, Pamela Martin, David Kim, Neil Doshi, and David Montgomery.

People came into my life along the way who were perhaps more angel than mentor, and who supported me when I thought this project would never see the light of day. They read the entire manuscript and never once complained when I inundated them with requests and swallowed their time. Steve Caton took me in at Harvard University when it mattered most, and offered invaluable comments and advice that have vastly improved this text. Lara Deeb has been there for me as mentor and friend at key stages during this project and pushed me in new directions. I am forever in debt to her for all her kindness, patience, and deep engagement with my work. Michelle Obeid, my friend and intellectual confidant, has pushed me to get this project done, reading the manuscript multiple times, and giving me the confidence to keep writing.

I am also indebted to three other mentors-cum-angels: Debbora Battaglia who has been there to advise me in all facets of my career, but especially in maneuvering through the stages of a manuscript; Suad Joseph, whose guidance and care have been immeasurable, and who has supported and encouraged me throughout the painstaking process of producing this book, and Kirstin Scheid, who has been a dear friend throughout this process; and helped me navigate fieldwork, offering her invaluable experience and advice.

A group of colleagues and friends have, over the years, contributed in different ways to this book. Noora Kassem, Mayssun Sukkarieh, and Satya Mohapatra read drafts of chapters at various stages for which I am grateful. Ghassan Hage has been encouraging of my work throughout and I am always left in wonderment by his ability to read the world anew. Muzna Al-Masri, Maha Eissa, Sabine El-Chamaa, Bilal El-Amine, Elie Ghassan, Rania Masri, Helena Nassif, Rabih Salah, and Abdelrahman Zahzah opened Lebanon to me in ways I would have never imagined; I stand in awe of their knowledge. Ziad Abu-Rish, Tamara Al-Samerraei, Rayane Alamuddin, Asli Bali, Nadia Bou Ali, Omar Dahi, Rayan El-Amine, Hassan El-Houry, Sondra Hale, Samah Idriss, Darryl Li, Laleh Khalili, Munira Khayyat, Nicolas Kosmatopoulos, Maya Mikdashi, Jamil Mouawad, Yasser Munif, Mahmoud Natout, Eliane Raheb, Nisreen Salti, Mazin Sbaiti, Nadya Sbaiti, Maha Shuayb, Lisa Taraki, and Efstratios Sourlagas challenged my perceptions, questioned my ideas, and were there for me in so many important ways at different stages of this work. Nadia Abu El-Haj, Lori Allen, Ilana Feldman, Laurie King, Jonah Rubin, Michal Ran, Fida Adely, Ajantha Subramanian, Naor Ben-Yehoyada, and Jessica Winegar have been like a second family in the final phase of this project. They have offered breaths of fresh air for me to pursue other passions and have energized me through our various collaborations and conversations. To all, I offer my deep and profound appreciation and love.

My entire extended family has been the inspiration for this project. Their trials, terror, and pain, their joy, pleasure, and resilience inscribe these pages and my thoughts. Without them this entire work would have no meaning or motivation, and I hope I have done justice to their memories of war past and future. Dalal Hermez, more older sister than paternal aunt, deserves special mention for giving the manuscript one last deep look, challenging my biases and tightening my language.

My siblings, Ziyad and Sarah Hermez, made my world lighter when sometimes it got so heavy. I hope this book allows them a window into what I do. I love them more than they know and wish to thank them for always being there for me.

My parents, Samir Hermez and Velma Ekmekji, were with me every step of the way. Reams of paper, filled with the most beautiful of words, could never express my gratitude for their support and belief in me when my life choices didn't always make sense to them. They are an amazing team, and together, have allowed my siblings and me the freedom to pursue our worlds and find our passions. In their presence and from their love I gain peace of mind.

Diala Hawi, my life partner, has had to endure me talking about this project for so many years now. At every step, she had been patient, listening to me test my analyses and theories, shooting some of those theories down before I could ever embarrass myself in public, and being by my side as I wrote this book, even when my frustrations and anxieties became unbearable. I hope, therefore, that she is satisfied with this final product, and I offer her my deepest love as we watch our beautiful kids grow together.

And finally, Alia, my daughter, has given my world meaning. From her I've learned to smile at the mundane and be excited about waking before the birds chirp. I look forward to walking alongside her and her brother Samir (who has just arrived into our life as this book goes to press) as we struggle for a better world.